When Killing
Is a Crime

When Killing Is a Crime

Tony Waters

LYNNE
RIENNER
PUBLISHERS

BOULDER
LONDON

Published in the United States of America in 2007 by
Lynne Rienner Publishers, Inc.
1800 30th Street, Boulder, Colorado 80301
www.rienner.com

and in the United Kingdom by
Lynne Rienner Publishers, Inc.
Gray's Inn House, 127 Clerkenwell Road, London EC1 5DB

Library of Congress Cataloging-in-Publication Data
Waters, Tony.
    When killing is a crime / Tony Waters.
        p. cm.
    Includes bibliographical references and index.
    ISBN-13: 978-1-58826-514-2 (hardcover : alk. paper)
    ISBN-13: 978-1-58826-539-5 (pbk. : alk. paper)
1. Murder—Case studies. 2. Homicide—Case studies.
3. Manslaughter—Case studies. I. Title.
HV6515.W33 2007
364.152—dc22

                                                2007020777

British Cataloguing in Publication Data
A Cataloguing in Publication record for this book
is available from the British Library.

Printed and bound in the United States of America

        The paper used in this publication meets the requirements
∞   of the American National Standard for Permanence of
        Paper for Printed Library Materials Z39.48-1992.

    5   4   3   2   1

Contents

Illustrations

Figures

Tables

Photographs

Acknowledgments

OF THE BOOKS I'VE WRITTEN, THE PRESENT ONE HAS GENERATED SOME of the most interesting discussions among my peers and students. People are interested in violence and killing, usually want to know more, and are eager to share their own thoughts about the subject. In this respect, they are no different from most people throughout history. After all, murder, killing, and vengeance are often at the heart of mythologies, national stories, and holy books like the Bible and Quran. Such fascination is reflected in modern popular culture by movies, books, newspapers, and even the Internet, which often focus on the nature of murder and discussions about appropriate societal responses. I have appreciated the thoughts of everyone who has pursued these discussions with me, and I of course share this fascination.

This book emerged out of my experiences teaching criminology at California State University, Chico. In 1999 or so, when Laurie Wermuth was chair of the Sociology Department and I was a new faculty member, she suggested that my lecture and reading assignments about killing might form the basis of a book. She pointed me to Randall Collins's article that is so important to Chapter 5. Around the same time, my "three theory" approach to the study of killing gelled in one of my criminology sections. The students in this section included Dan Baraz, Scott Bowden, Suki Dhaliwal, Heather Fleming, Gabriel Frutos, Heather Gibson, Sara Green, Ty Hollins, Brian Joy, Carolyn Lara, Noah Lauermann, Samuel Llamas, Jonathan Mendez, Becky Olwin, John Pizzo, Katy Pors, Luis Ramirez, Norma Servin, and Demetrius Steward. Other students who helped me think about these issues were David Pratt, Rachael Justice, Judy Vang, Nicole Storman, Marcelo Escobedo, Danielle Guildner, Dywayne Hurst, Nou Vang, Moria Santino, Joel Rainey, and Jaime Luevano. If they happen to come across this book, I hope that it emphasizes for them how the classroom can be more than a sum of a professor and individual students. And of course I hope they learned new ways to think about killing and murder as a result of our classes. I certainly did.

The Department of Sociology at CSU, Chico, has been a great place to teach, write, and read. Credit for this goes to a fantastic set of colleagues, including Olga Bright, Nandi Crosby, Clark Davis, Andy Dick, Carol Edelman, Liahna Gordon, Al Jensen, Kathy Keiser, Maureen Knowlton, Janja Lalich, Paul Lopez, Jerry Maneker, Bill Martin, Homer Metcalf, Brian Paciotti, Dan Pence, Gwen Sheldon, Cynthia Siemsen, Chunyan Song, Janna Waligorski, and Moon Jee Yoo.

Other students also contributed significantly to the ideas in this book. Bill Travers carefully read Mark Cooney's works when I started the project. Annie Abramson helped with a number of research-related tasks several years ago. Liz Barrett e-mailed me great references while I was living in Tanzania in 2003–2004. I also benefited from conversations with Brian Paciotti about the nature of violence in Tanzania, California, the American South, Seattle, and elsewhere.

Karla McLaren became perhaps the person most engaged in conversation with me during the writing of this book. She quickly grasped the theoretical concepts I was exploring and helped me to think about the role that third parties play in shaping violence—an idea that became a common thread throughout the book. A thoughtful and enthusiastic assistant, Karla suggested several of the examples, and she injected what little humor may be found in this textbook on an otherwise stern topic.

Concepts of justice and reciprocity embedded in our legal system today have their origins in Judeo-Christian thought, and so I owe thanks to two people at Peace Lutheran Church in Grass Valley, California, who offered their insights. Richard O. Johnson assisted with the material on W.T.C. "Rough" Elliott and sparked thoughtful discussions of the Old Testament during Adult Sunday School. Dean Eatman, the associate pastor, also answered my odd questions about the Old Testament.

Intellectual debts are sometimes not always apparent from a book's footnotes and citations. In the case of this book, the debts I owe to Mark Cooney, Max Weber, Travis Hirschi, Michael Gottfredson, Emile Durkheim, Kai Erikson, Benedict Anderson, and Randall Collins should be obvious. Less obvious are the contributions of Cooney's mentor, Donald Black, who developed the sociology of law that both Cooney and I take advantage of. Lawrence E. Cohen first pointed me toward ecological theories in general, and his routine-activities approach in particular; Chapter 3 very much implicitly reflects his thoughts. Reaching back to graduate school at the University of California, Davis, I recall how Jack Goldstone taught me about the strength of the comparative method, which has become implicit in much of my work. This is the first book I have written that compares theories. The principles for doing this relate very much to Goldstone's two courses on comparative methods. Frank Hirtz first directed me to the sociology of law when he was my dissertation adviser, and this conversation has continued at Chico with Cynthia Siemsen and Andy Dick.

A final note of thanks is due to the administration of California State University, Chico, and in particular to our provost of the past thirteen years, Scott McNall. He emphasizes the importance of the "teacher-scholar" model in cultivating a committed university faculty. The longer I have been at CSU, Chico, the more I have appreciated this. The teaching keeps my feet on the ground and, I hope, keeps my writing accessible—if not always to "the general public" then at least to our undergraduates, who, after all, are an important portion of the general public. The rewards and respect that such scholarship receives at CSU, Chico, have contributed a great deal to my own personal professional development. I hope that these effects are also apparent in my teaching and in whatever impact on the discipline of sociology this book may have.

—Tony Waters

Introduction

MURDER IS THE MOST HEINOUS OF CRIMES, FOR WHICH SOCIETY reserves the strongest of punishments. Perhaps because of this strong reaction, most people think that they can recognize a murder when they see it. Indeed, within their own society and in their own time, they usually can. Even so, whether a killing is defined as a murder or not is a process specific to time and place. The process of defining a particular killing as murder involves not only a victim and a perpetrator, but also a social context established by others. In other words, murder is always a social act that involves not only killing, but also judgment and evaluation by society at large. Thus, if the phenomenon of murder is to be understood sociologically, analysis must venture beyond the finding of guilt or responsibility in a particular case. A deeper understanding of how society separates general killing from criminal killing needs to be developed. This sorting out of legitimate killing from illegitimate killing occurs in a process known as *criminalization.*

The subject of killing and murder seems familiar; most people have witnessed thousands of killings via film, television, newspapers, and literature. By applying social theories to their understanding of what does or does not constitute murder, undergraduates can learn to use these theories to explore the nature of crime. More broadly, the skill students will gain in applying the sociological perspective can in turn be applied to a range of intuitively familiar phenomena in the study of deviance, social problems, and other subfields of sociology.

How This Book Came to Be

Each society has a process through which killings are described as legal justifiable homicide, illegal unjustified homicide (i.e., murder), or just plain killing. The process varies not only with a technical or legal capacity to assign blame but also with the capacity of a particular society to respond in a manner it defines as decisive and appropriate. This *response* to killing is the process through which a particular killing is identified as a murder, and not as an accident, self-defense, act of war, or execution. When viewed through a sociological lens, this response to killing offers a window into how a society perceives broader issues of social status, fault and innocence, the nature of blame, and agency.

Murder and the Sociological Imagination

In sociology, it is clear that crime (and all other social phenomena) is a "social construction." This means that acts are "constructed" as crimes only when there is a consensus that the acts are wrong and that the broader society has the right and responsibility to respond. Without the context of such a judgment, a violent killing is just that—a killing. As a sociologist, I have taught criminology classes since 1997, and I have consistently focused on the importance of *social context* in crime. Both crime and criminals are defined as such only when the broader society judges them to be so. Crime is different from what is often presented in the popular media, wherein a particular individual is thought to have a psychological predisposition to crime, or a particular act is defined as clearly illegal.

Indeed, there is a wealth of data indicating that most acts that are criminal are never identified with a particular person. This fact becomes intuitively obvious to students when I point out that they themselves may have committed many illegal acts of drug use, theft, assault, and so on, for which they were never punished. Because they were never connected with their crimes, they can present themselves in class as "students" rather than "criminals." Indeed, on the anonymous self-report surveys I administer in my classes, typically about 90 percent of students admit to committing an act that in a literal positivistic (and legal) sense is criminal. On a gut level, students understand that the main difference between themselves and someone who commits the same crime (but is caught) is that the ill-fated person has been somehow "criminalized," while (to their own relief) they have not.

Nevertheless, murder is still an extreme crime that engenders a special horror. While many students can imagine being a petty thief, a drug dealer, a brawler, or a computer hacker, they assume that murder is inherently "criminal" and therefore different from more mundane criminal acts. Murder is not different, though. Similar rules apply to the criminalization of murder as to the criminalization of marijuana use, petty thefts, assaults, drug sales, robberies, burglaries, or drunk driving. I have found over the years that the best way to help students understand the social context of all criminalization is to focus on the unexamined "taken for granteds" that individuals have about the crime of murder. These include the presence of states, legislatures, police forces, prosecutors, and court systems that spend a great deal of time deciding which acts are worthy of a response and which are not.

The Criminalization of Killing

There are two advantages to using killing to explain processes of criminalization. The first has to do with the inherent interest of murder in all societies and times. Murder figures more prominently in novels, film, and television than, say, drug use, domestic battery, influence peddling, shoplifting, or check fraud—no doubt due to the irrevocable consequences for the victim.

The second advantage (and my reason for writing this book) is that this focus on murder provides a meaningful alternative to traditional criminology texts and their explanations of crime and criminalization. Over the past thirty to forty years, the US federal government has invested billions of dollars to evaluate techniques for preventing crime, reforming neighborhoods, and rehabilitating criminals. Much of this money was well spent, and some programs have prevented violent and criminal acts that otherwise would have occurred. But such research, which sees crime as a problem to be solved, inevitably assumes that there is a specific and identifiable criminal population that can be treated, and a set of discrete acts that can be prevented.

Consequently, the standard criminology text moves crime a step away from important questions about when, how, and why laws are created to define illegal acts. Typically, such books assume a "psycho-legal" approach to crime, as does the popular culture.[1] The psycho-legal approach focuses on the individual thoughts of people who commit crime, which is particularly interesting in a society that emphasizes individual intent when assigning legal culpability. But it also pushes aside questions about how patterns of enforcement develop, perhaps because many of these texts spring from a police subculture that assumes certain people are by nature "criminal" while the rest of us are not, and the process of criminalization gets overlooked (or at best reduced to a sidebar or subchapter).

My interest in the process of criminalization, combined with the dearth of relevant undergraduate texts, led me to develop my own teaching materials about killing. This book is a summary of the arguments I have used to describe criminalization in my classes, and reverses the traditional order found in most criminology textbooks. I do not start with a description of the criminal as a special case, but instead focus on the nature of one crime: murder. Murder is conceptualized as an *action* and a *reaction*. Both the act and the reaction to murder are defined in the context of other related actions, both criminal and noncriminal.

Nevertheless, I do agree that conventional statistics about murder and violence are important, particularly in defining specific issues, teaching about killing and killers, and offering insight into how the influential people who collect statistics think about killing. But these statistics are not central to the study of the criminalization of killing; therefore, statistical tables and graphs are mainly found at the end of this book (see Appendix 1). Murder must be understood as a social phenomenon and a social construction. It is not simply a statistical fact generated by government bureaucracies.

Organization of the Book

Chapter 1 establishes the theoretical basis for the study of murder and delineates between the act itself and the reaction of a broader society. In order to focus sociological thinking, this chapter explores how certain acts become defined as murder while others are defined as violent death—by assessing killing and murder from three different perspectives:

1. *Third-party theories,* or the process by which a society comes to define particular types of killing as criminal, and other types as not.
2. *Social ecology theories,* which describe how most murder is an unintended consequence of interpersonal conflict or combat gone awry.
3. *Durkheimian labeling theories,* or the argument that social reactions to killing occur in a manner that reaffirms the integrity, mores, and continuing existence of a society.

Chapter 2 explores the ways in which different societies define killing as justifiable or not, and how they seek to control illegitimate killing. This chapter discusses the nature of killing in stateless societies that do not have a legitimated and all-powerful third party to make judgments of guilt, fault, and compensation—and it describes the tendency toward violent feuding in such societies as victims seek righteous justice through revenge attacks. Such feuding happens in a wide range of circumstances, including among the hunting and gathering Ju/' Hoansi of Namibia; the upper-class planters in the pre–Civil War US South; the forest-dwelling Ache tribe of Paraguay; the modern-day mountain-dwelling Albanians; and the street gangs of some modern US inner cities. The chapter also explores what the comparison between such stateless societies and modern states tells us about the rule of law in the control of killing and the definition of murder.

Three case studies illustrate how feuds and revenge killings escalate in the absence of a powerful third party: Albanian feuding and blood revenge; the killing of Ken McElroy on the streets of Skidmore, Missouri, in 1981; and a story about death and witchcraft from Cameroon.

Chapter 3 examines the fact that killing is not typically the result of careful complex planning but is rather one consequence (and a rare one at that) of interpersonal violence. This chapter introduces social ecology theorists who point out that, in the modern United States, most murders occur in the context of an argument or fight. The fatal event is often the result of a conflict in which one or both protagonists engaged many times before, the difference being that in the final instance, the victim ends up dead instead of only scared or hurt. Social ecology theorists assert that the only difference between an assault and a murder may be the trajectory of a fist or the availability (or accuracy) of a gun, knife, or even a blunt object. The perpetrator's intent to hurt or maim the victim is the same. Ecological theorists point out that the difference between murder and assault can even reflect conditions outside the immediate control of the perpetrator. For example, the speed of an ambulance or the willingness of a witness to intervene can mean the difference between an assault and a murder.

Three case studies are included in Chapter 3: how murders escalated in a neighborhood near the US Capitol in the 1990s, a story of death and justice on the rural California frontier in the late 1880s, and a murder among Sacramento's small Mien community in 1991.

Chapter 4 explores the range of responses societies have to acts they define as murder. Not all killing is deemed equal. For example, in the United States the intent and context of the person holding the knife or gun matter a great deal. So do the social status of victims and perpetrator. Indeed, contemporary court trials focus a great deal on "looking into the head" of defendants and parsing issues like intent and malice to determine appropriate sentences. The punishment for first-degree murder (killing with forethought and malice), second-degree murder (killing without forethought but with malice), and manslaughter (killing without forethought or malice) varies, irrespective of the fact that the victim suffered the same consequence: death.

The world's societies have developed a wide range of official and unofficial responses to killing, such as ignoring the death, labeling the death accidental, celebrating the death, gossiping about the death and perpetrator, sentencing an accused perpetrator to prison, torturing the perpetrator, or executing the perpetrator. These responses reflect, among other things, status distinctions of the murderer and victim, imputed motives, and the capacity of a society to punish perceived wrongs. The common thread in these responses, though, is a need to reassert a moral order that has been damaged by the killing. Likewise, the response is administered in a manner that ensures that the victim's kin will not seek retribution on their own, for this would lead to a potential escalation of unsanctioned violence.

Three case studies are included in Chapter 4: a description of a vigilante killing in western Tanzania in the 1990s, the story of a rural Chinese settlement in which ten people were killed in 1928, and discussion of attempts by an Indiana prosecutor to try the Ford Motor Company for manufacturing a defective vehicle that led to the death of three girls in a fiery automobile accident.

Chapter 5 examines how states themselves are involved in killing, and the prospects for the long-term control of state-sanctioned violence in different countries, as well as attempts to control genocide and war crimes by the international community. States are among the most prolific killers; this reflects the fact that assertions of state power are necessary factors in the establishment of social order. The elites holding power in a state often use killing to maintain their political authority and use the lethal power of the state to do so. The range of killing undertaken by states includes execution, war, massacres, and genocide. Such killings occur in a unique context in which killing may become bureaucratized. Salient sociological issues include the nature of nationalism, the capacity of the state to legitimate killing, and the creation of command killers.

Three case studies illustrate the range of state-sanctioned killing. The first is the Rwanda genocide of 1994, in which 500,000 to 800,000 people were killed during a span of three months. The second focuses on the 5 to 8 million deaths in the Congo Free State from 1890 to 1910 that occurred as part of the industrial policy of Belgium's King Leopold II. The third case describes the famous Milgram obedience experiments, wherein normal people obeyed orders to torture and even kill fellow citizens.

Chapter 6 points out that while private violence has decreased substantially during the past 500 years, there is an increasing risk of state-sponsored lethal violence as states become more powerful. Sociological theory is effective for highlighting this trend in ways often missed by the legal and psychological theories used by modern law enforcement. The surprising conclusion from this analysis means that future long-term attempts to restrain violence significantly will focus on how to restrain states from using violence to subdue potential opponents.

My assessment of how killing becomes criminalized is primarily qualitative. However, the conclusions I draw depend on a wide range of studies using statistical techniques. Thus, many of the tables on which the arguments in this book are based are included in Appendix 1. A second appendix presents legal definitions of murder and homicide, including definitions of the legal codes of California and Texas. These codes provide a window into the values of a particular society, including issues of how its members evaluate life, childhood, sexuality, crime, deviance, abortion, and other issues.

Together, these six chapters and two appendixes introduce students of criminology to the nature of criminalization. By focusing on the criminalization of killing from a sociological perspective, it is hoped that students will begin seeing crime not only as an individual act but as one best understood in a social context. In the process, students will become discerning consumers both of scientific data from the criminal justice system and of popular entertainment. This is important because, as will be clear by the end of the book, both scientific and popular views continue to shape public policies about deviance, law development and enforcement, and social control.

Note

1. Indeed, Cooney (1997a:153–154) questions whether "crime," embedded as it is in culture, is even useful as a theoretical concept.

CHAPTER 1

The Criminalization
of Killing

Sociology and Murder

Criminology is the subfield of sociology relating to the study of crime. According to criminologist Lawrence Sherman (1992:xi), criminology is the study of the consequences of rule definition, rule-making, rule-breaking, and rule enforcement. In effect, Sherman is saying that the sociology of crime is concerned with the mechanisms through which rules are defined and created, the situations that make rule-breaking more likely, and how the enforcers of the rules are able to maintain their legitimacy. Sometimes these rules are formally codified as "law," and sometimes they are not. Many volumes have been written about why crime rates fluctuate, the psychology of criminals, criminal law, the relationship between crime and poverty, effective policing and crime, why punishment is effective (or not), crime sprees, case studies, and so on.[1] Many of these studies are interesting because they appeal to our general fascination with the faults of others and are used to illustrate what logically happens to people who do wrong.

Murder is the most heinous of crimes and as a result is, I think, the most interesting. Murder is also discussed frequently in morality tales—to illustrate what is right, wrong, fair, or just in human relationships. We talk about murder, read about murder, and use murder as an example in political discourse; weekly television shows and films focus on murder at least as much as any other crime. This happens even though (as criminologists point out) murder is an uncommon crime. Stealing, assault, fraud, illegal use of drugs, and many other acts are far more common. In essence, as far as rule-breaking goes, murder is infrequent and unusual. Nevertheless, because it is so prominent in the cultural imagination, a disproportionate amount of energy goes into deciding how rules against murder are created and enforced. This book takes advantage of this fascination to investigate how some killing becomes criminalized as murder or homicide while other killing

1

does not. This focus on killing helps to uncover the very nature of rule-making, rule-breaking, and rule enforcement.

The Problem of Defining Murder

The definition of *murder* is seemingly self-evident: it involves one person killing another unlawfully with premeditation and malice.[2] A definition along these lines is found in dictionaries and in modern US legal codes. But such a definition presumes much; in particular, it assumes a legal code that denotes some killings as lawful and others as not. This definition also requires a means of seeing into another's mind to identify whether there is malice or premeditation. Both conditions are culturally situated and vary with time, place, and society. In addition, while all societies have some type of formal or informal legal definitions regulating killing, the capacity to apply the definitions varies a great deal, depending on the presence of an authority able to assert its will.

Not all killing of humans is murder under legal codes emphasizing premeditated malice.[3] For instance, at extremes, killing in war on behalf of a state, particularly for a victor state, is not murder. State executions are also not murder, because they are not "unlawful." To use a sociological term, state executions are "legitimate." However, between this legitimated individualized killing by the state (execution) and the more general killing of an anonymous soldier (war), there is in fact a great deal of ambiguity. Grappling with the ambiguity of what is or is not legitimated killing is a focus of this book and what ultimately makes the study of the criminalization of killing so interesting. In grappling with this ambiguity we not only better understand the sociology of murder but also acquire a sociological framework useful for the study of crime in general.

The following cases illustrate a range of killing, how it became defined, and how a government might respond:

- In nineteenth-century United States, deaths from dueling were considered legitimate and excusable; indeed, dueling was a requirement for upper-class males (see, e.g., Cooney 1997b; Benton [1826?]).
- Definitions of justifiable homicide have tightened over the past 100 years as laws about the illegitimacy of fighting have been passed and enforced. But, in the nineteenth century, the survivor of a barroom brawl might suffer no legal consequences—and be bought a round of drinks (McGrath 1984; Lundsgaarde 1977).
- In Texas until 1974, a man who killed his wife and her lover *in flagrante delicto* was considered provoked, and the killing therefore excusable (Lundsgaarde 1977:149, 212).[4]
- Killing in the context of "feuding" is legitimate, justifiable, and

even required in a wide range of societies (Waller 1988; Cooney 1997a, 1997b; Lee 1979; Bates 2001:42–48).

- In most years, only about two-thirds of the known homicides in the United States were solved, meaning that in one-third of the cases, someone has literally gotten away with murder (Uniform Crime Reports 2004).
- Recently in Cameroon, a man was convicted of bewitching a python that killed a small girl, a crime to which the man confessed. The man was placed in the local jail under antiwitchcraft statutes, where he died after being mistreated by the police, and his death was considered excusable (Fisiy 1998).

On a more general level, there are also patterns in how different types of killing are responded to. Among them:

- There are persistent differences in punishment for murder, depending on the assumed psychological condition of the killer and other issues. These conditions are typically specified in legal proceedings evaluating issues such as intent and premeditation, and the weapon used. Age, gender, and race can also be relevant.
- In the US legal system, the difference between a murder drawing a life term and an assault drawing a suspended sentence is often dependent on circumstances beyond the control of the perpetrator or victim, such as ambulance response time, medical skill levels, weapon functioning, and bystander intervention (Gottfredson and Hirschi 1990).
- Murder and attempted murder have been punished as the same crime in Australia under the assumption that the perpetrator had the same intent, whether he or she was successful or not (see Daly and Wilson 1988:13).
- Business executives who knowingly create policies and market products that kill predictably and regularly, such as automobiles and cigarettes, may be held responsible for deaths in civil court, but typically not in criminal court. Likewise, businesses that do not install required safety equipment can be sued in civil court for wrongful death, but they typically cannot be prosecuted in criminal court (see, e.g., Erikson 1978; Strobel 1980; Curran 1993; Lee and Ermann 1999).

The disparities in descriptions of murder described are attributable to the varying ways that different societies wrestle with the definitions of what is lawful, what is not, what is intent, and what is malice. Understanding how societies confront these questions, arrive at definitions, change definitions, and evaluate individuals in the context of these definitions is what the criminalization of killing is about.

Different Ways of Looking at Murder and Violent Death: Act and Reaction

With few exceptions, studies of murder start with an act, "the crime." But this is typically a legal category defined by a government, not a sociological definition. As a result, studies start with an assumption that what the state has defined as illegal and criminal is what is interesting. Thus, similar examples in which no legal judgment is rendered are ignored, and the process of rule-making and discretion in enforcement are left unaddressed. Even the process of deciding whether a killing is first degree, second degree, manslaughter, war-related, genocide, self-defense, accidental, or due to natural causes is typically brushed aside.[5]

For example, consider the most extreme category of murder: genocide. There is much to learn by broadening the examination of genocide to include mass killing. Indeed, the term *genocide* only emerged in order to classify the most extreme type of state-sponsored murder in which entire ethnic groups are killed, and this legal category was created only in the twentieth century and became important as a twentieth-century legal term. Courts use the term to distinguish different types of massacres, particularly those undertaken by a state. As a crime, genocide is frequently used to distinguish massacres by Germany (1930s and 1940s), Cambodia (1970s), Rwanda (1990s), Bosnia (1990s), and Turkey (1910s) from less systematic types of killing by governments.

However, while the word *genocide* is new, the phenomenon of targeting groups for massacre is not. For example, the massacres by Belgian King Leopold II's Congo administration between about 1890 and 1910 (Hochschild 1998) were genocidal in nature but have not been categorized as such. Nor typically are the massacres of American Indians by Europeans and their descendants, or the destruction of entire cities by Genghis Khan's forces. Similarly, the victims of the Aztec empire's mass human sacrifices are not typically listed in histories of the world's genocide.[6] Nor for that matter are the killing fields in Angola in the 1980s and 1990s, or in the southern Sudan, where ethnic groups were probably targeted for death in the 1980s and 1990s. However, each act did occur, and even though King Leopold II (and many others) died powerful and unindicted, it is plausible that a study of his reign in the Congo can help us understand the institutions and structures that are necessary to organize the mass killing that is today defined as genocide. For this reason, several of the case studies in this book should be included in a study of the nature of genocide, even though there has been no specific finding of guilt by a legal system, such as has been done on behalf of Jews, Rwandans, and Bosnians. By the same token, the brutal killings undertaken by feuding clans that are beyond the effective reach of modern legal systems are also of interest for understanding how law enforcement comes to restrict violence.

The Reaction: Guilt, Innocence, and Violent Death

The problem of varying responses to human-caused death is not restricted to genocide. Other types of violence have been evaluated in ways that, to the modern American ear, might seem paradoxical. Gunfighters in the nineteenth-century gold-mining town of Bodie, California, often saw their "lethal combat" end with a drink for the victor, although an unlucky few instead ended up at the wrong end of an ad hoc "vigilance committee's" rope (McGrath 1984). Jim Jones, who perished in Guyana with over 900 of his followers in a "murder/suicide" in 1978, is difficult to classify; was Jonestown a suicide or murder? (Hall 1989). Damiens, the man who tried to kill the French king Louis XV in 1757, was drawn and quartered in a gruesome execution for the crime of "regicide," even though the king recovered from his wounds and reigned for twenty more years (Foucault 1976:3–5). And what about coal mine owners in the United States during the twentieth century who did not install safety equipment because it was too expensive? Or Ford Motor Company, which failed to make modifications to gas tank design in the 1970s Pinto, even though the change would have prevented lethal explosions? Or cigarette manufacturers who lied about the consequences of tobacco use in the 1960s? Are they to be considered "good businessmen" even though they knew that their actions would lead to disease, injury, or death?

Note that the examples in the preceding paragraph implicitly compare and contrast the *reaction* of the society to each of these acts of killing or attempted killing. It is important to understand that in different times and places, some acts will be criminalized as murder while similar acts will not be criminalized. The focus of the criminalization of killing is to ask how a particular act becomes defined as criminal in some circumstances, but not in others.

The Sociology of Murder and Violent Death

Much of the study of murder is focused on different typologies of murder, specific murder cases, patterns of murder across time, descriptions of murderers, and stories of how murder cases were solved. Many of these stories are interesting in their own right. However, all share a particular flaw that sociologists call "sampling on the dependent variable." This term means that you are studying a particular phenomenon by only looking at cases that have already been attributed to that phenomenon. In the case of murder, it means you are studying murder by only looking at cases that have been classified as murder by the government. This means that you leave out "negative cases" of a broader phenomenon.

Thus, in the case of murder the broader phenomenon is specifically killing, and more generally, violence. From a sociological perspective, it is relevant to study murder as a subcategory of killing and violence and ask, "What type of killing and violence ends up being categorized as murder?" For example, if we understand violent fighting in general, we can begin by asking what it is about violence that sometimes leads to murder and other times does not. This question can be asked on two levels. First, how do some acts that start out as a fight end up as a killing? And second, why are some killings that result from fighting classified as murder, while others are classified as justifiable homicide? What are the differences, the social contexts, and the social definitions that make one killing more serious than another?

Culture and Murder: Act and Reaction

Television, movies, and novels typically make murder seem simple. A death at the hand of another—and a seemingly self-evident judgment of fault by a fictional character—are all that is needed. In other words, there is an *act* and a *reaction*, and in that order. In fact, between these two seemingly self-evident actions is a great deal of ambiguity in which very human judgments are made, usually without a great deal of precision. In other words, both the act and the reaction to the act can vary independently. The approach that a group of people take to defining killing, being killed, and framing the situation tells us something very elemental about how authority is wielded in that particular society.

Consider each of the two elements: the act and the reaction. The *act* can be analyzed in terms of how it is done, who does it, who dies, and so forth. The act might occur in a private social context involving only the person who kills and the person who is killed. But the *reaction* is about a judgment that involves an interpretation of intent and responsibility that *always* occurs in a broader social context. This reaction also implies an ability to make righteous judgments that others recognize as legitimate. Thus, since judgments are involved, another person or party must be recognized by the social group as capable of reacting appropriately. This outside party might be the friends and kin of the persons who kill and were killed. But in modern society, the outside judge is most often the government.

When the arbiter of a judgment is a government, it must be recognized by a social group as the only valid referee for the resolution of the most personal type of grievance. In modern society, this legitimacy means government has a "monopoly" on policing power or the use of "legitimate coercive force." The differences between societies wherein the kin of the killer and victim react, and societies wherein a powerful government restricts the right to react to itself, will be discussed later in this chapter.

Likewise, the "legitimacy" of the state can also vary a great deal; and while it is true that this legitimacy is partly rooted in raw coercive power (i.e., who is stronger or has the more powerful weapons), more subtle application of state power requires a broader consensus.[7] This consensus is difficult to develop and maintain, and it is at best imperfect, even in the modern United States. Examples of areas where (even in the United States) there is not a monopoly over the legitimated use of coercive force include street gangs, ethnic communities where police are distrusted, and remote areas where police presence is slow to arrive and therefore seen as weak. In all of these situations, people are less likely to appeal to the police if they are wronged, and as a result they are more likely to seek "justice" (or revenge) on their own.

The *reaction* also varies in regard to the social status of the perpetrator and the victim. This variation is often reflected in the resources invested in different types of homicide investigations. High-status victims (politicians, movie stars, or middle-class high school students) merit more strenuous efforts to resolve their deaths and mete out punishment. Low-status victims (for example, a victim of a botched drug deal) or criminals who die while in custody might merit only a cursory police investigation and little investigative effort. The same variation holds true for potential perpetrators. High-status suspects who can afford expensive private defense lawyers (for instance, O.J. Simpson) are treated with greater care than lower-class suspects. Defendants released from Illinois death rows due to the inadequacy of their counsel in the late 1990s are an example of poor defendants for whom little care was taken despite the seriousness of their punishment (*Economist* 1999).

Finally, there is the fact that in the modern United States, only about two-thirds of all murders are resolved. Approximately 15,000 murders are reported to the Federal Bureau of Investigation (FBI) annually, which means that about 5,000 cases each year go unsolved and unpunished (*Uniform Crime Reports,* various years). However, despite such a seemingly dismal record, the reaction to the resolved murders is very important. This reaction to those caught reassures the public that the state can respond legitimately and restore a sense of righteousness when such a serious crime has been committed. Sociological theories can tell us why this reassurance is important, and even why it works to help control overall rates of violence (which in turn leads to lowered rates of killing).

Where This Is Headed:
Social Theory and the Study of Murder

Three general approaches to evaluating the data about when violence becomes murder (and when it does not) are discussed in this chapter. While there are other sociological approaches to the criminalization of killing, these three approaches provide insight that is simple in structure, can be applied to many conditions, and can explain a great deal of cross-cultural data about how and why killings are criminalized.[8] The robustness of each approach for describing the crime of killing is developed more fully in Chapters 2, 3, and 4.

The Criminalization of Killing: Three Social Theories

The definition of a particular killing as murder requires the presence of a "third party" that has the social power to label the killing as morally reprehensible.[9] This labeling in turn requires a consensus among those involved that this third party is the only party with the legitimate right to take action. This consensus means that the disputants give up the right to seek revenge or justice on their own. In modern society, this third party typically includes a government, formal law, police, and the courts that have what sociologist Max Weber (1948:78) calls a legitimated "monopoly of the use of physical force within a given territory." This is in contrast to societies that do not have a powerful government and where, as a result, disputes are settled in confrontations between the two parties and the friends or kin of each. In such societies where there is no powerful third party, disputants, their friends, and their relatives often rely on a "code of honor" that emerges between groups that are roughly matched in terms of weapons and warriors. Codes of honor can result in feuds in which revenge and counterrevenge killings between such roughly matched groups in turn lead to high death tolls.

A second way of looking at killing is advanced by criminologists Michael Gottfredson and Travis Hirschi (1990), who point out that murder is typically a subset of other events such as fighting and arguments. Their research into homicides reported to the police in the United States shows that most murder occurs in the context of interpersonal conflict. In their formulation, murder is understood as the extreme by-product of a broader category of arguments and altercations.[10] They point out that in the modern United States, about 50 percent of all homicides are a consequence of interpersonal conflict, with 20 percent being a by-product of robbery or burglary that began as one crime but ended as murder. As a result, Gottfredson and Hirschi correlate levels of murder and violent death with how effectively interpersonal conflict is controlled within a society. They point out that the regulation of interpersonal conflict often occurs in contexts beyond the control of particular disputants.

A third sociological view is that which emerges from the tradition of the French sociologist Emile Durkheim. He pointed out that society itself is impossible without a reaction to crimes that identify what is considered right and wrong. From this line of reasoning, it follows that punishment for murder (or any crime) is necessary for the restoration of a moral order that is violated by unsanctioned killing. Such Durkheimian theory asserts that the amount and type of punishment undertaken in a particular society reflect a need to maintain a moral order as much as they reflect a demand for "justice" for a particular offender or victim.

Sociologist Kai Erikson has been particularly articulate in pointing out, in Durkheim's tradition, that the extent to which crime is punished in a particular society is often a function of how secure the ruling elite is. If the elite is insecure, the threat offered by an internal or external threat is likely to be highlighted, and a campaign to protect morals and "the people" is likely to be embarked upon. In cases where an internal threat emerges to the existing power structure, that society is likely to respond by righteously criminalizing acts that might have been ignored at other times in a way that focuses punishment on the marginalized and deviant. In cases of external threats such as war, the society's punitive ferocity is focused outward, and the actions of its own members are less likely to be found deviant. In either case, the moral order is maintained through the act of declaring someone, either an insider or outsider, in violation of a particular moral standard. In this context, Durkheim and Erikson write, laws evolve. For example, as a result of such evolution, honor killings that were defined as justifiable in the nineteenth century because they were committed in the context of a duel or fight were redefined as manslaughter or murder in the twenty-first century.

Explanatory comments throughout this book explore the ways in which each of these three theoretical approaches can be used effectively in particular cases. Some of the implications of each approach will be explained in further detail, beginning with the theories of Max Weber and Mark Cooney. In later chapters, these three approaches will be explored in depth using case studies.

The Criminalization of Murder and the State: Cooney and Weber

If the act of killing is only defined as murder when there is a public reaction, how do the act and reaction get joined? Based on anthropological and sociological data from many societies, Mark Cooney (1997a, 1997b, 1998, and 2003) concluded that a reaction of a powerful and legitimated third party is what distinguishes ordinary noncriminal killing from murder.[11] What is more, Cooney argues that this reaction is usually a good thing; particularly in transparent and democratic societies, a predictable and reliable third-party judgment is consistent with overall *lower* levels of violent death. In other words, at least some justice systems work to control violence. Cooney's assumption is that when there is a general understanding that an appeal is made to a powerful authority figure, a slight, accident, or issue of honor is *less* likely to be settled privately. If a powerful third party is present, the incident is more likely to be dealt with through nonviolent means such as avoidance, negotiation, or simply toleration.

To understand why third parties or governments are important to the maintenance of order, it helps to also understand how justice works when there are only two parties, that is, disputants without a legitimated third party. Cooney (1998) writes that this essentially is what happens in societies beyond the effective control of a chief, king, or state. In these societies, everyday disputes are more likely to lead to extended feuds between two groups because both groups judge independently the slight and because they are also in a position to exact the righteous vengeance they deem appropriate. Such judgment inherently involves a conflict of interest, and peaceful strategies of avoidance, toleration, or negotiation become less likely.

Cooney documents that in such stateless societies there is a higher rate of violent death than societies where a government successfully asserts its legitimated monopoly over the use of force (Cooney 1997a; Weber 1948:78). If there is no government or effective third party, anyone suffering an affront must seek justice on his or her own behalf. In such cases, if an assault occurs, the person feeling the grievance does not go to a third party such as the police or the courts, but seeks righteous revenge on his or her own. Or, perhaps the elder of the offended person seeks compensation for the attack from the family of the person causing offense. If the compensation is refused, victims and their kin may seek compensation through force and attack. This in turn is an assault on the honor of the person attacked, and a feud between the two parties results. Particularly if the two parties are evenly matched in their capacity to deliver a violent response, such feuds can last a long time without a surrender. In such a context, even if the original grievance is forgotten, victims from each side seek to protect their own honor in the context of ongoing attacks, some of which may be lethal.

The classical sociologist Max Weber (1948:78) wrote that the advantage of having a legitimated, effective, and powerful third party is that for all potential parties, the "state is considered the sole source of the 'right' to use violence," not only presumably in issues of justice but also in the collection of taxes, military draft, compulsory school attendance, power of arrest, punishment, incarceration, and even execution.[12] In effect, instead of it being normative to respond violently in the interest of your group against another, the dispute is handed over to a third party (the state), which is ideally assumed by both parties to be neutral, incorruptible, and powerful enough to have the final word. In the process, the conflict of interest inherent to two-party feuds, in which judge and jury are typically kin, is resolved.

What Cooney is saying is that in most cases, when a legitimated police and court system (i.e., a third party) becomes powerful, the overall level of violence in a society declines.[13] This is because the third party has the capacity to efficiently, forcefully, and legitimately enforce the laws, or, more generally, because "civilization" defines particular acts as criminal and illegitimate not only for the two parties but for society.[14] In the case of killing, this means they can define some killings as murder worthy of official response while labeling other killings as justifiable homicides. Cooney's point is that when this happens, a member of a particular society is *less* likely to die by someone seeking revenge who takes action into his or her own hands. Cooney explains this by comparing what happens in states that have a legitimated government with what happens in two types of small societies where there is no legitimate government. The first type is the classic stateless area beyond the boundaries of conventional governments. The second type is areas *within* jurisdictions where there is a strong state, but the police are distrusted. He calls these areas "virtually stateless."

An example of a remote stateless society is the Ju/' Hoansi of southern Africa (Lee 1979; Cooney 1997a), which Cooney uses to illustrate how issues of honor and blood revenge lead to high rates of killing. Among the Ju/' Hoansi, an attack on one member of a clan is considered to be an attack on the entire clan. In this context, retribution is sought, and these clans may feud for many years. Cooney (1997a) observes that the rates of violent death in the Ju/' Hoansi and other such populations are extraordinarily high because each assault results in a new call for blood revenge. This means that the shedding of blood by one group should lead to the shedding of compensatory blood by the other. Other research has shown that when such feuds become particularly intense, as many as one-third of all adults will die violently.[15] What is more, something like two-thirds of the survivors have participated in a killing. But such high mortality from private killing occurs only in groups beyond the control of governments, which do not have a legitimated third party to judge conflict and to pass judgment on who is at fault. The result is that all confrontation (lethal or not) is between two parties, and a formal code of honor rather than the rule of law is the arbiter. In these stateless societies, many members of each clan become both victim and victimizer.

But statelessness and the problem of two-party feuding is not found only in remote hunter-gatherer and horticultural societies. Cooney's point about the importance of a third party is also well illustrated by the concept of "virtual statelessness" found in the inner cities of the United States and other modern countries. In these cases, a strong state with a monopoly over the use of coercive power is not by itself enough. The state must also be *legitimate* if it is to be accepted as an effective third party. For example, in most areas of the United States today, arguments and fights that can escalate to feuds are much rarer than among groups like the Ju/' Hoansi. In part, this is because when a confrontation begins, often a threat to call the police is enough to strike fear into the hearts of the disputants and their kin. But even in the United States there are social areas that are "virtually" stateless, in which the threat to call the police works imperfectly because the police are distrusted or ineffective. In these places, even though police patrol cars and weapons may be available, combatants still appeal to friends and kin for revenge or protection, rather than to the police and courts of justice.

In the modern United States such virtual stateless areas include socially isolated minority communities who fear that the police will be arbitrary in the settlement of disputes, people who fear racial bias in the police response, and groups engaged in criminal activities, such as gangs. In such circumstances, honor and protection become justifications for violent behavior. Cooney uses the following quote to illustrate what happens when law is effectively unavailable and affronts are settled in the context of an urban code of honor:

> Don't be pushed around; if somebody insults you, assaults you, or steals your property, handle the problem yourself; do not run to the police because if you do, you might get into more serious trouble on the street [where the police are not perceived as an all-powerful, legitimate third party]. If the law does get involved in the case, it is all right to lie to officials to avoid going to jail or to send your enemies there. In capsule, law is the enemy; stand up for yourself. (Cooney 1997b:394–395, quoting from Anderson 1992)

Such virtual statelessness can be found within any population where police legitimacy is suspect. Members of criminal gangs might victimize each other, but because they cannot make an appeal to the police, they often seek revenge themselves and escalate the level of violence. This happens as people seek to resolve feuds and affronts of honor via two-party honor codes in a manner similar to the Ju/' Hoansi.

Killing and Interpersonal Conflict: Gottfredson and Hirschi

Murder is a personal act. One person causes another to die, and a murderer is often identified and held accountable. Modern law for this reason focuses on the intent of the individual. But from a sociological perspective, this is only part of the story. Also relevant is the context or "ecology" in which the violent act occurs. It is a matter of established criminological fact that murder is more likely to occur in some contexts (in bars, out-of-doors, in the presence of alcohol use, during summertime, on weekends, etc.) than in others, and that some types of people (young males, the intoxicated, and the poorly socialized) are more likely to kill and be killed than others.

Gottfredson and Hirschi (1990) indicate that killing in today's United States most often occurs as the consequence of unplanned interpersonal conflicts that escalate to a point that was not intended before the fight, argument, or altercation started. Typically, about half of the US homicides reported each year to the FBI result from such interpersonal conflict. An additional 20 percent start out as robbery or burglary but escalate to killing when the perpetrator becomes nervous or impulsive and/or the victim resists. Similar to killings that start out as interpersonal conflicts, these deaths were not intended before the event started; they were a by-product of events set in motion by a lesser criminal act. In other words, in the modern United States, about 70 percent of all murders reported to the police are unintended by-products of what normally would be lesser crimes, altercations, or arguments. Using this line of reasoning, Gottfredson and Hirschi conclude that homicide is often the unintended consequence of a confrontation by people with "low impulse control," a condition often exacerbated by alcohol or drugs. A good example is a case of fatal domestic violence, which typically is the consequence of ongoing fights and arguments within couples, of which only the last one is fatal.

Gottfredson and Hirschi's research points out that a typical murderer is a brawler, or, in other words, a person who impulsively solves problems through violence. The only difference between assault and murder is that one day the odd punch lands, and a neck is broken. Or, in the context of a domestic dispute where a couple has had numerous violent confrontations ending in trips to the hospital, police reports, and 911 calls finally ends fatally, perhaps because a loaded gun was handy. The homicide is only different in its consequences from this couple's "next-to-last" fight, which ended with two living disputants, rather than one dead victim and an incarcerated murderer. The lack of impulse control and the intent of the assailant to harm were the same in each of the two incidents. But one ended in murder.

Gottfredson and Hirschi note that the availability of weapons is an important part of the ecology of murder. In the case of handgun violence (the most common weapon inflicting lethal wounds in the United States), homicide is an ecological by-product of having a loaded weapon available, and of the precision of aim. In the case of domestic violence, the ecology might reflect the weight of the frying pan picked up for a "final" swing. In the case of a knife fight, the fact that an ambulance arrives two minutes late can be the ecological difference between a charge of homicide (when the victim bleeds to death) and a charge of assault (when the victim survives).

The power and authority of third parties are also part of the ecology of a situation. If a strong third party is available, individuals are less likely to take a swing during the heat of anger. Perhaps most troubling, the difference between an assault and a murder is also dependent on the ecology of the bystander, or how long a witness takes to call the police (Rosenthal 1964[1999]). There is often little difference in thought, intent, or character of a murderer, batterer, fighter, or armed robber. All that is different is the ecology of the situation leading to the victim's death. The case of assault or battery becomes a case of homicide due to the outcome of the situation; in other words, what varies is not the perpetrator but the consequences for the victim and the reaction of the state.

The mundane nature of most violent death is Gottfredson and Hirschi's main theme, and it is an important one, as it points out that most murder emerges out of situations—and not a murderous intent exclusive to those who actually kill. The logical conclusion is that if homicide is to be controlled, the situational nature of interpersonal violence can be regulated by limiting access to weapons, drugs, and alcohol, and restricting situations that lead to violence. Gottfredson and Hirschi assert that a particular level of interpersonal combat in a society—and the same availability of weapons—will result in a fairly constant number of violent confrontations that will end up lethal.

An example of the ecology of violence is illustrated by the argument that initiated the Hatfield and McCoy feud in 1882 (Waller 1988:71–73; MacClintock 1901). This is an old case, but it resonates with the type of conflicts that turn fatal, even today. The incident occurred on election day in Kentucky, a day liberally lubricated with drinking and brawling, when Tolbert McCoy asked Bad 'Lias Hatfield to repay a debt of $1.75 so that he could buy some more whiskey. Hatfield claimed he didn't owe the money. A fight ensued but was broken up by law enforcement officers. Ellison Hatfield, a relative of Bad 'Lias, responded by calling Tolbert McCoy a "coward" and challenging him to a knife fight. McCoy accepted, and the fight ensued. As Ellison Hatfield gained an advantage on Tolbert McCoy, a second McCoy joined in with another knife. In the melee, Ellison Hatfield was about to crush Tolbert McCoy's head with a rock when a third McCoy pulled out a pistol and shot Ellison in the back, inflicting the wound that ultimately killed him.

Social ecology theorists look at fights like this one and point out that a number of almost random circumstances came together to turn a minor disagreement over $1.75 into a killing. This ecology included the customs of nineteenth-century Appalachian elections that brought together guns, knives, alcohol, and male bravado. If the principals had been sober or unarmed, the fight might never have started—or would have concluded, as most fights do, without escalating to homicide. This ecology of weapons, alcohol, and male bravado leads to fights and potential killing not just in Appalachia but in modern bars, modern sporting events, and even college parties that have a similar ecological mix. As a result, social ecology theorists point to the regulation of such circumstances as a practical means to control the seriousness of violence. If you can remove potential weapons, alcohol, or the youthful bravado that contributes to this ecology, the likelihood of impulsive assault and fighting will decrease.

Indeed, modern society already regulates the social ecology of potentially violent situations by restricting access to alcohol and weapons at potentially volatile events. Some modern-day ecological regulations include restrictions on drinking ages, driver licensing, liquor licensing, enforcement of open bottle laws, enforcement of antiprostitution laws, curfew laws, gambling restrictions, vehicle registration requirements, and prohibiting the carrying of concealed weapons. These are all examples of government regulation aimed at controlling the ecology of potentially violent situations by extracting one "ingredient" that makes a normal situation more likely to turn violent, or even lethal. By the same principle, private means of controlling the ecology of such situations include the use of locks and security services. The point of such efforts is not to make a large number of arrests, but to limit the access of potential perpetrators and lessen the number of volatile situations such as easily started cars, unsecured property, situations of honor, and potential combatants.[16]

Why Definitions of Murder Are Different
Across Time and Place: Durkheim and Erikson

Sociologists Emile Durkheim (1895) and Kai Erikson (1966) both wrestled with the question of why, at different places and times, definitions of crime change. They believed that even in a "society of saints," something somehow would be defined as wrong and worthy of response by the group. This response is what the group uses to define who is a member in good standing and who is not.

For example, in the United States it is well established that legal definitions of homicide have shifted over the past two centuries. Two hundred years ago, dueling was legal and normative in many states. Indeed, Andrew Jackson killed or wounded several people in duels before becoming president of the United States. Today, meeting on a "field of honor" and killing an opponent is an open-and-shut case of first- or second-degree murder that would typically result in a life sentence. Many of the killings committed during the nineteenth century in the context of fighting, brawling, dueling, and "self-defense" would today result in prosecution. Certainly participation in a duel would be questioned in any political campaign, particularly one for the presidency.

New definitions of what is self-defense and what is not result from what Durkheim called the "normal evolution of morality and law" (Durkheim 1895:68–69). As social customs that were formerly normative become reprehensible, there will be expressions of moral outrage and efforts by "moral entrepreneurs" to stamp out a particular practice. Both morality and law may change in response. Durkheim asserted that crime is necessary for such changes in morals and definitions of crime to occur:

> Imagine a society of saints, a perfect cloister of exemplary individuals. Crimes, properly so called will there be unknown; but faults which appear venal to the layman will create there the same scandal. . . . If, then, this society has the power to judge and punish, it will define these acts as criminal and treat them as such . . .
> *Crime is then, necessary*; it is bound up with the fundamental conditions of all social life, and by that very fact it is useful, because these conditions of which it is a part are themselves indispensable in the normal evolution of morality and law. (quoted in Erikson 1966:26)

Though Durkheim asserted that crime is necessary to the development of new standards for normative and legal conduct, he did not believe that crime is desirable. Rather, he asserted that the *reaction* to crime is necessary to the development of law and social order. Understanding why crime is necessary is key to understanding why definitions of murder and self-defense changed so much during the past 200 years. By understanding this point we will come to see how the United States gradually changed from a society in which lethal duels were normative (and practitioners even eligible for the honor of the presidency) to one today, where the same act would well result in the dishonor of a life sentence in the state penitentiary.

Durkheim's point is best illustrated in Kai Erikson's book *Wayward Puritans*, which concerns deviance in Puritan Massachusetts in the seventeenth century. The Puritans very explicitly tried to establish an exemplary society in which there would be no deviants and no crime. They excluded from Massachusetts anyone they considered to be criminal by refusing them passage from England. And yet, as Erikson's book shows, challenges to this vision of an ideal society nevertheless emerged, as Durkheim's theory would predict. In the case of the Puritans, Erikson writes, the deviance that emerged was focused on crimes against the religion that was at the heart of Puritan identity. Erikson claims that there were three major "crime waves" within the first sixty years that the colony was in the New World: (1) a theological dispute in 1636–1637 that resulted in the expulsion of dissenters; (2) an "invasion" by Quakers in the late 1650s and 1660s during which severe punishments were exacted, including banishment, ear amputation, whipping, and hanging; and (3) an attack on "witches" during the period of the

Salem witch trials in 1691 in which nineteen persons were hanged and three others died. In each of these three examples, the "crimes" were, by modern standards, imaginary. This drives home Erikson's (and Durkheim's) central point that in a society where there is no crime, it is necessary that *something* emerge that will help define what is moral and what is not. In the case of the Puritans, the "crimes" that emerged were focused by religion, including theological disputes, Quakerism, and witchcraft.

In each case, the criminalization of these behaviors resulted in a wave of punishment or a moral panic that became more extreme over time and finally disappeared as the behaviors were either eliminated or permitted to become normative. For example, despite the persecution of Quakers in the late 1650s and early 1660s, Quakerism was legalized by the end of the 1660s, and witchcraft was eliminated as a capital crime just a few months after the Salem hangings.

The irony in Erikson's examples is today revisited whenever a new policy is labeled as a "witch hunt." For example, in the twentieth-century United States, both the anticommunism impulse of the 1950s and the Prohibition-era ban on alcohol were similar attempts to declare previously normative behavior as deviant. In each case, the focus of these moral panics became normative again after the government found out that the "enemy" could not be beat. Notably, by such reasoning, it will not be surprising if the "War on Drugs" conducted in the 1980s and 1990s will suffer a similar fate.

Erikson asserts that it is just as important to evaluate a society's reaction to and definition of deviance as it is to evaluate the deviant act itself. Crime is necessary, but the whole apparatus of law enforcement can collapse on itself if it crosses the invisible line between when it is legitimate to vigorously enforce laws and when it is not. And herein lies a lesson for understanding why and how concerns about criminal assault and murder seem to rise, even when rates of overall interpersonal violence fall. What happens is that as one form of violence disappears (e.g. dueling), society searches for another act that will be identified as venal and deviant so that a new moral crusade can begin. This crusade is as much about the need to reinforce the moral order as it is about what has come to be thought of as venal.

A good example is the case of domestic violence, which was considered to be beyond the interests of the government as recently as the 1960s. One result of such official disinterest was that there were low rates of domestic violence reported to the police since it was often considered illegitimate for the police to intervene in a family dispute, even a violent one. However, particularly in the 1980s, feminists and law-and-order conservatives alike began a crusade to criminalize domestic violence, and both reports to police and arrests rose. It is unclear as of this writing whether this crusade against domestic violence will effectively limit this form of violence as indeed dueling was limited. It is apparent, though, that violence once considered the business of the family is now reacted to much more aggressively by the law and police. Most jurisdictions report rises in the rates of arrests and victim reports, even as the actual number of incidents of domestic violence (reported and unreported) may well be declining.

So a society's definitions of crime and murder change or, to use Durkheim's word, "evolve," and behaviors that were once declared deviant (e.g., dueling, fighting, domestic violence, and even witchcraft) first come to be seen as common but then disappear. However, when the older form of deviance disappears, a new form must be defined. This evolution can have both good and bad consequences. On one hand, a general decline in the amount of violence between the nineteenth century and today, or between hunter-gatherer groups and modern societies, is in part explainable by the fact that more types of violent death are considered criminal now than in the past. On the other hand, when a society looks for new activity to criminalize, it can do so on the basis of arbitrary social traits, including race, political viewpoints, ethnicity, and religion. Indeed, Durkheim's approach also explains what happened when Adolf Hitler and the Nazi Party sought to redefine venality; they identified the Jewish population as deviant and adopted the policies leading to the Holocaust.

When the Third Party Kills: State-Sponsored Violence

The biggest purveyors of violence in the twentieth century were governments. Governments killed in the name of war, revolution, discipline, business, development, and racial superiority. Much of this killing has been purposive, in the form of genocidal policies, penal policies, laws, and war. But victims have also ended up dead when killing is incidental to policies of forced migration, agricultural reform, consumer product safety decisions, or military decisions inflicting "collateral damage" on civilian populations. However, as Cooney points out, the rates at which different types of governments kill vary. Those with high levels of totalitarian state control over citizens' lives are more likely to carry out policies of extermination of particular groups; open democratic capitalist societies, in contrast, are less likely to carry out such policies. But such societies also have a tendency to become involved in wars with high death rates.[17]

Summary

In this book the criminalization of murder is explored in two ways: first, by looking at murder as the act of killing and the reaction to it; and second, by using three social theories to look at these phenomena from different perspectives. These three theories are:

1. Third-party theories, focusing on the nature of the state and its interest in controlling illegitimate violence by establishing a legitimate monopoly on the use of violence. Such theories imply that societies where most people believe in the fairness, effectiveness, and legitimacy of police action are more peaceful than those lacking such beliefs.

2. Social ecology theories, focusing on the actual act of homicide. Social control theories assert that most murder is the result of impulsive acts that occur in the context of a fight, argument, or altercation in which elements such as alcohol, a weapon, and male bravado are present. Data from the modern United States indicate that most homicide is of this nature. An important point made by these theories is that murder is a subset of violent crime, and not usually the result of planning or forethought. That is, most murder is a by-product of a situation in which an argument, assault, robbery, burglary, or other altercation occurs. Social ecology theorists point out that the murder rate is a function of a much larger assault/altercation/robbery rate in which only a limited number of incidents become fatal. The fact that incidents are fatal, these theories assert, is not so much an issue of intent but is often due to ecological factors, such as the fact that a lethal weapon was handy, a witness did not react quickly, or a gun was loaded.

3. Durkheim's and Erikson's theories, focusing on how laws and the definitions of crime change. These theories emphasize the social reaction to murder (or any other crime), and how that reaction reaffirms the integrity of the social order. This means that it is important to pay attention to how different types of killing are judged as either justifiable, wrong, evil, good, or necessary. Durkheimian theory asserts that the definition of murder (or any crime) changes over time in response to a society's capacity to control a particular type of behavior. This theory is useful for explaining how killings that were once permissible become illegal and subject to severe penalties.

While these theories do not exhaust the theoretical approaches to understanding crime or killing, they are useful in understanding both the act of murder and the broader social reaction to murder. The three theories are applicable to many situations, and they help to explain a great deal of data about murder and killing.

Finally, although the subject of this book is murder and killing, these theoretical approaches can be used to evaluate how rule-making and rule-breaking occur for acts of less import, such as assault, drunk driving, alcohol prohibition, or different types of theft. Everything that is today defined as being criminal has been through a criminalization process at some time. By understanding how the most heinous of crimes—murder—has been criminalized, it becomes possible to understand how and why an act that was normative (or merely deviant but not illegal) becomes a focus for control by the government.

Notes

1. The statistics of murder are included in Appendix 1.

2. Miethe and Regoeczi 2004:15–23 discuss effectively how different types of biological, psychological, and sociological approaches have been used to study homicide. Most relevant here are their point about how the "definition of the situation" inheres to the issue of killing and homicide, as well as any other criminological issue.

3. See Appendix 2 for actual examples of legal statutes, in this case from Texas and California.

4. The Texas statute in part reflected varying legal definitions of "insanity" rooted in the unusual western concept going back at least to the 1843 case of Daniel M'Naghten, who tried to kill the prime minister of England but instead killed his secretary. M'Naghten was not considered guilty in the legal sense because of his insanity (see Daly and Wilson 1988:261–269).

5. The main distinction in the official FBI reports is in justifiable and nonjustifiable homicide. No systematic legal distinction is made between different types of homicide; the statistic generated lumps together first-degree murder, second-degree murder, and several types of manslaughter. In the 2001 FBI reports an exception, "act of war," was added as an asterisk following the September 11, 2001, terrorist attacks in Washington DC, New York, and Pennsylvania. These deaths were excluded from 2001 homicide statistics. In contrast, the 168 deaths in the Federal Building in Oklahoma City, Oklahoma, in 1995 were categorized as homicide and were included in the statistics reported by the FBI the following year. The FBI statistics are reflected in Appendix 1.

6. For a partial exception, see Diamond 1991.

7. Donald Black (1976, 1993) has written a great deal about how the quantity and quality of law affect social control in any particular society. My analysis here follows in this tradition.

8. The shorthand way to describe the utility of any theory is to evaluate its parsimony (i.e., simple in structure and description), robustness (i.e., applies to many conditions), and accuracy (i.e., makes predictions and generalizations that match the known data). The way to challenge a theory is to find a more parsimonious, robust, and/or accurate way to explain the same data or problem.

9. The term *third party* as used here is consistent with what Cooney (1997a) and Black (1993:95–124) write.

10. Cooney (1998) makes a distinction between moral and predatory killing. By moral killing he means killing that emerges out of personal feelings of being wronged due to a verbal or physical slight. Predatory killing is the planned stuff of movies and drama in which killing is done to further a financial or other form of profit. Cooney points out that moral killing accounts for 70–80 percent of the homicide cases in the United States. Predatory killing constitutes the remainder.

11. Cooney is a student of Donald Black (1976, 1993), who has written a great

deal about the role that law plays in ordering social action. Particularly relevant for this book are Black's ideas about the strength of the law and legal systems in social control. Black's studies introduced the use of anthropological data in assessing how law is an effective means to create and regulate modern society. This book follows in that tradition.

12. John Locke (1690), writing in the same tradition as Thomas Hobbes, emphasized that order created by a sovereign was necessary for a civil society. In other words, the power is the source of civil order.

13. Cooney also discusses the relationship between states with "too much" power (such as totalitarian states) and violent death. See Chapter 5.

14. Recently, Cooney (2003) has described how both Elias (1939) and Black (1993) have developed this point.

15. See Hill and Hurtado's (1996) description of violence and mortality among the Ache in Paraguay/Brazil.

16. An interesting way to think about this principle is to look at the nature of "third party" auto insurance, which is in fact a means of controlling the ecology of a confrontation. Requiring all drivers to have a deep-pocketed third party means that in the event of an accident, it is not necessary to use a threat of retaliation to extract just compensation; rather, the third party automatically assumes responsibility for the consequences, no matter who was at fault.

17. No continent or people has had a monopoly on state-sponsored cruelty. Since 1492, victims have often been a by-product of Europe's colonial expansion. But, in the long run, as Jared Diamond (1992) points out, the phenomenon is found on every continent, and in many types of societies.

CHAPTER 2

The Invention of Murder: Killing and the Law

The Difference Between Killing and Murder

Historically, killing has not usually been considered criminal. Courts, judges, and the rule of law are not universal, and as a result, a formal definition of crime is not found at every time and in every place. In fact, formal crime is a relatively recent innovation in most parts of the world. To have the rule of law and the judges and legal statutes that go with it, a government that will react by forcing compliance when necessary and prevent others from taking the law into their own hands is necessary. Indeed, philosophers like Thomas Hobbes, John Locke, and Jean-Jacques Rousseau believe that if one person harms another, the person wronged has a natural right to compensation.

This chapter is concerned with how and why people all over the world surrender their personal right to seek righteous revenge and grant it to powerful governments who through their legal systems seek justice on the behalf of victims. This is a great benefit much of the time; when a powerful government emerges, individuals no longer need to guarantee their own safety or seek revenge when they are wronged. But, as will be seen, such institutions also carry great risks. The capacity to administer justice includes the kind of power that can create malevolent or violent elitist rulers. At extremes, this power creates brutal but legal regimes like Nazi Germany and Joseph Stalin's Soviet Russia, where substantial proportions of the population died violently as a result of wars and mass executions conducted by the state.[1]

Mark Cooney (1997a, 1998:22–66) graphed the relationship between state power and found that it followed a "U" shape (see Figure 2.1).[2] This graph shows how in places where there is little state power, every clan or family fends for itself when it comes to insisting on its own rights and privileges. In the event of a dispute, the only way to seek righteousness is to

Figure 2.1 Cooney's "U" Describing the Relationship Between State Power and Violence

When state authority is absent, rates of lethal conflict are absent due to on-going feuding and attacks by small kin-based groups. When state authority is strong, rates of lethal conflict rise again as totalitarian and authoritarian states seek to preserve the power of elites through the use of execution and war. The most peaceful type of societies are democratic ones where elites must seek the consent of the governed. Such states can control anarchy, but without resorting to the excesses of authoritarian/totalitarian rule (Cooney 1997a).

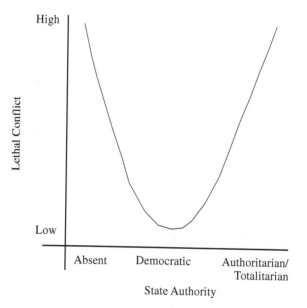

engage in a two-party negotiation, avoidance, or negotiation (Black 1993:74–96). There is no recourse to a powerful "third party" judge to resolve the issue. When this happens, extraordinarily violent feuds between two groups that are evenly matched in terms of warriors and weaponry tend to emerge. This is why in "stateless" societies, rates of violence are high. When a government emerges that is strong and close to the people governed, overall violence rates tend to drop.

Such closeness to the ground is what is found in modern democracies where governments are deposed through an election or other peaceful political means focused by law. This "just right" balance between the power of the state and its responsiveness to the people is, according to Cooney, as important for lowering levels of violence as is the presence of effective law. But what happens when state power becomes more all-pervasive, and the government begins to regulate daily routines of the citizens? In this circumstance, the distance increases between those who rule and the citizens. In such circumstances, governments seek control through the use of fear, extreme violence, and a pervasive sense that it can monitor and see everything. Such was found in totalitarian states such as Germany during the Nazi era, the Soviet Union, and Cambodia under the Khmer Rouge. And the overall violence rate begins to approach what is found in stateless societies, where chaotic feuding is so common.

Therefore, this chapter will first explore the reasons why anarchic stateless societies seek to establish governments as a way to control violent behavior and, hence, killing. In effect, this chapter describes the left side of Cooney's U-shaped curve, thereby showing how and why judicious application of criminal law results in a more peaceful society. (Chapter 5 will describe the right-hand side of the curve, wherein state-sponsored violence, including that of the modern era, can kill at horrific rates.)

Underlying this chapter is what sociologist Max Weber (1947:78) called the "monopoly of the legitimate use of physical force within a given territory." This monopoly maintains an order that protects people from being attacked, protects private property, exacts righteous revenge on behalf of crime victims, and prevents victims (and their kin) from taking revenge on their own behalf. The monopoly over the use of force (or violence) is typically legitimated by a population that willingly surrenders the right to take personal revenge, because the alternative—anarchy—is so threatening. In turn, this monopoly is maintained through a mix of respect and/or fear of the government, which as Weber points out is inherently violent. It is only under such circumstances that killing is reframed as the formal crime of murder. When this happens, governments are created that give officials—be they patriarchs, chiefs, nobles, kings, judges, or bureaucrats—the final word in the legitimate punishment of criminal offenders.

When a government has a monopoly on the use of physical force in a given territory, it becomes what Cooney calls a third party that can step in and settle disputes on behalf of the victimized (Cooney 1997). In criminal courts, governments do this in the form of arrest, public conviction, and punishment. In such a system, the victim or the victim's kin cannot take "self-help" retribution. Anyone doing this challenges the state's right to rule, and the state will punish such individuals for taking the law into their own hands, irrespective of the justice of the precipitating incident.

However, for the monopoly over the use of coercive force to be effective in restricting such two-party violence, it is necessary for the state's power to be taken for granted by the population or, in other words, be considered *legitimate*. What is more, the population must comply willingly with the implied use of force if a more complex legal order, in which "criminals" can be systematically identified and punished, is to be successful. This legal order is one in which individuals are of equal status with accusers and jurors (or, in the words of the United States Constitution, peers) before the law. In such a legal system it is assumed that everyone will be held similarly accountable in a fair fashion, and that if there is a transgression, the powerful third party will seek a just compensation in order to right a wrong.

But there is a catch. Raw coercive power is not enough to create a civil society. A government that is careless, arbitrary, or cruel in the use of coercive power risks the loss of its legitimacy. A loss of legitimacy, or even a weakened legitimacy, means that taken-for-granted cooperation with the government (including the collection of taxes and appeals to the state for the settlement of disputes) becomes more difficult, and revolt is risked. When this happens, small groups form to assert their rights and protect themselves against others doing the same, irrespective of the wider sense of governmental justice or law. In the well-known words of sixteenth-century political philosopher Thomas Hobbes, an ethic of "all against all" emerges, and life becomes "nasty, brutish and short." That states *usually* avoid all such challenges to legitimacy is an important testimony to both how important governments are in the modern world and how fearsome anarchy is. Nevertheless, the granting of coercive power to a government is always a tenuous thing; the capacity of a government to coerce compliance can wax and wane. Thus, when legitimacy increases, citizens are more likely to use the state to settle disputes and are less likely to seek compensation or revenge on their own behalf. But the opposite is also true. In places where the legitimacy of the law decreases, people are more likely to ignore the state and seek revenge on their own behalf. A contemporary example of how important legitimacy is in the policing of a society is provided by Iraq, which the United States invaded in 2003. The greatly feared—but legitimated—authority of Saddam Hussein was easily swept away by the US forces. But legitimacy and trust were not automatically transferred to the militarily victorious Americans and their allies. Indeed, when the Americans were unable to effectively mediate between competing groups, they lost control over the monopoly over the use of coercive force. Civil war broke out, and secretive revenge killings and executions became common.

Anarchy, Statelessness, Legitimate Authority, and Cooney's "U"

In Hobbes's description of a society of all against all, there are no rules, much less someone to enforce them. Therefore, there is no trade, strangers are dangerous, and any personal encounter is potentially violent. In such a society, personal strength is the most important thing, and loyalty is only assured among immediate kin. According to Hobbes, this creates a life that is nasty, brutish, and short, particularly during times when food is lacking, or when land or resources are in short supply. The thought of living in such a society engenders fear, and it is not particularly surprising that people everywhere seek a powerful third party to administer justice.

A good way to think about how the third party works (and doesn't work) is to look at three different types of statelessness, and the patterns of violence that emerge in each. These include traditional stateless areas where there is no government, societies in which the state is weak and cannot regulate powerful elites, and the virtually stateless areas of modern societies.

Traditional Premodern Stateless Societies

Premodern stateless societies are groups in which there is no state and never has been one. These are the foraging, horticultural, and pastoral societies in which there is no legitimate king, queen, or chief to appeal to when someone is wronged. Until the first chiefdoms—the earliest form of government—began emerging in horticultural societies about 5,000–7,000 years ago, all human societies were stateless. Such societies were equal in the sense that there were no extremes of wealth, and all members hunted, farmed, herded, or gathered. Such premodern societies were small but typically had very strong norms of loyalty, kinship, and group identity. In issues of justice, individuals appealed to friends and family in order to assert their position. And this probably worked as long as the small group stayed isolated from strangers (see Signe and Willis 1988). Nevertheless, such isolation from nonhostiles was often difficult to sustain across long periods, and ongoing feuding between small groups of kin and attacks from unrelated neighbors were often a major cause of death. What leadership there was often reflected the skilled use of personal violence and displays of courage by "big men."

Transitionally Stateless Societies

When societies first create a state, the monopoly on the use of coercive power is weak because the people do not yet have routine access to courts or police. People continually negotiate between traditional norms and the new power of the state. This was the case in early modern Europe and in some parts of the third world today, where older systems of justice exist side by side with an emerging state in a condition known as *legal pluralism*. Often, such societies have a high degree of inequality. Elites are still good fighters—although they may be military officers who organize others to fight, rather than having only personal fighting skills. But as individuals, they are beyond the reach of both the new courts *and* traditional law due to their high status. The lower classes may well display less violence due to fear and/or respect for the new monopoly over the use of violence. In this situation, violence among elites often remains high, as such "big men" still seek to prove themselves through the use of violence and displays of personal courage. These displays are usually denied to commoners, whose access to weapons is limited by law; the common people are subject to arrest in the event that they use violence. In many such transitional societies, the elite are likely to engage in unpunished feuding, brawling, dueling, and lynching; and the coercive power of the new state is directed at the lower classes.

The Modern World and Its Virtually Stateless Areas

Virtually stateless areas are found in modern urban bureaucratized societies, including the United States. Despite well-financed and strong systems of law, there are areas where a lack of legitimacy, or a difference in customs, means that police cannot easily resolve disputes. Typically, this occurs among the poor and marginalized people who are the focus of the laws and prohibitions emerging from conventional, mainstream society.

In the modern world, conventional areas of society—including the vast suburbs of middle-class America—are relatively peaceful (Baumgartner 1988). Even though they rarely do so, suburbanites believe they can take advantage of policing and courts, and that these institutions will treat them in a just fashion. As a result, even when provoked they will rarely confront a deviant. In such circumstances, conventional people abhor personal displays of violence by the elite or anyone else, and they avoid personal confrontation. The few confrontations that do occur are dealt with on a personal level and rarely escalate to an ongoing lethal feud.[3] What is more, they believe that if they take matters into their own hands, they will be arrested by the government. These same beliefs and assumptions are not shared at the margins of these societies, where there is often distrust and hostility toward the idea of involving police and courts in dispute resolution. In marginalized and virtually stateless areas, people do not believe that the police will seek justice on their behalf, and they are therefore more likely to engage in "self-help justice." Or, as Donald Black (1993:11) characterizes it, law, whether from a third party or elsewhere, becomes less available. In modern cities, this includes

- Neighborhoods where ethnic minorities and immigrants are distrustful of the law, the police, and the courts
- Remote areas in which the presence of the police is absent due to lack of communication and transportation
- Cults that rely on a single charismatic leader and seek guidance in matters of justice only from that person

- The social space between drunk persons, which is often stateless as the alcohol gives each individual a heightened sense of control in a potentially violent situation
- Youth and low-status individuals, who often distrust the police and the legal system
- The social and emotional space between lovers, spouses, parents and children, and siblings, which makes it difficult for the law to intervene
- Two states that each have their own monopoly on the use of legitimated force (which is why border areas can be more anarchic than other parts of a country)
- Prisoners, who often have their own informal codes for behavior and prefer to handle their own disputes—despite the fact that guards are nearby and have ready access to lethal weapons
- Street gangs, which do not appeal to police for the resolution of disputes
- The social space between individuals undertaking criminal activity, which is always stateless

Reciprocity, Righteousness, and Justice

At the heart of all justice systems is a belief that when a person is wronged by another, he or she has a right to seek compensation. Indeed, such a need for justice is at the heart of many religions traditions. Much of Islamic, Judaic, and Christian scripture concerns rules of compensation that must be applied in the event of a wrongful death, theft, adultery, injury, and a wide range of other offenses. Under such codes, if an object is stolen, the thief must compensate the victim for the loss. If a domestic animal is killed through negligence, the negligent person must compensate the owner. If someone is unjustly insulted, the perpetrator should offer an apology and an acknowledgment of fault. And finally, if someone is unjustly killed, a life should be offered in compensation, whether in the form of slavery, execution, or a life of imprisonment. Perhaps the best known of such compensation codes is the Old Testament assertion that just compensation requires an eye for an eye, a tooth for a tooth, and a life for a life. Implicitly, the alternative to this just compensation is a righteous rage in which forceful restoration of rights is legitimate.[4]

The concept of righteous compensation or moral reciprocity may well be found in all societies. But how "wrongful" events are interpreted is embedded in cultural expectations, which means that the devil is in the detail of individual and group-based interpretations. Even in societies with a body of written laws and powerful courts to enforce them, it is not likely that every situation will be resolved to the satisfaction of all. As a result, technical investigations are undertaken by judges trained to identify the "truth" relative to the law. This truth is used to decide who owes what to whom, or who has a right to receive righteous compensation.

Traditional Statelessness, Transitional Statelessness, and Two-Party Justice

In asking why some third-party justice systems work to temper violence, it is useful to think about what happens in the absence of any government. That is, what are two-party justice systems like? How is social order maintained in the traditional premodern stateless society? To review, in stateless areas, group identity is extremely important, because only the small, intimate kin group is trusted and asserts rights to compensation when a member is wronged. Disputes are not settled by powerful outsiders, but by disputants (and their kin) who often are unable to agree on whether a field, hunting territory, wife, or fishing ground belongs to one person or group or to another. This most often happens when there is either an environmental catastrophe or a rapid increase in population. The result is that loyalty to kin becomes more important than loyalty to an abstract law or ethic. In such a situation, any stranger is a potential enemy and therefore a potential threat; safety is only found among people with whom there is a close personal bond.

Justice and Kinship: Traditional Statelessness

The most obvious place that two-party justice systems are found is in societies that are beyond the effective control of any state. Today such societies include only small hunter-gatherer societies, remote scattered villages involved in horticulture, and pastoral societies that follow herds of domestic animals in remote areas. Such stateless areas have shrunken and almost disappeared, as the power of the modern state has spread rapidly, particularly during the past 500 years.[5]

But for much of history, such statelessness was the feature of most societies. Alliances to seek rights and compensation formed along clan lines, and in the process they also reinforced clan divisions. Cooney (2003) calls these societies "group oriented," because offenses against one member of the clan are considered to be an offense against all. What is more, when punishment is meted out, it is against the clan, and not necessarily against the individual who actually committed the offense. In such stateless societies there are no prisons; after all, prisons are not found in places without fixed buildings, and in fact they are found primarily in rich societies that can afford to feed a nonworking population.

In recent years anthropologists reconstructed the mortality rates among people living in remote areas beyond the reach of states. What they found is that violence in such societies is so high that it is common for 30–40 percent of the adult males to die violently, often across a period of decades. Table 2.1 is a compilation of data from studies about such stateless societies.[6] For comparative purposes the table includes statistics generated for societies with strong centralized governments, such as the Soviet Union and Nazi Germany. (Table 2.1 will be referred to again in Chapter 5.)

Consistently, the finding is that males who live to adulthood in stateless communities stand a high chance of killing and/or being killed. This is because fights, once initiated, become long-running feuds in which raids, brawls, and ritualized gladiatorial contests continually lead to serious wounding and even death as men seek to prove their fighting prowess. No particular battle has a high casualty rate, so there are few mass graves filled with bodies as might be found near modern battlefields, even though studies show that the persistence of feud violence leads to a high rate of violent death across many years or even decades. This is because the wounded, their kin, and the kin of those who have died demand the revenge they believe is their due—including another life. This demand for compensation is of course resisted by the opposing group, which often has a wholly different view of the balance sheet of fault and injury. This different view is why, in the absence of a legitimated all-powerful authority, feuds may persist over long spans of time.[7]

This type of statelessness can be described by looking at two very different modern stateless societies: the Ju/' Hoansi of Namibia, and the Ache of Paraguay. Both societies had high levels of violence in the twentieth century (some of which inevitably became lethal), despite the fact that they lack complex weapons.

The Ju/' Hoansi. The conclusion that many stateless groups in fact had high levels of violence was perhaps most surprising for those studying the Ju/' Hoansi, including anthropologist Richard Lee. The Ju/' Hoansi are a small population of hunter-gatherers who live in the Kalahari Desert in Namibia and speak a "click" language (thus the unusual transliteration of their name). Until recently, they had only casual contact with government authorities; indeed, it was only in the 1950s that the South African colonial government ruling Namibia sent officials into the area where the Ju/' Hoansi lived. The group was very peaceful in the 1960s, when Lee first studied and lived with them, and the initial impression presented to the anthropological world was that they were "the harmless people."[8] The fact that they had no firearms further contributed to this view. Such a view was sympathetically received in the West, which had recently endured World War II and was contemplating nuclear warfare.

However, stories collected from the Ju/' Hoansi by Lee[9] revealed that

Table 2.1 Violent Death Rates in Various Societies

	Time Period	Percentage of Adults Killed
Stateless Societies		
Waorani (Ecuador)	5 generations	61
Gebusi (New Guinea)	1940–1962	39
Males		
Achaura Jivaro (Ecuador-Peru)		59
Highland Albania	1901–1905	40
Yanomamo (Venezuela-Brazil)	1964–1987	30
Grand Valley Dani (New Guinea)		28
Mae Enga (New Guinea)		25
Huli (New Guinea)		13
Females		
Achuara Jivaro (Ecuador-Peru)		27

	Time Period	Deaths per 100,000 per year
Stateless Societies		
Gebusi (New Guinea)	1940–1962	683
Omu (New Guinea)	1896–1946	620
Goilala (New Guinea)	1896–1946	533
Anyana (New Guinea)	1924–1949	420
Murngin (Australia)	1906–1926	330
Yanomamo (Venez-Brazil)	1970–1974	166
Ju/' Hoansi (Botswana)	1920–1955	42
Societies with States		
France	1900–1990	58
Great Britain	1900–1990	26
United States	1900–1990	13
Democratic	1900–1987	10
Authoritarian	1900–1987	210
Totalitarian	1900–1987	400
Communist	1900–1987	420
Rwanda	1971–2000	167–334
Bodie, CA	1880s	116

Sources: Cooney 1997; McGrath 1984:253–255.
Note: Statistics for Rwanda assume the deaths of 500,000–800,000 in a population of 7–8 million.

from the 1920s to 1955, these small bands of hunter-gatherers had been torn by fighting. Survivors recounted 81 disputes, including 10 major arguments without blows, 34 involving fights without weapons, and 37 with weapons (Lee 1979:90). Fifteen of the 22 killings recounted to Lee involved feuding in which one killing was related to a previous lethal offense, or in other words revenge. As a result of this fighting there were at least 22 fatalities, and many more major woundings. This is an extraordinarily high death rate in a society that by 1968 included only 569 individuals (Howell 1979:45). What such a statistic means is that about 9.5 percent[10] of the males between ages 15 and 59 died violently during the period. By way of contrast, 0.7 percent of American deaths were from violent assault in 2002–2003.

The most lethal series of incidents among these "harmless people" began over a man's (Debe's) desire to take a girl (Tisa) as a second wife. This feud proceeded across many years as a series of brawls in which individuals, none of whom were associated with the original disputants, became renowned for being particularly cruel in their vengeful attacks. There were a total of nine killings during this particular feud, which occurred over a period of about twenty years from the 1930s to 1950s. Here, Debe and Kashe (Tisa's brother) describe one of the brawls:

Debe: We were all living together at Nwama. Bo started it by refusing me a wife. I wanted to marry Tisa and her mother and father gave me permission, but Bo had already married Tisa's older sister, and wanted to take [Tisa] as a second wife, so he refused me.

There was a big argument, and fighting broke out. Bo yelled at my younger sister, "What is your brother doing marrying my wife? I'm going to kill you!" He shot [a poisoned] arrow at her and missed. Then Bo came up to me to kill me, but my father came to my aid. Then Samkau came to Bo's aid. Samkau shot at me but missed; my father [Hxome] speared Samkau in the chest under the armpit. Samkau's father, Gau, seeing his own son speared, came to his aid and fired a poisoned arrow into my father's thigh. I was shooting at Bo but missed him.

[Kashe continued the story]:

Kashe: Then Debe's father, Hxome, stabbed Gau with his spear. Gau put up his hand to protect himself and the spear went right through it. Samkau rushed at Hxome with his spear and tried to spear him in the ribs. At first the spear jammed, but then it went all through.

In the meantime several side fights were going on. My older brother dodged several arrows and then shot Debe's sister in the shoulder blade (she lived). I dodged arrows by two men and then hit one of them in the foot with a poisoned arrow.

After being hit with a poisoned arrow in the thigh and speared in the ribs, Hxome fell down, mortally wounded. Half-sitting, half-lying down, he called for allies. "I'm finished, my arms are stilled. At least shoot one of them for me."

But no more shooting happened that day. We went away and came back the next morning to see Hxome writhing in his death throes. He had been given cuts to draw off the poison, but the poison was in too deep, and he died. We left Nwama, and came back [to camp] at Xai-xai. (Lee 1979:93–96)

In this particular brawl there were friends and relations nearby, some of whom as an expression of loyalty immediately joined in. Many were hurt and wounded, irrespective of whether they participated in the original offense. This immediately created more grievances, and each wounding intensified the fear, anger, and need for retribution. There was also a fatality, and considering the anguish and anger the slain Hxome's relatives (and the many wounded bystanders) must have felt, it is not surprising that feuds such as this one continued for many years.

Interestingly, Lee indicates that at least twice in the thirty-year period he studied, "this egalitarian society constituted itself a state and took upon itself the powers of life and death." In both instances, former Ju/'Hoansi enemies came together to informally pronounce a death sentence over men whose violent natures were a threat to the larger group. In the first case, a man named Twi, who had killed three people, was ambushed by his own community in broad daylight. Each of the men present took turns shooting arrows at Twi until "he looked like a porcupine." After Twi was dead, each of the men and women stabbed his body with a spear, so that the responsibility for the execution would be shared.

The second execution was even more dramatic and ended the feud Debe described earlier, some ten years after the death of Hxome. This death sentence involved Gau, a man who had also killed three people (including Hxome). Debe's account recalls a conversation with his uncle as they contemplated the appropriate response for their clan. Note the emphasis on seeking reciprocity as they contemplate whom to attack:

Debe: [I said] "You are right to seek revenge. I am going to kill Bo who started it all."

"No" [my uncle said] "Bo is just a youngster, but Gau is a senior man . . . and he is the one who has killed another [senior man], Hxome. I am going to kill him so that [senior men] will be dead on both sides."

One evening [my uncle] walked right into Gau's camp and without saying a word shot three arrows into Gau, one in the left shoulder, one in the forehead, and a third in his chest. Gau's people made no move to protect him. (Lee 1979:96)

The critical point in this account is that in a "normal" two-party justice system, Gau's people were responsible for protecting Gau and his clan by attacking Debe's uncle. That they did not was a silent acknowledgment by

Gau's family that despite clan loyalty, Gau was at fault, and a righteous compensation for his "crimes" was his execution. In such a small society all protection from arbitrary attack comes only from one's own immediate kin, and not a powerful "third party." This required great courage by Debe's uncle, who by all rights should have been immediately counterattacked. But because this counterassault was not made, the feud was over. As Lee writes, for only the briefest of moments there was a consensus that violence could be used without contestation.

The Ache of Paraguay and club fights. The Ache were a stateless group of hunters and horticulturalists living in remote areas of Paraguay. They came into systematic contact with the outside world in the 1970s, although before then there had been sporadic contact with Paraguayan ranchers. Anthropologists Kim Hill and Magdalena Hurtado studied the Ache for seventeen years and developed comparative data about Ache violence relative to the Ju/'Hoansi.[11] Hill and Hurtado noted that before 1971, 17.4 percent of all Ju/'Hoansi deaths between the ages of 15 and 59 were caused by accidents or violent feuds and brawls. But the totals for the Ache were even higher. Before contact with the outside world in 1971, about 55 percent of all Ache died from violence, including infanticide (Hill and Hurtado 1996:174). Among the latter group were children who were victims of child sacrifices, typically burial with a deceased adult.[12] For adults, 45.6 percent of 15- to 59-year-olds died of violence and accidents. But the most common type of violent death before contact was from what Hill and Hurtado call "inter-tribal fighting," which accounted for 36 percent of the deaths of all males. Much of this involved retaliatory violence by Paraguayan farmers and ranch employees who believed that the Ache killed horses or cattle, raided manioc fields, or had other reasons to fear Ache arrows. In short, it was combat between indigenous groups and invaders, in which neither had a legitimated monopoly on the use of violence over the other (Hill and Hurtado 1996:168–169).

In addition, there was a third significant source of violent death among the forest-dwelling Ache bands, stemming from inherited traditions of "club fighting." Club fighting is an excellent example of how two-party justice works in the absence of a formal state. Surprisingly, this violence occurred in a society in which Hill and Hurtado never observed a loud argument, scolding, or scuffling. Instead, ritualized club fights with wooden staves were the only socially acceptable way for males to confront one another. Such fights could arise spontaneously during a dispute, they could be the result of chance encounter, or they could be called after a perceived slight from another group. Events precipitating these fights might include the capture of a child by Paraguayans, or even a freak accident like a lightning strike. In some instances there were no precipitating events; club fights were called just because "we wanted to."

The most dramatic ritual was a formalized club fight. Runners would be sent to clearings where different bands of Ache lived, announcing the gladiatorial event. Up to 200–300 men would arrive in a clearing the night before the fight and cut and sharpen clubs made of hardwood and measuring about two meters long. The day before the fight provided a chance for each man to figure out which of his enemies he would attack. Male honor was at the center of the conflict, and often the focus was on slights over blatant or assumed sexual affairs, or animosities stemming from the previous club fight. Elaborate rituals were involved. The "uniform" for the fight involved black body paint decorated with white feathers. Kin groups and allies would rush onto the fields together in a manner designed to terrorize potential opponents. But the actual combat was a free-for-all in which there were two rules: hit any man you disliked, and protect your close kin and friends. The fight itself began about eight o'clock in the morning and continued until about three in the afternoon. Women and children watched from the sidelines; children would even climb up into trees to get a better view of the combat.

The days after the club fights were miserable for everyone. All of the fighters were sore and bruised, and a few would die after each fight. For those who lived, they were so sore that they were unable to provide for their families. In this environment, the men's families became hungry because no one hunted or tended their fields. The men and their families also began to nurse new grudges based on what had happened during the contest. In short, the club fights created new problems rather than solving older ones.

Hill and Hurtado point out how the immediate cause for issuing the challenge to fight did not explain the enthusiasm with which some men chose to participate. Rather, they found that the club fights existed so that the men could simply "display one's strength . . . to show how strong we are" (Hill and Hurtado 1996:71). Thus, the ritualized club fight was a way to seek status and admiration within the broader social group. Most Ache men had many scars on their heads, including dented skulls. As a means of dispute resolution, club fights were much worse than that of the modern state. The melee that ensued in a mass club fight simply resulted in new grudges that led to the next fight.

More examples of premodern statelessness: between war and peace. Studying stateless societies is inherently difficult because they are generally obscured from trained observers, leave few written records, and are always suspicious of strangers. The data from the Ju/' Hoansi and Ache are among the best there is, primarily because these societies have remained stateless and isolated until recently. But how representative are they of the premodern world?

Jared Diamond (1992:228) would not be particularly surprised by the high death rates among the Ache or Ju/' Hoansi. He notes that among most small tribal groups, including those he worked with in New Guinea, each village, band, or family group is a political unit living in a perpetually shifting state of war, truces, alliances, and trade with neighboring groups. Distrust of strangers in such situations is common even as human needs for sociality and trade are pursued. In Weber's (and Cooney's) terms, these groups live in an area where there is no third party powerful enough to monopolize coercive force. As a result, every slight, unintended or not, is evaluated as a potential attack that may need to be responded to personally. In such societies, leaving the confines of the village is terrifying. A short day trip through another group's territory is always dangerous, because your brother or cousin might have offended someone there. As a result, you might be a target for retaliation because the conditions for statelessness existed not only within your group but also between groups.

This condition of one against all in premodern stateless societies has been perhaps best summarized by Stephen LeBlanc (2003), an archaeologist, who studied settlement sites around the world. He points out that defensibility (and not practicality) was often the primary criterion for selecting a village site. LeBlanc found that practical considerations like access to good soil or water seemed to be secondary considerations in stateless societies. In fact, the most fertile valleys were often depopulated "no man's lands" because it was difficult to defend them from attack. One of the excellent examples LeBlanc provides is of native peoples in the American Southwest who lived in cliffside dwellings accessible only by a series of quickly removable ladders. Living in such a dwelling was very difficult, since villagers carried water, food, and other materials high up the cliffside. The choice and development of such sites, he points out, make sense only in societies where there is a strong belief that attack can occur at any moment.

For that matter, defensibility is why castles along the Rhine River in Europe were on hilltops, and not along the river where water was more readily available. Such stone castles were first and foremost designed for defense (not tourism). They were a place where harvests could be protected from potential invaders, and where farmers could take shelter in the event of invasion. Whether in medieval Europe, the American Southwest, or New Guinea, people in the premodern world were consistently vulnerable to violent attack.[13]

Transitional Statelessness: Elite Violence

In modern societies, evidence indicates that lower-status people have higher rates of violence than higher-status people. Simply put, murder rates are higher among the poor, criminals, and marginalized people than among the conventional upper-, middle-, or working-class people. This is markedly different from the egalitarian Ju/' Hoansi, Ache, and New Guinea tribes, where violence permeated society because there was no third party available to settle disputes with finality. As will be seen, this leads to a paradox that Mark Cooney described in his 1997 article "The Decline of Elite Violence." Data indicate that in societies where a centralized state is emerging—and an elite led by chiefs, notables, or even elected officials develops—elites engage in violence routinely, enthusiastically, and personally in much the same way the Ache did in their club fights. In this way, the mastery of personal violence enhanced the social status of knights, nobles, and other elites during Europe's feudal times. Indeed, fighting was so high-status that it was permitted only for the noble classes. This is in large part why it was socially acceptable for "big men" to engage in violence. Knights in medieval Europe were such big men, as were many tribal leaders from around the world. American politicians engaged in duels and brawls well into the nineteenth century and, like President Andrew Jackson, could nonetheless hold high office. As with the Ache, elaborate tradition often shaped the challenge and structure for the "gentlemen" who engaged in activities like jousting or duels.

Cooney's paradoxical observation is that when the third party begins to assert itself, its pacifying effects are first felt most strongly by the less powerful, that is, the group that is most easily taxed, policed, and intimidated into compliance by a government asserting its power. Thus a peasant could easily be shamed and punished in a formal public trial by a powerful court for initiating violence even against another peasant. While this may have meant that arbitrary arrests of poor peasants rose, it also meant that violence fell more rapidly among these groups as violence itself became a crime not only against the clan but against the all-powerful monarch.

But what of the elites who themselves made up the nobility and court officials of the state? Cooney points out that in these circumstances there is no one to forcefully regulate disputes between the powerful. Such elites monopolized the violent use of weapons and dominated noble courts but were not necessarily answerable to a higher political authority in the way the peasants were. What is more, they themselves controlled the means of violence: horses, armor, and the weapons of the knight. The importance of violence in the assertion of status is perhaps most obvious in the elaborate rituals of chivalric honor that were so important to the relationships between medieval knights. Roughly equal in status and personal military prowess, such knights were vulnerable to challenges to their honor.

But, ritualized or not, chivalric traditions were surprisingly lethal. For example, between 1589 and 1610 in France, roughly 10,000 people were killed in ritualized duels, which Wolfgang Schivelbusch (2003:130–131) describes as "the French aristocracy's final rebellion against the absolute authority of the [new centralized French] crown." In short, dueling and violence were a way for the French elite to emphatically demonstrate that, unlike the peasantry, they continued to be above the law and were not accountable to the crown. But the exchange for this was lethal dueling customs. And indeed, in the end the French aristocracy's rebellion against the crown's absolute authority failed, and they were reduced to dependence on the crown.

Cooney (1997b) divides this elite violence into four types: elite brawling, elite feuding, elite dueling, and lynching. Unlike the cases of the Ju/' Hoansi and Ache, all presume the presence of state power.

Elite brawling. The type of policing that emerged in thirteenth-century England provides an indication of how such imperfect legal systems control elite violence. By that century, local lords and clan chiefs had ceded power—and paid taxes—to a king. He in turn protected England in its wars with the Norman French and others, organized markets in which strangers could exchange goods without fear of being cheated, restricted the interclan warfare that had been endemic, and established uniform laws for the punishment of individuals who violated the king's peace. An important result of monarchical rule was that traders could travel between localities without fear and peasants could farm the fertile areas that had previously been abandoned due to their susceptibility to attack. Moreover, no longer did the local clan chief have absolute control over the administration of his territory. Rather, he was subservient to the king's representatives, among the most important of whom were the king's *eyre*.

The eyre were traveling judges from the Royal Court at Westminster. They would pass through each locality every few years, review the decisions that the local lord had made, and examine the records of the king's tax collectors. They would also try all serious crimes, of which murder was the most important. The eyres' power to try murderers was important for the local population because it meant that they could not, should not, and would not take punishment into their own hands, especially since under the king's law, the estate of any convicted murderer reverted to the king's treasury, not to the clan. Judging from statistics presented by James Given (1977), it seems that the introduction of the eyre system had the effect of lowering homicide rates among the peasant masses.[14]

But there was a problem with the emergence of groups like the eyre, who traveled the countryside without fear: how would the eyre themselves be contained by the king's law? Given (1977:72) notes that "it can be suspected that the rolls may not give a complete picture of violent activity among the aristocracy. If any group was able to avoid being accused of homicide by the jurors, it would have been this one." For example, the records of Bishop Oliver de Sutton describe a series of violent incidents over "prebends," which are the right to levy a tax in the name of the king:

Bishop Oliver de Sutton of Lincoln in September 1292 collated [appointed] Master Thomas of Sutton, one of his relatives, to the Thames prebend. A royal clerk, Edward St. John, disputed this collation [appointment], claiming a prior papal provision for himself. Sutton declared the provision invalid. This did not prevent Edward and his followers from seizing the church by force in early November. Either at this time or shortly thereafter, one of St. John's followers, Peter of Wyresdale, was killed. The bishop excommunicated St. John and his men. Thomas of Sutton managed to regain the church, but St. John returned to the attack. With an army of 200 men he assaulted the church, piled timber in the porch, lighted it, and pulled stones from the church walls so that arrows could be fired at the men within. His forces eventually managed to enter the church and wounded two clerics. . . . St. John's followers broke into the neighboring church at Long Cretendon during [a church service] and beat the officiating clergy. They also attacked the monastery of Notley. . . . In October 1294 the king ordered the lands and prebends restored to Thomas of Sutton and issued a general pardon to all those involved in the killing of Peter of Wyresdale. (Givens 1977:71–72)

Contrast how the modern United States government would have dealt with the highly unlikely event of a freelance army of 200 men that assaulted a church: the leader likely would have been arrested and very publicly tried. Explicitly or implicitly, exemption of the elite from the English king's peace was to continue for several *hundred* years more. Cooney (1997b), quoting Lawrence Stone, describes the brawls that would occur in London in the sixteenth century:

In London itself the fields about the City and even the main arterial roads were continued scenes of upper-class violence. Bloody brawls and even pitched battles occurred in Fleet Street and the Strand. . . . It was in Fleet Street that there took place in 1558 the armed affray between Sir John Perrot and William Phelippes, supported by their retainers; in Fleet Street that John Fortescue was beaten up by Lord Grey and his men in 1573; in Fleet Street that Edward Windham and Lord Rich carried on their repeated skirmishes in 1578; in Fleet Street that Lord Cromwell got mixed up in an armed affray in The Strand that Edward Cecil, future Viscount Wimbledon, lay in wait with ten soldiers to catch Auditor Povey. (Cooney 1997b:390)

Such brawling permitted high-status men to exhibit their physical prowess and could be an entrée into politics and power well into the nineteenth century both throughout Europe and in the United States. Future US president Andrew Jackson was well-known for his personal courage in dueling and brawling on the Tennessee frontier where he lived. The following story of a fight that left a wounded Jackson in bed for three weeks in 1813 is a good way to close this section on brawling:

Andrew Jackson was an excitable sort with a famously loose rein on his temper. A survivor—barely—of several duels, he nearly got himself killed following a meeting in which he was merely a second, and in which one of

the participants, Jesse Benton, had the misfortune to be shot in the but-
tocks. Benton was furious, and so was his brother, future U.S. Senator
Thomas Hart Benton, who denounced Jackson for his handling of the
affair. Not one to take denunciation placidly, Jackson threatened to horse-
whip Thomas and went to a Nashville hotel to do it. When Thomas
reached for what Jackson supposed was his pistol, Jackson drew his,
whereupon the irate [and wounded] Jesse burst through a door and shot
Jackson in the shoulder. Falling, Jackson fired at Thomas and missed.
Thomas returned the favor, and Jesse moved to finish off Jackson. At this
point, several other men rushed into the room, Jesse was pinned to the
floor and stabbed (though saved from a fatal skewering by a coat button), a
friend of Jackson's fired at Thomas, and Thomas, in hasty retreat, fell
backward down a flight of stairs. Thus ended the Battle of the City Hotel.
(Drake 2004:3; see also description in Kane 1951)

At the time of this altercation, Jackson had already served as a judge,
US senator, and major general in the Tennessee militia. He was a prominent
man who meted out justice to those who he commanded. And yet, when it
came to his interpersonal relations with people like the Bentons, no other
authority was powerful enough to step in to arrest Jackson or his partners in
the botched duel, or the brawl that followed.

Elite feuding. Stateless groups like the Ache and Ju/' Hoansi engaged in
feuds.[15] Feuds are ongoing violence between clans in which a slight against
one member of the clan is responded to with an attack on the offending
clan. But as chiefs or other nobility emerged to coordinate social activity, it
was in the interest of all concerned that this sort of general violence be controlled, and that the authority of the chief or his representatives be legitimated as the final arbiter in disputes. This legitimation offers a number of practical social consequences that benefit the new nobility and commoners
alike. Besides making the roads safe for travelers, the "no man's land"
between feuding groups could be settled, particularly in agriculturally
promising lowlands that were difficult to defend from raids. This means that
larger amounts of food could be produced, and villages could be established
nearer sources of food, water, and transportation routes rather than in
remote places selected for their defensibility. Production of grains and other
products increased as a result, permitting commoners to have more children,
and the nobility to reap higher profits from the lands they controlled. Settled
lands were profitable for commoner and noble alike. But this says nothing
about the level of violence between the elite who still contested territory.

Elite feuding occurs in societies where government control is incom-
plete and where patriarchs are still able to maintain a status above the law.
Punishment of poor or marginalized miscreants might be undertaken by the
state and a court system. Indeed, attacks by people of low status on those of
high status are dealt with in extraordinarily harsh ways. A good example is
in the pre–Civil War American South, where the court system was very will-

ing to punish slaves, free blacks, and others of low status while turning a blind eye to the planter elite, which was rarely brought before a court of law to answer for lethal acts. To illustrate, I will cite two cases, one fictional and one historical, that are both very familiar to Americans. The first is the Shepherdson and Grangerford feud in Mark Twain's *Huckleberry Finn*, and the second is the Hatfield and McCoy feud that took place on the river border between Kentucky and West Virginia in the 1880s and 1890s.

Many of the stories Mark Twain wrote about rural Missouri in the 1840s concern the nature of justice in places where the central state was weak but there was a local aristocracy. The best illustrations of this are in Twain's satirical novels *Huckleberry Finn* and *Tom Sawyer*. In *Tom Sawyer*, the high-status Dr. Robinson and the low-status ne'er-do-wells Muff Potter and Injun Jim team up to steal money that had been buried in a coffin. In a scuffle, Dr. Robinson is stabbed to death by Injun Jim, who turns and blames Muff Potter for the killing. The public excitement and drama of the court trial are exactly the type of strong third-party response needed to guarantee that Dr. Robinson's friends and family will not take justice into their own hands, possibly initiating a feud. The full righteousness of the township is cited in explaining how Muff Potter must hang for the murder of Dr. Robinson. Indeed, Twain describes the formal courtroom rituals that Potter is subjected to before it is dramatically revealed by Huck Finn that Potter is innocent, and the real murderer is Injun Jim. So the blame for the murder is placed on Injun Jim, who escapes and eventually dies in a sealed cave, a broken and disgraced man. In this instance, the legal system worked, at least in this case involving two socially marginal characters and the family of the high-status Dr. Robinson.

But in 1840s Missouri, the power of the law was limited; there were still large social areas where the sheriff and prosecutor dared not assert their authority. Contrast the strength of the law in dealing with Muff Potter and Injun Jim with the situation that emerges when Huck and Jim land in the middle of a feud between two families of "gentlemen," the Shepherdsons and Grangerfords in *Huckleberry Finn*. Despite the fact that the two clans have taken potshots (many of them lethal) at each other for years, there is never even a suggestion of involvement by a sheriff, prosecutor, or posse—as there was for Muff Potter. This is because gentlemen in such a circumstance are effectively above the law. They handle their clan disputes personally, with one result being that rates of lethal violence escalate (as they did among the Ju/'Hoansi and the Ache). Twain has his character Buck explain how this works:

> "Well," says Buck, "a feud is this way: A man has a quarrel with another man, and kills him; then that other man's brother kills *him;* then the other brothers, on both sides, goes for one another; then the *cousins* chip in—

and by and by everybody's killed off, and there ain't no more feud. But it's kind of slow, and takes a long time." (p. 144)

I don't think that Ju/' Hoansi feudists like Debe or Kashe would have objected to Buck's way of characterizing a feud. One can only imagine what would have happened in this situation if, at an early date in the feud, one of the Shepherdson or Grangerford patriarchs, or at least a portion of their followers, had been placed in the defendant's dock, as Muff Potter was. Would the feud have developed if a powerful state had been able to exact retribution on behalf of the first victim? A realistic test of this hypothesis can be made by examining the actual feud between the Hatfield and McCoy clans in the 1880s. This long-running feud actually did end after Kentucky arrested ten Hatfields and executed one low-status Hatfield kin. (As you may recall, this case was briefly discussed with reference to the social ecology of killing in Chapter 1.)

The Hatfields and McCoys were large families—clans—who lived on opposite sides of the Tug River, which formed the boundary between West Virginia and Kentucky in the nineteenth century. They were a lusty lot who had large families, frequently intermarried, and, before the Civil War, made their living primarily through farming and hunting. What little cash they had typically came from whiskey sales. As the population expanded after the Civil War, though, individual patriarchs accumulated wealth in the form of formal land titles and timber concessions. Two men who were able to do this well were Ranel McCoy and "Devil Anse" Hatfield. Both were successful men living on opposite sides of the Tug, tied together through marriages. Despite the fact that both had limited education (Hatfield was illiterate), they became important men in their communities because they could mobilize kin for farming and the harvesting of timber. They accumulated the titles of the local aristocracy (such as justice of the peace), controlled large blocs of votes in local politics, and even engaged in protracted litigation over land deals. Although the state was established in the area and was an effective arbiter in many cases, its capacity to monopolize the use of violence was to be tested by a mixture of traditional status, romantic entanglements, and ultimately killings. This case provides a good example of how feuding can reassert itself in the presence of a weak state.

The Hatfield-McCoy feud is variously traced to a number of affronts against honor involving (depending on the source) theft of hogs, a grudge carried from the Civil War, a love affair between a Hatfield daughter and McCoy son, or a drunken fight. Sam McCoy, who wrote his memories down at age seventy, remembered the time as being one of "boisterous arguments, and horseplay that seemed to turn brutal almost accidentally with the use of knives and guns" (Waller 1988:239). However, what preceded the most important incident is not in dispute: it was a brawl lubricated by alcohol, in

The Hatfield clan posed for this picture in 1897 at the behest of a local storekeep-er. The feud had ended a few years previously, but the Hatfield clan had achieved a national notoriety, which is perhaps why there is such a prominent display of firearms in this and other portraits they posed for. Devil Anse Hatfield is seated at the center. The other males are from Devil Anse's extended family and friends. His wife, Levicy, is seated in the background in the doorway of the log house.
Reprinted by permission of the West Virginia State Archives.

which Devil Anse's son Ellison was shot in the back by Pharmer Hatfield. The immediate response of the law was to arrest three of the McCoys who were involved in the brawl and incarcerate them in a Kentucky jail. The response of the Hatfields was more unusual. They organized a raid to cap-ture the prisoners and bring them back to West Virginia for a "death watch" over Ellison. When Ellison died, the three McCoys were tied to bushes and shot to death while twenty Hatfields watched.

Eight more years of feuding but no arrests followed, with as many as twenty deaths on both sides. A number of Hatfields were eventually cap-tured and imprisoned by the state of Kentucky. One man, a low-status ille-gitimate nephew of Devil Anse known for his mental slowness, was hanged for the murder of one of the McCoy women, even though there was little evidence that he had pulled the trigger. Notably though, the organizers of the feud—including the respected patriarch most guilty of organizing the killings, Devil Anse—were never arrested for murder, only for occasional violations of liquor laws. Indeed, Devil Anse Hatfield died of old age at home in 1921. An implicit deal was made between the states of Kentucky and West Virginia and Devil Anse Hatfield, wherein Devil Anse would recognize the authority of the state, and the state would give him one last pass for his defiance of their monopoly on the use of violence (see Waller 1988:72–76).

Elite dueling. Dueling provides a ritualized way for gentlemen to display courage and their capacity for violence. Such rituals have advantages over the types of brawls described earlier, the most important being that the event becomes a one-on-one affair in which the rules are made clear before the confrontation. As noted by Senator Thomas Hart Benton below, there is also an interval when compromise about the underlying issues can be reached. In contrast to brawling, formal dueling seemed to provide combatants with the possibility of a fair fight. Senator Benton defended the practice of the formal duel as a way to prevent the brutality that emerged out of the type of brawls he had with Andrew Jackson. Note that buried in Benton's description are assumptions about the role of an elite, the nature of honor and vengeance, and the role of lethal violence in maintaining high social status:

> Certainly it is deplorable to see a young man, the hope of his father and mother—a ripe man, the head of a family—an eminent man necessary to his country—struck down in a duel; and should be prevented if possible. Still this deplorable practice is not so bad as the bowie knife and the revolver, and their pretext of self-defense—thirsting for blood. In the duel, there is at least consent on both sides, with a preliminary opportunity for settlement, with a chance for the law to arrest them, and room for the interposition of friends as the affair goes on. There is usually equality of terms; and it would not be called an affair of honor if honor was not to prevail all round; and if the satisfying a point of honor, and not vengeance, was not the end to be attained. Finally, in the regular duel, the principals are in the hands of the seconds (for no man can be made a second without his consent); and as both these are required by the dueling code (for the sake of fairness and humanity), to be free from ill will or grudge towards the adversary principal, they are expected to terminate the affair as soon as the point of honor is satisfied, and the less the injury, so much the better.
>   The only exceptions to these rules are where the principals are in such relations to each other as to admit of no accommodation, and the injury [to their honor] such as to admit of no compromise. In the knife and revolver [brawl] all this is different. There is no preliminary interval for settlement—no chance for officers of justice to intervene—no room for friends to interpose. Instead of equality of terms, every advantage is sought. Instead of consent, the victim is set upon at the most unguarded moment. Instead of satisfying a point of honor, it is vengeance to be glutted. Nor

does the difference stop with death. In the duel the unhurt principal scorns to continue the combat upon his disabled adversary; in the knife and revolver case, the hero of these weapons continues firing and stabbing while the prostrate body of the dying man gives a sign of life. In the duel the survivor never assails the character of the fallen; in the knife and revolver case, the first movement of the victor is to attack the character of his victim—to accuse him of an attempt to murder; and to make out a case of self-defense, by making out a case of premeditated attack against the other. And in such false accusation, the French proverb is usually veri- fied—the dead and the absent are always in the wrong. (Benton [1826?])

Formalized elite dueling of the type that Benton idealized was dis- cussed widely because of the drama involved as well as the prestige and power that so many disputants enjoyed. But it also illustrates the limitations of a weak legal system in policing those who hold power, even when cases

This mass-produced engraving of the duel between the leader of the Federalist Party, Alexander Hamilton, and US Vice President Aaron Burr was widely distributed in the nineteenth century. This depiction reflects the view of Hamilton's partisans that he pur- posely shot high whereas Burr took direct aim. Hamilton died as a result of his wounds. Library of Congress

of killing are involved. That the practice has disappeared in the United States and Europe is an important indication of how the rule of law can eventually restrict the behavior of even the powerful.

Elite lynching. Lynching is the fourth type of elite violence identified by Cooney. Lynching is a form of vigilante justice in which a community rises up and challenges the authority of the state's monopoly to punish offenders. In the United States elite lynchings were most common in the post–Civil War South, where the legitimacy of Reconstruction-era governments was challenged by Southern white elites, and in the American West, where the authority of police, courts, and law spread widely only in the late nineteenth century. By a conservative count, between 1882 and 1968 there were 4,730 recorded lynchings in the United States, and 73 percent of the victims were African American.

In lynchings, "vigilante committees" typically emerge to assert the power of elites who are unconvinced that conventional law preserves the status quo. Such vigilante committees are often secret sources of power that emerge to enforce law or tradition in the form of paramilitary militia, or more spontaneously, in the form of lynch mobs. In the American South, such vigilance committees often emerged in the context of lynchings organized by clandestine white elites like the Ku Klux Klan and other secret organizations that did not recognize the legitimacy of the United States government.

The demise of the type of society that can produce lynching is very recent. Indeed, investigations and trials of elderly American men who engaged in vigilante violence in the 1950s and 1960s continued even into the twenty-first century. For example, the trial of Edgar Ray Killen, an eighty-year-old former leader of the Ku Klux Klan in Mississippi who organized the killing of three civil rights workers in 1964, ended in a guilty verdict for manslaughter in 2005. Until then, it was believed that no jury in Mississippi would convict a man who had been an important community leader, and in the world of 1964 Mississippi, above the law.

In the American West, lynch mobs often arose in the context of a weak policing system that was perceived as illegitimate and corrupt. As in the South, mobs emerged, broke into jails, and marched defendants out to be summarily hanged. In the South and the West, the state rarely responded by arresting the lynch party, whose members were not only well-known but often prominent. This can of course be perceived as a moral failing, but it can also be understood as being a consequence of a weak state. The final lynchings in the West occurred in the 1930s, and the last in the South in the 1960s.[16]

One of the last lynchings in the West was undertaken in 1933 in downtown San Jose, California, apparently by students from Santa Clara University (Farrell 1992). Brooke Hart, a Santa Clara student and heir to a local department store chain, was kidnapped and murdered. Two suspects were captured in nearby Alameda County (where Hart's body was found) and put in the Santa Clara jail. A mob of thousands, led by Santa Clara University students, used a battering ram to break into the jail and remove the two suspects, who were then stripped of their clothes and hanged from trees in a nearby park. Thousands were present for the lynching, and a number of them even had their pictures in the newspapers of the day. But no one was ever tried for the extrajudicial killings.[17] Despite the obvious challenge to conventional state authority, the consensus was that a trial of the killers was not appropriate.[18]

Modern Virtual Statelessness

Implicit to all legal legitimacy is trust. The people served by the law must believe that a sense of righteousness will be sought on their behalf if they are wronged. Furthermore, they must believe that if they take justice into their own hands, they can be legitimately prosecuted. When large numbers of people share such beliefs, vast areas become peaceful, and ways to avoid physical confrontations emerge. Someone who believes that a powerful third party will seek vengeance on his/her behalf is less likely to throw a retaliatory punch, grab a weapon, or organize his/her relatives to seek self-help justice. This social psychology of "civilization" exists in vast stretches of the modern world where punches are commonly pulled, words are left unsaid, and the rights of others are respected. This is related to the strength of the state, or what sociologist Norbert Elias (1939:266) described in this way: "It is by more than a coincidence that in the same centuries in which the king or prince acquires absolutist status, the restraint and moderation of the affects . . . [that is] the 'civilizing' of behaviour, is noticeably increased."

In the United States, the middle classes have this type of civilization, where despite their fears, individuals rarely see a fight in which weapons are used, and killing is rare. In the modern United States it also exists in the upper classes, where individuals are confident that their position will be maintained and protected without the need to establish their own reputation through the use of personal violence. The result, as Cooney has posited, is that in modern countries the reach of the law is so pervasive that the highest rates of violence are typically found among the poor, immigrant communities, and marginalized minorities, and not the elite.

What do third-party theories have to say about the relatively high violence rates among marginalized ethnic and racial minorities in modern society? Cooney (1997a) says that a "virtual statelessness" emerges when the police cannot effectively monitor a community. These virtually stateless areas exist on the periphery of conventional society, or in the most private corners of personal life. In these areas, just as it was with the Ju/' Hoansi or elite duelists, careless words and acts are more likely to lead to righteous personal violence in which protagonists take matters into their own hands. These are pockets of modern society where the appeal to law is not effective. Some of these areas are commonsensical. Drug dealers, gangs, prisoners, embezzlers, and individuals routinely engaging in criminal activities are unlikely to appeal to the police for protection, and as a result they are more likely to take demands for righteousness into their own hands. As with the Ju/' Hoansi, when this happens there is a potential for retaliatory violence. Other stateless areas are on the margins of society, where the police and law are not well understood and are mistrusted. This is why immigrant groups and minorities who are discriminated against are more likely to experience gang activity and other forms of self-help justice (Cooney 1998:124–129).[19]

Finally, there is a surprising place in society where virtual statelessness is found: in the privacy of the conventional home. In intimate relationships between partners, romantic couples, parents, children, and siblings there is an assumption that the unkind word or violent punch will not result in an appeal to a third party for resolution. As a result, relationships that are usually loving can take on all the characteristics of a Ju/' Hoansi brawl or a Hatfield and McCoy feud. This impulse toward righteousness is perhaps best understood by reflecting on the virtually stateless areas between siblings, or for that matter, the virtually stateless areas between teenagers and their parents. In both spaces, extremes of emotion are generated and cannot be diverted by appeals to the police or any other outsider. The result can be ongoing conflicts triggered by trivial matters.

The virtual statelessness of the household also explains why police are often reluctant to intervene in domestic violence cases. Their intervention is not viewed as legitimate by the disputants, be they victim or perpetrator.[20] In fact, both parties potentially perceive the role of the police in such situations as illegitimate. The emotions and anger felt in such situations are probably not that different between disputants in an ongoing Ju/' Hoansi feud.

Criminals, Gangs, Cults, Prisoners, and Drug Dealers

Street gangs are a good example of virtual statelessness. A modern street gang is typically composed of young males (and a few females) who feel marginalized from conventional society. They are most often found in poor neighborhoods and among stigmatized racial and immigrant groups. Gangs are often an "oppositional subculture" whose identity is rooted in the rejection of the established conventional power structure, especially the third party represented by the police. Gangs also often become "total institutions" in which members are separate from the larger society, and what is normative becomes "bounded" by the small group (see Lalich 2004). Leaders are often charismatic and able to exact a high level of loyalty to the small group to the exclusion of the broader society in which formal law dominates. Such gangs assert themselves as an alterative to the third party, through a medium of fear that is exacerbated by a generalized belief that the police can do nothing if a victim complains. America's leading gang expert, Malcolm Klein, recognized this when he attributed the following joke to gang members:

> *Question:* What's the difference between the cops and everyone else standing around at a murder scene?
> *Answer:* The cops are the only ones who don't know who did it. (Klein 2004:188)

The reason that the cops do not know who did the crime is that witnesses in marginalized communities are distrustful of the capacity of the police to protect them if they come forward. In other words, the perception is that the police do not have a plausible monopoly over the use of violence, and potential witnesses fear attack. This is why witness tampering is such a serious crime; it threatens the authority of the third party. In the virtually stateless areas created by street gang activity, there is likely to be a street ethos with its own code of honor focused on the same manly courage emphasized in premodern societies like the Ju/' Hoansi and Ache.

Cult members organized around an ideology and charismatic authority rather than illegal activity are also unlikely to take advantage of the third party, and as a result can become violent. As long as a charismatic leader controls members, violence may remain low. However, should the power of the leader deteriorate, or his or her position be challenged, acts of violence against other groups—or even within the cult—may escalate. Extreme examples of such lashing out include incidents like the mass suicide/homicide in Jonestown in 1978, mass suicide of the Heaven's Gate cult in San Diego in 1997, and sarin gas attacks by the Aum Shinrikyo cult on Japanese subways in 1995 (see Lalich 2004). Osama bin Laden's followers in Al-Qaeda can be thought of in a similar fashion. Cults effectively reject the authority of the conventional third party, creating a virtual statelessness focused on their leader, who is believed to be above the laws of the larger society. Honor is achieved through obedience to the cult leader, not to a broader system of law.[21]

Prison inmates present yet another kind of virtual statelessness because, by definition, they are distrusted by and distrust the authorities. As a result, independent codes of honor often develop inside prison walls. Prisoners walk a fine line between cooperating with the power of the state (represented by the prison authorities) and following the prisoners' honor code. As an example, one former prisoner explained the need for racially based gangs inside California's prisons:

If a black inmate attacks a white inmate in prison, it is considered the responsibility of other white inmates to respond. This provides some measure of protection for those inmates who are not members of any gang but who do not wish to become prey for those who are, [even though] there may have been other black inmates who thought that what these "youngsters" had done was stupid, but they were obliged to back them up unless a representative from the white side met with a black "rep" and tried to get it resolved. But before any discussion could be had, skinhead whites demanded that the blacks leave. When they refused, a fight broke out.

After the fight, the yard was cleared and the inmates were returned to their cells. The whites concluded it was all caused by the blacks, and the blacks blamed prejudiced skinheads for ignoring the proper channels for "justice." Tension climbed, and the next day a full-scale riot broke out.

Staying neutral is not allowed in such circumstances. (Englehart 2005:B13)

Note that the situation in this prison is not so different from the type of social structure that emerges to protect groups in other two-party systems of justice, such as that described by Mark Twain. The observations of the white inmate in a California prison also mirror those of the elite senator Thomas Hart Benton, who earlier justified the necessity of two-party dueling. Enforcement of the prisoners' code means that threats of violence between prisoners are often carried out, particularly when a competing prison group challenges the hegemony of a senior group.

Subordinated Minorities and Immigrant Communities

Minorities who have experienced systematic discrimination from the police and courts are more likely to take demands for righteousness into their own hands than are individuals who share ethnic solidarity with the police and courts.[22] In the United States, the long history of systematic discrimination against blacks in policing and court decisions makes it less likely that interpersonal disputes will be referred to the police, particularly in marginalized neighborhoods. Years of confrontation, discrimination, and crime mean that poor blacks often see themselves in opposition to the power of the law, and self-fulfilling prophecies emerge. Police officers become distrustful of the black community and resort to stereotypes in making discretionary decisions about when to enforce laws. This appears discriminatory to such communities (as indeed it is), and the people come to believe that the police are ineffective, racist, and corrupt. One of the ironies in criminological research is that complaints to the police are often more frequent than in more conventional areas. However, this does not mean that the police necessarily have a legitimated monopoly on the use of violence in these neighborhoods. Rather, the police are treated as a bargaining chip to be played by disputants. Cooney (1997b:394–395) summarized attitudes of young black interviewees who existed on the edges of society in the following manner:

> Don't be pushed around; if somebody insults you, assaults you, or steals your property, handle the problem yourself; do not run to the police because if you do, you might get into more serious trouble on the street. If the law does get involved in the case, it is all right to lie to officials to avoid going to jail or to send your enemies there. In capsule, law is the enemy; stand up for yourself.

In the context of this subcultural ethos, the presence of the police is not equated with the presence of justice; the police represent a hostile government seeking to reinforce a distant (and illegitimate) power structure. The presence of the police represents fear of hassle and discrimination rather than reassurance of order.

Poor immigrant groups in the United States also may feel that law is unavailable to them. Since they are new to the country, they are not likely to be familiar with the formal and especially informal legal culture. Language difficulties create further barriers between immigrant and host communities. As a result, immigrant groups may rely on traditional norms of social control that require obedience to elders. However, in modern societies these norms quickly break down, and a cultural divide created by the legal pluralism emerges, wherein neither group trusts the police:

> The young ones won't pay attention to our traditional councils anymore, because the government doesn't permit them to have any authority. . . . We can't enforce our will. In Laos, they would have had to listen to their elders, or they would have been severely beaten. Here the government won't let us enforce [beat the children], though. So the kids run wild. They are good students in elementary school and junior high school. But then in high school everything goes wrong, and suddenly the American kids are doing better than ours. Please explain to the government that if we were permitted to handle our own problems everything would be much better, and our young people would be good citizens and students. (quoted in Waters 1999:149)

In short, the immigrant community slides into a virtual statelessness because of systematic misunderstandings about who is responsible for what, and how discipline is to be administered. In such an environment, the police are perceived as being ineffective, and the level of violence escalates as it would in any other stateless situation.

Intimate Spaces

The family and related intimate spaces are a final stateless area where there is a reluctance to invite the involvement of the police. When victimized by a spouse, sibling, or parent, few people appeal to the state or courts for a judgment; instead, they take matters into their own hands. The emotional bonds of intimates, as well as the financial dependence of a child or partner, make it difficult for an outsider—a third party—to intervene.[23] Indeed, this is why police officers hesitate to become involved in domestic abuse cases. There is a treacherous stateless area between intimates, where both parties (victim and perpetrator) may turn on the investigating officer. Likewise, victimized partners and children are often unwilling to testify in court due to fear, love, or any number of other complicating emotions. This reluctance to testify emasculates attempts to legitimate the monopoly over the use of police force in the social space between the victim and abuser. Just as in a feud among the Ju/' Hoansi, recrimination and retaliation escalate, often far beyond the scope of the initial dispute.

A Final Comment on Two-Party Justice

The common thread among these diverse examples of stateless areas is that the government does not always easily intervene legitimately in disputes that turn violent. Because stateless people believe (rightly or wrongly) that the state will not respond, they take their demands for justice—righteousness—into their own hands. But whether this self-help justice occurs in the premodern world of the Ache or in the world of the modern United States, the result is an escalation of violence. Third-party justice is not considered as an option, because the police and courts are *perceived* as being too distant, low-status, unable to protect witnesses, inherently corrupt, incompetent, or too intrusive.

Two-party justice always implies that one's own small group is the most important, and it is from the group—and not the state—that justice and protection are sought. The problem is that this kind of group solidarity leads to tense standoffs in which mutual distrust begets feuds divorced from either the original grievance or law. Instead it is embedded in a morality of loyalty to kin. From such a context it is not surprising that the protection of a state with a monopoly over the use of coercive power is so desirable. The legitimated state provides freedom from fear, a chance to travel widely, a promise that trade can be undertaken, and the assurance that traders are permitted to arrive and depart with wealth. Finally, there is a promise that when the law is breached, righteous compensation will be sought by a powerful state.

But these benefits come at a cost: ceding the monopoly over the use of legitimate violence to a third party. A legitimated state can lead to large communities where strangers live peacefully together and do not engage in ambushes, duels, brawling, lynching, or feuds. These communities are the

vast modern-day working- and middle-class suburbs of culturally homoge-
neous neighbors who have a stake in protecting a system where they feel
safe. In such circumstances, vast numbers of people go for years without
dealing violently with one another and only rarely feel compelled to assert
the authority of law or the police (Baumgartner 1988).

But the danger for such complacent middle classes is, as Cooney points
out, that excesses of state power that are as lethal as—or even more lethal—
than anarchy become possible. As you may recall, the right-hand side of
Cooney's "U" indicates that as state power increases, the potential for citizens to die violently from wars and mass executions also increases. Indeed,
this is what happened in the Soviet Union and Nazi Germany. Both were
countries with modern industrial and agricultural market systems and powerful governments. But both also suffered greatly from governments in
which power was concentrated in the hands of a few. In this context, as
Table 2.1 indicates, legalized violence carried out by the state itself led to
death rates similar to that of the Ju/' Hoansi or even the Ache. The mechanisms of how and why this happened will be discussed in detail in Chapter
5. Only the right kind of state power, not state power in and of itself, leads
to lower death rates.

Why Third-Party Theories Are Important

Third-party theories of criminalization are important because they discuss
the very foundations of the relationships between the state, law, and justice.
It is a robust theory that helps us look at why killing is a crime in a wide
variety of places and contexts. Understanding the nature of the third party
means that we also understand why law is so important to maintaining civil
order; by studying third-party theories of criminalization, we come to see
that it is not law itself, or policing itself, that limits private violence and
crime. Rather, it is a plausible belief that the state can and will step in to
reassert a sense of righteousness if you are a victim. But it is at the same
time about the fear that if you take matters into your own hands—if you
violate a legitimated monopoly on punishment—you become a criminal
yourself. Both the belief in and fear of the state are important elements of
legitimacy.

To understand this, it is useful again to return to Max Weber's classic
definition of the state in order to analyze its elements, particularly as it
refers to the nature of legitimacy and the fact that the use of legitimate coercive force is monopolized. To quote Weber in full:

"Every state is founded on force," said Trotsky at Brest-Litovsk.[24] That
is indeed right. If no social institutions existed which knew the use of violence, then the concept of "state" would be eliminated, and conditions

would emerge that could be designated as "anarchy." . . . Today the rela-
tion between the state and violence is an especially intimate one. In the
past, the most varied institutions—beginning with the sib—have known
the use of physical force as quite normal. Today however, we have to say
that a state is a human community that (successfully) claims the *monopoly
of the legitimate use of physical force within a given territory.* . . . The
right to use physical force is ascribed to other institutions or to individuals
only to the extent to which the state permits it. The state is considered to
be the sole source of the "right" to use violence. (Weber 1947:78)

Two terms in this formulation are particularly important for understanding why it is important to have a state as a third party. These are "monopoly
over the use of physical force" and "legitimacy." These are discussed
briefly in the following two sections.

Monopoly over the Use of Physical Force

The monopoly over the use of physical force means that *only* the agents of
the state can use violence and coercion to generate compliance. If anyone
else uses violence, no matter how just the cause, he or she is accountable to
the state. Neither you nor your brother can use violence to reestablish righteousness; only the state that holds the monopoly can. Individuals, siblings,
families, clans, tribes, and all others surrender their freedom to seek
revenge for legitimate grievances when the state asserts its monopoly over
the use of coercive force. However, to be effective, the state must step in
and use this power only in a manner that is perceived as *legitimate*.

Legitimacy

The maintenance of a monopoly on the use of coercive power rests on an
amorphous term, *legitimacy*. Legitimacy is the unspoken power that a people cede to an institution to represent them and administer matters, including justice, on their behalf. Legitimacy can be gained through the fear of
anarchy, or fear of violence as in an authoritarian society. But legitimacy
also comes from the implied consent of those who are policed and governed, often through elections or other democratic mechanisms. There are
also elements of patriotism and love of country in legitimacy. Whatever the
source of legitimacy, in the modern world it can lead to the vast areas where
strangers deal with each other peacefully, and without fear that a revenge
attack will occur.

As Weber implies, for most of human history, violent killing was not
considered equivalent to the modern crime of murder. This is because a legitimated third party with a monopoly over the use of coercive force must be
present in order to judge a violent death not only as an offense against a clan

or family but as an offense against the larger social order. And a state must be present to make this judgment that a particular crime becomes murder.

For this to happen, issues of intent are necessarily judged, and in the process the severity of the challenge to the broader society is evaluated. Among the relevant issues of intent are questions about whether the death was accidental, self-defense, or the consequence of a legitimate challenge. Or was the killing undertaken in the name of the legitimate government? Evaluating such intent is necessary for determining whether the state responds. Such judgments, though, are often difficult and ambiguous; even where there is intent to kill, some types of killing are not murder. Today, killing by police and prison officers performing their duties is killing but not murder. Killing by soldiers is only on rare occasions defined as murder.

These are obvious cases, but there are still others where killing is never criminalized. Less obvious, but just as real, are the killings that occur between inner-city gangs and do not attract the attention of the police, accidental deaths in which there is inadequate evidence to prosecute, killing in remote unpoliced areas, and killings that for whatever reason the government is not interested in. Because the police do not become involved, these are not murders, just killings. In short, without a powerful government prepared to assert its monopoly over the use of coercive violence and to insist that a violent death is criminal, justice in the name of a larger abstract law is not sought, and the death is therefore not a crime. This is the real story of how a reaction by the state becomes important in evaluating whether killing is a crime or not.

Notes

1. This "great compromise" between the catastrophe of anarchy and the catastrophe of great central power was discussed at length by Enlightenment philosophers like Hobbes, Locke, and Rousseau, who described it as a "social contract." Such a contract in effect requires the granting of individual natural liberty to a sovereign for the freedoms (i.e., civil liberty) that emerge when a sovereign guarantees the sanctity of agreements between individuals. But this power in turn tempts the sovereign with despotism.

2. Cooney's U-shaped diagram follows closely on ideas about the availability and strength of law proposed by Donald Black and his students. See, e.g., Black 1976, 1993.

3. Baumgartner (1988:10–13) refers to this as "moral minimalization."

4. Schivelbusch (2003:129–130) notes that moral reciprocity is deeply rooted in human affairs but does not only apply in the case of vengefulness. Closely related norms of reciprocity are found in cases of gift-giving, expressions of gratitude, and revenge. The economist Adam Smith (1776) even went so far as to claim that such a need for reciprocity was inherent to human nature. The impulses for trade, gift-giving, and revenge represent different goals, but because they are all embedded in

assumptions of reciprocity, they are also intertwined impulses. See also Marcel Mauss ([1954]2000), *The Gift,* for a discussion of reciprocity.

5. However, pockets still remain where tribal councils administer justice in deference to traditional norms. Among the most notorious today are societies in Pakistan and Afghanistan where councils of elders may prescribe death by stoning or gang-rape in cases of adultery or other offenses. Indeed, women who have been victims of such sentences have become celebrities in the West, where such practices are viewed as a violation of human rights (see, e.g., Nicholas Kristof's 2004–2005 columns in the *New York Times*). More common perhaps are groups of elders in remote areas of the Third World who mete out punishment in the form of beatings and fines. Such penalties are often assessed in the context of preserving the peace between clans, rather than as a sense of individual justice.

6. See also Appendix 1.

7. Signe and Willis (1988) emphasize in their writing that such societies are not always violent, and that particularly in the short run (even a period of decades) a number of remote societies are peaceful and develop excellent ways of defusing potential conflict.

8. *The Harmless People,* by Elizabeth Marshall Thomas, was one of the earlier books about the Ju/' Hoansi, published in 1959.

9. See Appendix 1 for a summary of the killings that Lee recorded.

10. Such estimates are always rough. Hill and Hurtado (1996:68) claim that 17.4 percent of all deaths between the ages of 15 and 59 were violent. The 9.5 percent figure is very conservative, and I generated it in the following manner. I assumed half of the population (285 people) is male and that the population has a life expectancy of 30–40 years. Of these males, 30 percent die before the age of five and will not become combatants, leaving, conservatively, 200 males. Nineteen of the 200 males, or 9.5 percent, actually did die violently. Keep in mind that this is a conservative figure that assumes that the census taken in 1968 can be projected into the past, before the Ju/' Hoansi had access to modern medical care. In fact, the total population from the 1920s to 1955, when the killings actually occurred, was probably smaller than in 1968. This means that violence was a major threat to the men of "the harmless people." In a later study, Nancy Howell (1979:68) found that nine out of sixty-eight deaths to husbands between 1963 and 1973 were due to trauma and violence. This figure includes accidents and was calculated after the feuding had ceased.

11. See Appendix 1 for a comparison between Ju/' Hoansi and Ache death rates from various causes.

12. Important adult men who died were typically buried with young girls under age five. Typically these girls were orphans or other children who were marginalized socially (Hill and Hurtado 1996:68).

13. Nevertheless, all was not war in such societies at all times. As Signe and Willis (1989) stress, if such aggression is seemingly innate to human nature, so is a drive for sociality. Aggression and violence are sociality gone awry. Situations gone awry of course are more likely to emerge in times when resources are stressed as a result of any number of environmental conditions. Societies can be peaceful in times of plenty, a situation that has persisted for decades within a particular society, if not longer. The Semai of Malaysia, for example, have a long history of peacefulness. As Robarchek and Denton (1988) discuss, the point is not whether the Semai are inherently aggressive or not. Rather, it is that norms for group cooperation and sociality can develop that emphasize peaceful resolution of conflicts. They report seeing very little conflict in the years they were with the Semai, a condition they attribute to

conditions where the small band of 100 individuals is the "sole source of nurturance and security. . . . Peacefulness does not require suppression of individuality. . . . It is simply the only sensible way for people to behave" (Robarchek 1989:43).

14. See also Appendix 1 for a summary of the different homicide statistics available from England between the years 1200 and 1900.

15. See Appendix 1 for a summary of the rates at which the Ju/' Hoansi and Ache died violently.

16. Plausible charges of lynching into the 1980s are occasionally made in the press.

17. Earl Warren, who later became chief justice of the US Supreme Court, was district attorney of Alameda County during the Brooke Hart case. He decided not to pursue the case against the lynch mob in court, apparently due to the general public feeling that "justice" had been served (Farrell 1992).

18. Lynchings continue to occur in many places of the world where there is a distrust of police departments and the justice system. Lynchings often happen spontaneously as a form of mob-based "street justice," such as when a thief is caught and beaten by a mob, or when extralegal tribunals are organized by secret societies (see, e.g., Paciotti and Borgerhoff Mulder 2004).

19. See also Appendix 1 for a comparison of the rates whites and blacks have been homicide victims in the United States across time.

20. For statistical accounts of these issues, see Appendix 1.

21. This is the case unless the cult is organized as a militia in overt violent opposition to the government with an ideology emphasizing the legitimacy of the law. But few cults are organized in this fashion.

22. See, for example, Appendix 1 for a comparison of homicide rates between whites and blacks in the United States.

23. For a description of the relationship between policing and domestic violence in Minneapolis, see Appendix 1.

24. Leon Trotsky was the negotiator for the new Russian Communist (Bolshevik) government at Brest-Litovsk in March 1918. The Treaty of Brest-Litovsk resulted in the withdrawal of Russia from World War I and the cession of eastern territories to the powers allied with Germany, and led to the creation of the Soviet Union. Trotsky, besides being important in the founding of the Soviet Union, also wrote a great deal about the nature of government.

Legitimizing the Third Party: Albanian Blood Revenge

During the early twentieth century the small Balkan country of Albania was first a remote corner of the Ottoman empire, then a principality ruled by a warlord king after World War I, and finally occupied by Italy during World War II. For most of the second half of the twentieth century Albania was a reclusive Stalinist state sealed off from the rest of the world and ruled by one of the most severe, controlling, and totalitarian governments. But since 1991, Albania has become an anarchic state, in which the government lost legitimacy, and a range of mafias, clans, and businesspeople assumed control. It is an unusually good example of the roles the state plays in controlling violence. Principles dealing with the role of legitimated third parties, two-party justice, and the threat of totalitarian violence (i.e., a strong third party) are well illustrated.

As is the case in many places where the government becomes weak, extragovernmental institutions emerged in Albania in the 1990s. These include norms and rules to both further peaceful relations between groups and provide compensation when an offense occurs. The *kanun* of Albania is a code of traditional rules for feuding, which are contained in books and oral traditions. But there are no courts for the kanun; each side in a dispute is left to evaluate the rights and the wrongs visited upon them. This system is inherently imperfect, and as a result each clan traditionally had a three-story stone tower known as a *kula* to which the men would retreat when a dispute was unsettled. They were "locked" inside the kula because if the offended party encountered them outside it, they could be killed. This traditional practice of blood vengeance had been effectively stamped out by the Communist government, which dismantled the kula towers and ruled with an iron fist from 1945 to 1991. Indeed, during the Communist days, the penalty for a kanun-based attack was that the perpetrator was buried alive with his victim.

In 1991 the Communist government fell, and an anarchic period in Albania began. Thus in the 1990s, the kula towers were gone even as the kanun was revived. As a result, the members of the clan against which there is a kanun declared were still effectively "locked" because they restricted their movements to areas close to home, or risked death. Even in the 1990s, wandering about in town could be a fatal mistake, as will be described.

An Albanian Feud:
The Kanun and the Death of Shtjefen Lamthi

Scott Anderson (1999) described the murder of Shtjefen Lamthi on a street in Shkoder, Albania, in 1998. Some 200 people witnessed the killing in which Leka Rrushkadoli pumped thirty-one bullets into Lamthi in retaliation for the killing of his father by Lamthi's father in 1985. No one cooperated with the police to make an arrest even though the identity of the killer was well-known. Indeed, the identity of the killer was so well-known that Anderson, a foreign reporter, was eventually able to find and interview him and publish his picture in the *New York Times Magazine*. Anderson found that death delivered on the open street to people like Lamthi had its origins in a modern kanun that could not be controlled by the weakened Albanian government.

The kanun killing of Shtjefen Lamthi had its origins during the Communist period when state control was strong. Shtjefen's father, Preka Lamthi, was an official in the government. One day in 1985, Noue Rrushkadoli, a neighbor and fellow member of the Communist Party, visited to play cards and drink *raki* at his friend's house. There was a lot of drinking, and Noue, who was known for his temper, ended up turning over the table of his host, a particularly strong Albanian insult. Preka, the elder Lamthi, ordered him out of the house, but Noue Rrushkadoli responded by attacking Lamthi's son Shtjefen, stabbing him six times. Following this, someone—it is not clear who—stabbed Noue. The knife hit his heart and he died. A government inquest into the death of Noue Rrushkadoli decided that regardless of who held the knife, the killing was in self-defense. No case was prosecuted, and Shtjefen survived. But Noue's sons Leka and Angelo Rrushkadoli quietly nursed their grudge, wary of a man they perceived to be a powerful government official of an all-powerful state.

In 1988, with the control of the Communist Party slipping in Albania, Leka Rrushkadoli made his first revenge attack, stabbing Preka Lamthi in one of the town lanes. In response, the two families became warier of each other, even while Albania was changing quickly. Both families moved to a new town and entered the new freewheeling capitalist economy. Then, in 1997, the economy collapsed, and Leka began to nurse his old grudge against the Lamthi family again. He bought a Kalashnikov automatic weapon and waited. Shtjefen crossed his path on August 3, 1998, and Leka shot him in the marketplace. From the Rrushkadoli perspective, the score was now even, but they knew that the Lamthi family would seek revenge. As a result, all of the males of the Rrushkadoli family found themselves "locked," afraid to be seen in public. One member of the Rrushkadoli family who had emigrated to Canada ten years previously and returned found himself "locked" and unable to return to Canada.

Assessing the Kanun of the Lamthi and Rrushkadoli Families

In 1999 when Anderson published the story in the *New York Times Magazine*, the score was one Lamthi and one Rrushkadoli. But both clans still felt wronged. So the end result of Noue Rrushkadoli's 1985 death was a feud in which fourteen years later, two entire clans had removed themselves from the broader community, afraid to move about or engage in other types of normal social and economic activity. But this was not an inevitable result. Examples of the "what ifs" in this situation highlight some of the broader social conditions that led to the murder of Noue Rrushkadoli in 1985 becoming framed as part of a kanun, and not another way.

For example, what if the death of Noue Rrushkadoli had occurred in 1955 instead of 1985? The strong Communist government would have effectively stopped Noue's sons from responding. In the event that a revenge killing had occurred, the all-powerful Communist government would have stepped in, buried Leka with Shtjefen, and the feud would likely not have gone further.

What if there had been a more powerful government installed in Albania in the 1990s, as indeed there was in a number of ex-Communist countries at that time? Preka Lamthi (or whoever held the knife that killed Noue) might have been tried for manslaughter, sentenced to prison for a few years, and the passions of the Rrushkadoli sons cooled. Alternatively, if the central government had been more powerful, they would not have been hesitant about arresting Leka Rrushkadoli after he fell from grace, and perhaps try him for the crime.

What if the Albanian economy had boomed, and all had held good jobs? Would the Rrushkadolis' minds have turned to revenge? Even had Leka killed Shtjefen, perhaps his family would have turned on him and handed him over to the police so that they could get back to the business of prosperity.

The biggest "what if" question is about the role that revival of traditions like kanun play in the assertion of what is right, wrong, and moral in a society undergoing rapid social change. Following the collapse of any established order, a new one emerges. This is often contested, as the society struggles to establish new norms for understanding itself. The attempt to assert (or reassert) an old tradition like kanun becomes a potent tool to define who is part of whatever group is emerging, and who is not.

Further Reading

Anderson, Scott (1999). "The Curse of Blood and Violence." *New York Times Magazine*, December 26.

Vigilante Justice in Skidmore, Missouri

Ken McElroy was shot and killed while sitting next to his wife, Trena, in a Chevy Silverado in downtown Skidmore, Missouri, in August 1981. At least thirty-five people were present at the time of the killing, including law officers, the mayor, and other prominent people in the small community. At least two guns were used to shoot as many as fifteen rounds.

The shooting occurred in the afternoon outside the American Legion Hall following a meeting that had been called to discuss how Skidmore could protect itself against Ken McElroy. McElroy and his wife showed up, uninvited, at the meeting. Leaving after exchanging words with the men there, he and Trena returned to his truck. As he was sitting in the truck, he was shot by two different rifles. Despite the large number of potential witnesses and repeated investigations by local, state, and federal authorities, all reached the same conclusion: Ken McElroy had been killed by "persons unknown." All thirty-five people present claimed not to have seen anyone fire. Despite the coercive power of the courts to compel testimony, none present admitted to having seen who killed Ken McElroy. Town Marshal David Dunbar, who had earlier resigned out of fear of McElroy, would only comment twenty years later, "It's really a shame about the Silverado. That was a really nice truck."

Ken McElroy was born in 1934, the fifteenth of sixteen children born to itinerant sharecroppers. He never learned to read well and never held a steady job. McElroy lived outside of Skidmore, a town of about 500 people, with a succession of women—a harem, some writers called it, because frequently there was more than one teenage wife or girlfriend living there. Indeed, in the 1960s and 1970s McElroy regularly cased junior high schools, looking for new girls to replace those of whom he had tired. As a result, by the time of his murder in 1981, he had had at least ten children by four different women. He had been arrested twenty-two times and been tried only once (he was acquitted) but never served time in jail. Indeed, the event that precipitated his murder, a shotgun assault on a seventy-year-old grocer, resulted in only his first conviction and sentencing. He was free on bail when he was killed.

Ken McElroy married for the first time at age eighteen and moved briefly to Denver, Colorado. He could not hold a job, so he and his wife soon moved back to Skidmore. There, he began hanging out with his "coon huntin' buddies," men who shared his passion for hunting raccoons at night when the animals were active. His nighttime activities were to become his income—he became a cattle rustler in a remote corner of Missouri where cattle markets were poorly policed and there was no obligation to brand cattle. Nighttime stealth, a refined capability to harass and intimidate any witnesses, and an attorney who could be retained at a cost of $5,000 per felony kept him out of the courthouse and driving a succession of new pickup trucks. McElroy also developed a skill for brandishing weapons.

McElroy's first arrest came in connection with his wife-to-be, Trena, an eighth grader whom he first seduced in 1971 when she was twelve years old. McElroy already had two women, Marcia and Alice, living with him at the time. Nevertheless, Trena moved in, replacing Marcia. She dropped out of school in the ninth grade and was pregnant by the time she was fourteen. But then sixteen days after the birth of her son, she and Alice fled to Trena's parents. This lasted only a few hours. Brandishing a gun, McElroy forced the girls to return home with him, where as punishment he beat them and forced them to perform sex acts. After that, he returned with Trena to the home of her parents. McElroy shot the family dog, poured gas around the house, and burned it down.

Two days later, Trena took her newborn son to a doctor, who coaxed the story of the arson out of her. The doctor contacted the county social welfare agency, who put Trena and her baby into foster care. The case was taken to the district attorney. On the basis of Trena's testimony, McElroy was indicted for arson, assault, and rape. Even at $5,000 per felony, his attorney told him, it would be difficult for him to be acquitted. But McElroy did not relent. He found the foster home where Trena was living and began making threatening calls. The district attorney slapped on eight more felony molestation charges as a result of the trysts he had had with Trena beginning when she was thirteen years old.

But McElroy could still be charming. He arranged to divorce his second wife, Sharon, from whom he had been separated for several years, and marry Trena. More threats persuaded Trena's mother to give consent to the marriage, which in turn solved McElroy's legal problems. As his wife, Trena could not be compelled to testify against him in a case that was highly dependent on her cooperation for a conviction. McElroy had beat the charges.

There were more cases during the subsequent years. Many involved intimidation, whether it was over women, slights to McElroy's honor, or accusations of criminal activity. His last fight was in many respects just as trivial as the others. One of McElroy's children was chastised by shopkeepers Bo and Lois Bowenkamp for not having paid for a ten-cent piece of candy. Ken McElroy came to the store and found Bo Bowenkamp cutting open boxes with a butcher knife. A verbal altercation ensued, and Bowenkamp was shot with McElroy's shotgun. This time, despite the claims of McElroy and one of his hunting buddies that Bowencamp had threatened McElroy with the knife, Ken McElroy was sentenced to two years in prison. But, under Missouri law, he remained free on appeal; the only question in August 1981 was when he would begin his sentence. Stays were granted, during which McElroy returned to Skidmore to threaten witnesses, including the Bowenkamps. It was at this time the town called a meeting in the American Legion Hall. The conclusion of the meeting resulted in the still unsolved death of Ken McElroy by persons unknown.

Ultimately, of course, this is a story about the legitimacy of the law as it emerges from the people. Not even the power of the FBI could break the code of silence in Skidmore. To address the problem of Ken McElroy, the town of Skidmore briefly became a virtually stateless area. The townspeople's subsequent code of silence was as powerful as that in an inner-city gang, or any stateless area that is so difficult to police.

Further Reading

Krajicek, David (n.d.). Court TV Crime Library, online at http://www.crimelibrary. com/notorious_murders/classics/ken_mcelroy/index.html.

MacLean, Harry N. (1988). *In Broad Daylight: A Murder in Skidmore, Missouri.* New York: Dell.

Without Mercy (film, 2004).

Death by Python: The Deaths of the Girl Comfort and Samuel Betta

Witchcraft has long been a concern of governments attempting to establish the rule of law. Certainly, it was an issue for ministers in Puritan Massachusetts in 1691 who convulsed their own society with the Salem witchcraft trials. But it is still an issue around the world today, where it is an implicit competitor with modern elites seeking a centralized rule of law rooted in modern reasoning. Just how witchcraft—a force that is regarded by most modern people as completely imaginary—can threaten the modern state is revealed in the following story from the African country of Cameroon. This is why Section 251 of the Cameroon penal code was adopted, which reads in part: "Whoever commits any act of witchcraft, magic or divination liable to disturb public order or tranquility, or to harm another person, property or substance whether by taking a reward or otherwise, shall be punished with imprisonment for from two to ten years, and with a fine of five thousand to one hundred thousand francs."

The following paragraphs describe how this law was enforced in 1986 when the modern Cameroonian state challenged the authority of two men, Samuel Betta and Akama Epongo, who disputed control of a river near their village. To the modern ear, the story will sound odd. But keep in mind the beliefs that surround the incidents described here, and focus on the death of two people, a young pregnant girl named Comfort, and Samuel Betta himself.

As was the habit of villagers in that locale, Comfort went down to the Meme River to bathe while her mother was washing eating utensils. Her mother heard shouts and rushed to the river, where she saw her daughter being dragged away by a large python. The mother immediately went to search for help from the village. The villagers whom she sought told her that they were not surprised. They had anticipated that such an attack would occur since her common-law husband, Samuel Betta (Comfort's step-father), controlled the python that had been seeking to wrest control of the river from the chief of the village, Akama Epongo. Epongo in fact owned the river, which was patrolled by his crocodile. In his trial, Samuel recounted what had happened:

> I took the girl to the head of our witchcraft club who happens to be the village chief. When I offered the girl to him, he said he was going on a jour-

ney and that I should get back to him in four days. He got the girl and locked her up in a room and he alone has the keys. Up to this point the girl [was] still alive in the chief's witchcraft room. The price the chief asked me was a person and I gave him Comfort. Although Comfort is not my biological daughter, I have brought her up so far. Comfort [was] not yet dead, she [was] locked up in the chief's witchcraft room. I effectively offered the girl to witches. (Fisiy 1998:153, translation from French)

Confronted with this confession, the chief confirmed Betta's story, and both were arrested for having orchestrated the disappearance of Comfort under Cameroon's antiwitchcraft law, Section 251, because they had clearly used witchcraft to disturb the public order. This happened despite the fact that Comfort's body was never recovered. After a delegation from the village went to the police, the chief was arrested at the request of Comfort's mother in order to pressure him into releasing the girl. In order to generate more evidence about the case, the police beat and tortured the two defendants. Two weeks later Samuel Betta died in his cell and so was never tried for witchcraft. Akama Epongo was eventually tried and, on the basis of a confession that he did indeed own and control the crocodile of the river, was given a two-year sentence with hard labor.

Cyprian Fisiy goes on to note in his article about this case that "the feeling that one gets when reading witchcraft files is that alleged witches are treated as if they do not possess any civic or human rights; they are part of a dark force subverting the existence of the state." In effect he is saying that as long as witchcraft has a hold on the population, the monopoly over the use of coercive power is challenged. Belief in witchcraft by its very nature is indeed a challenge to the modern state. This is why the response in cases like this, whether in 1980s Cameroon or 1690s Massachusetts, is so strong and harsh.

Further Reading

Erikson, Kai (1966). *Wayward Puritans*. Boston: Allyn and Bacon.

Fisiy, Cyprian (1998). "Containing Occult Practices: Witchcraft Trials in the Cameroon." *African Studies Review* 41, no. 3: 143–163.

Fisiy, Cyprian, and Peter Geschiere (1990). "Judges and Witches, or How Is the State to Deal with Witchcraft? Examples from Southeastern Cameroon." *Cashiers d'études africaines* 118:135–156.

CHAPTER 3

The Ecology of Violence: From Hurt Feelings to Fatal Blows

MUNDANE IS THE WORD THAT CRIMINOLOGISTS MICHAEL GOTTFREDSON and Travis Hirschi (1990) use to describe criminal homicide in the modern United States. They describe homicide as ordinary and mundane because, while killings in the United States are relatively unusual, most occur in "normal" places and during the course of normal events. Such normal places include homes, bars, street corners, and the workplace. Even the relationships between the victims and perpetrators are normal. About 20 percent of killings occur between family members, and as much as 60 percent of the rest occur between people of at least casual acquaintance. Of the remaining 20 percent of American homicides, about half occur in the context of a robbery, which, while hardly routine for the victim, was not originally intended to result in death. Only in the final 10 percent do we find the homicides of popular entertainment—the contract killers, poisonings, psychopaths, serial killers, and bombers who make for a good story but do not reflect normal mundane homicide in the United States today.[1]

The events surrounding the 80–90 percent of killings that emerge out of such mundane "routine encounters" happen in a predictable fashion. They tend to occur on weekends and at night, and most even occur in front of an audience.[2] Well over half of all homicides in the United States in the late twentieth century resulted in an arrest within twenty-four hours of the incident, often with the perpetrator surrendering to the police. And finally, the actual event that results in a homicide often starts in the same way that any other verbal argument or simple assault does; it begins as a disagreement or squabble over a minor incident between two individuals who know each other. Most often, of course, such altercations do not end in death, but in insults thrown, or perhaps a physical assault of some sort. All that is different in a homicide is how the altercation ends, not how it starts. This is why, from a sociological viewpoint, murder is considered a subset of that mundane crime known so well to people who have had childhood squabbles with a sibling: assault.

Indeed, whether the victim dies or not following an assault is sometimes beyond the immediate control of the angry or drunk person wielding the gun or knife, irrespective of whether he or she has the legal intent to kill. The difference between events that end in words, fisticuffs, wounding, or death may depend on whether a loaded gun is readily available, a knife is handy, or the weight of the frying pan wielded is sufficient to cause a fatal injury. It may depend on whether someone has a cell phone to call 911 or knows CPR. One of the most terrifying cases described in American criminology classes is the rape and murder of Kitty Genovese. She was attacked two or three separate times in the early morning hours of March 13, 1964. Her screams in a middle-class section of New York City were heard by thirty-eight witnesses, only one of whom eventually called the police—forty minutes after the screams began. The police arrived quickly, but the violence of the final attack proved fatal (Rosenthal 1999). There is little doubt that had the police been called when she first screamed, the attack would not have been fatal.[3]

The speed of police and medical response, and what they do when they arrive, are thus also part of the ecology of a domestic disturbance. A fast ambulance may mean that someone's life will be saved and the perpetrator will be charged with assault. But an ambulance stuck in traffic may mean that the victim bleeds to death, and the charge will be homicide. The point is that many issues unconnected to the psycholegal intent of the perpetrator can contribute to whether a victim lives or dies as a result of a particular assault. The intent to kill may be the same for the person who grabbed an aluminum frying pan as a weapon, which causes a minor scalp wound, or a cast-iron frying pan, which fatally crushes the skull. What is different is not the psychology of the killer or the intent of the person wielding the pan, but the fact that someone died. Such a perspective means that who kills, and even who dies, are often beyond the immediate control of a killer. But if death is beyond the immediate control of the perpetrator, what is not is the amount of violence a particular individual commits. Ecological theorists point out that the more often a person is violent, the more likely it is that a death will result. Ecological theorists look at the typical mundane homicide as being the result of a gambling game. You can throw two ones if you roll the dice only once, but it is not too likely. But the person who throws the dice frequently is likely to eventually throw double ones.

This presents a different way to think about killing. Instead of looking at the process of criminalization as a function of state and law as I did in Chapter 2, the focus here is on the microsociology of killing. In the modern United States, what types of social situations are more or less likely to result in a violent death? Note that the killing described in this chapter is not between elites, armies, or chiefs. Rather, it is the type of killing typically found in modern societies, where violence is seen most often among the marginalized because the middle and upper classes are pacified.

Nevertheless, from the ecological standpoint, it is notable that the dynamics of violence remain largely unchanged. Andrew Jackson may have been a member of Nashville's planter elite during his brawl with the Benton brothers, but his brawling was as chaotic and purposeless as that of a modern urban gang, or even of a wife beater like Buck Thurman. Little was planned in such assaults; they were largely impulsive. The broader question is, how can a situation be regulated to make a lethal result less likely given that violent people are present? How does one element, the availability of law discussed in the previous chapter, affect the social interaction between two combatants? How does the presence of a weapon, alcohol and drugs, or a certain type of individual affect the situation? How do culture and issues of male honor contribute to the situation? What about the presence of young people, drunk people, or even prostitutes, or people who enjoy fighting and combat? These are among the ecological issues that determine whether confrontation, assault, and death will occur.

Criminologists thinking about crime in this way focus on the ecology of the situations. Thus they look at the availability of weapons and whether people in those situations are likely to control their impulse to lash out violently. This ultimately leads to questions about why a small percentage of people are frequently violent (and therefore more likely to kill), while most people are able to control their impulses and solve problems peacefully.

The Ecology of People: Murder and Young Males

Gottfredson and Hirschi (1990) specifically ask why some individuals refrain from frequent acts of violence (theft, drug abuse, and impulsiveness in general) while others do not. Data from every modern society, however it is measured, indicate that young males have the highest frequency of reckless and impulsive acts (see, e.g., Gottfredson and Hirschi 1990, Miethe and Regoeczi 2004, Cohen and Land 1987, and Daly and Wilson 1988).[4] Likewise, in every society the elderly commit fewer impulsive acts than the young, males commit more impulsive acts than females, and drunks are more reckless than sober individuals.

Why is it that when young males form groups with each other, they are more likely to be impulsive (and violent) than when they are with older people? How does the presence or absence of an authority figure (i.e., a third party) affect how they behave? In asking such questions, Gottfredson and Hirschi stand at the intersection of psychology and sociology; they are asking how social structure influences individual actions that result in violence. Figure 3.1 illustrates the relationship between violence and violent death as described by Gottfredson and Hirschi (1990).

Impulsive Acts and Age

Central to Hirschi and Gottfredson's ecological approach is that impulsive acts, whether legal or not, are relatively simple to commit. It is not difficult to assault someone, shoplift, get drunk, use drugs, steal, or burglarize a house, which is why they point out that the criminal mastermind of Sherlock Holmes novels and James Bond movies is exceedingly rare in the real mundane world of teenage (or twenty-something) criminals. In reality, much of the crime we see in society occurs as males jockey for status. This helps explain why as many as half of all homicides occur in the presence of an audience, and why a large proportion of both victims and perpetrators are young males.

Assuming homicide is a subset of assault, it is easy to conclude that young drunk males in the context of a fight, brawl, or general act of bravado are the most likely to kill. Young males are the people most likely to have a tendency toward rule-breaking, including assault and homicide. Gottfredson and Hirschi note that drunk young males are more impulsive and have less "self-control" than do people who are older, female, and/or sober. This focus on variations in self-control is central to Gottfredson and Hirschi's ecological theory. The more self-control there is, the less likely there is to be impulsive violence. The less self-control there is, the more likely there is to be impulsive violence. It is not completely understood what it is about the development of males that leads to a period in the life cycle when impulsive criminal acts are more common than later in life. But starting with the observation that young males are much more likely to commit

Figure 3.1 The Relationship Between Violence and Violent Death

Gottfredson and Hirschi (1990:31–34) make the point that homicide is a subset of interpersonal conflict resulting from a "loss of impulse control." The figure shows the relationship among frequency of events, legal classification, severity of victim injury, and legal response. For the overall category "interpersonal conflict," only a small proportion of incidents result in the death of the victim. This figure illustrates this point graphically. There are a great number of incidents where people lose "impulse control," but nothing worse than regretted words, often slanderous, are hurled. In a declining number of incidents, the loss of impulse control results in physical injury to the victim. Only in a very small number of incidents do these losses result in physical injury, the death of a victim, or what the law calls "homicide." Nevertheless, according to social control theory there is still a common factor, "lack of impulse control," on behalf of the perpetrator. As described in the text, this lack of impulse control is a necessary ingredient in the 70 percent of homicides resulting from interpersonal conflict, robberies, and burglaries. What is different is the "ecology" of the situation, for example, the fact that a gun, heavy frying pan, drunkenness, or other factor is present.

(continues)

Figure 3.1 continued

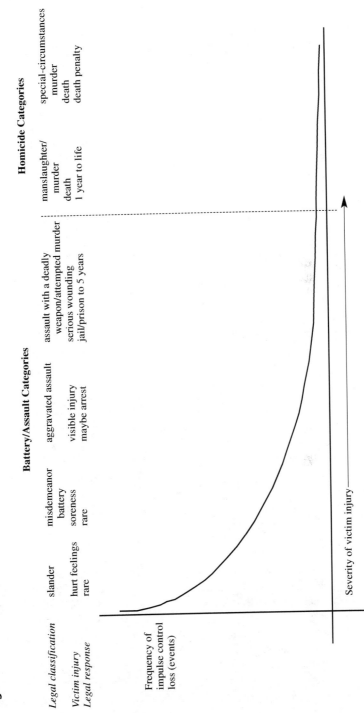

impulsive acts does point to an important element in the ecology of any situation. That is, in places where young males congregate, fighting, assault, and arguments over matters of honor are more likely than in places where they do not congregate.

This propensity for violent conflict is reflected in US homicide statistics. Robert O'Brien, Jean Stockard, and Lynne Isaacson (1999) analyzed statistics of individuals arrested for homicide in the United States from 1961 to 1995.[5] They found that usually the highest rates of homicide were among 20- to 24-year-olds. Such compelling data explain why social ecologists consistently point to concentrations of young males as being a factor leading to a higher likelihood that a violent act will occur. As with the availability of weapons, the presence of a person who because of his age is more likely to be violent contributes to the ecology of the situation and elevates homicide rates. Statistics show that homicide arrests for 15- to 19-year-olds rose especially rapidly in the context of an expanded illegal drug trade that infected American inner cities in the 1990s. These rates have since decreased somewhat, although the pattern of elevated rates of homicide arrests among 15- to 24-year-olds persists.[6]

Looking at the Social Ecology of Crime

Social ecology theorists focus on the context in which assault occurs, even when discussing homicide. The general assumption is that if you understand how, why, when, and among whom fighting and assault occur, you will understand rates of homicide in places like the modern United States. Data show that the strongest correlates of assault and violence are:[7]

- *Gender:* Males are more likely to engage in violence than females, and as a result they are more likely to kill, intentionally or unintentionally.
- *Age:* Most assault and homicide is committed by males between the ages of approximately fifteen and twenty-five, which is when males are physically their strongest and self-control has not yet been completely established.
- *Alcohol and drugs:* Alcohol and some drugs lower impulse control, which means that drunks and drug users are more likely to be violent than people who are sober.
- *Honor:* Issues of honor are most likely to lead to violence. Such issues of honor include slights, disagreements about debts owed, and the attention of females.
- *Badmen:* This term refers to individuals who impulsively seek revenge for slights on their own.
- *Weapons:* Guns are more lethal than knives, and knives are more

lethal than hands and fists. Automobiles are more lethal than motor-cycles, which are more lethal than bicycles. Guns and automobiles add to the potential lethality of a situation.

- *Third parties:* The presence of third parties affects the interaction. If authority figures such as the police, bouncers, teachers, or parents are believed to be present, a violent event is less likely to escalate. If only peers—be they rivals, intimates, or acquaintances—are present, violence is more likely to escalate.

To sum up, most assault—and most murder—occurs in groups of males who are between fifteen and twenty-five years old who drink alcohol or use drugs. Access to weapons (guns, knives, arrows, etc.) makes death more likely. Interestingly, assault is more likely to happen in the American South (as opposed to New England), even though the relationship among age, gender, and violence is the same.[8] Therefore, to control violence, it follows that laws and policies that remove any of these elements are likely to reduce the harm that can be done. In this respect, social ecology theories are very practical because they suggest specific laws and policies that can be adopted to control violence. Among the most obvious are:

- Careful regulation of alcohol use, including controlling its use by the young
- More careful policing of places where young males congregate, like sports events, bars, and high schools
- Arresting and incarcerating individuals who are more frequently violent, particularly during their youth
- Restrictions on the carrying and possession of weapons in places where violence is likely to occur

The Ecology of Killing and Personal Violence

The term *ecology* is most often associated with the biological sciences. However, focusing on the ways in which elements of a situation interact—which is at the heart of both biological and sociological ecology—helps assess how some circumstances lead to potentially lethal situations while others do not. To illustrate this point, I will explore five very different ecological situations: the ecology of bars in the California frontier town of Bodie in the 1880s, the ecology of modern street gangs, the ecology of domestic violence, the role of lethal weapons in homicide rates, and the role of "badmen," family, and socialization. These cases illustrate how the ecology of a situation leads to more or less lethal confrontation.

What they all have in common is an "ecology" in which violence thrives. As a result, the likelihood of a lethal incident increases because killing is a by-product of a violent environment. The more elements necessary for a lethal result that are present, the more likely it is that a particular event will end in a death.

Bars, Brawls, and Killing

Bars are some of the best places to explore the ecology of killing and social control. This is because young males gather in bars, alcohol is always present, and issues of honor frequently arise. In the modern United States, there is now an inherent recognition of the volatility of bars, which is why they are carefully regulated by law and custom. Among the common regulations that have emerged to control violence in bars are prohibitions on people under the age of twenty-one, laws prohibiting firearms, liability laws requiring bartenders to restrict alcohol to the obviously inebriated, mandatory closing times, and bans on prostitution. Third-party deterrents to violence include the hiring of beefy bouncers, ready access to police via 911 calls, and the willingness of witnesses to provide information to police in the event of a violent incident. Such simple and mundane regulations changed the social ecology of bars during the past 50–100 years. Just how well these regulations work is best understood by looking at what life in bars was like before they were instituted. The bars of the mining town of Bodie, California, provide a good illustration.

Bodie was a mining town in the high desert of eastern California in the late 1800s. Following the establishment of the mines, the town population rose from 1,500 to about 5,300 in the two years from 1878 to 1880. To accommodate the commercial needs of these miners, there were seventeen saloons, fifteen brothels, six restaurants, five general stores, a Wells Fargo office, and two stage lines (McGrath 1984:109). Most men carried sidearms at all times. Ninety percent of the population was male, most of whom worked in the underground mines outside the city.

Violence in Bodie's many bars was predictable every weekend, as liquored-up miners asserted their status as fighters. The *Bodie Morning News* of October 28, 1879, described the weekend nightlife among the miners in the following fashion:

> The latter half of Saturday night was a wild one. The consumption of bug juice [alcohol] was something wonderful. Fighters were as thick as blackbirds in a rice field, and were accommodated almost to a man. The downtown dance houses were scenes of numerous pugilistic passages, and pistols were several times drawn to enforce fistic arguments. No one had his measure taken, however, for a wooden overcoat, though the prospect at times looked as if it would develop into a bonanza for the Coroner and undertakers, but simmered down to a few rich "pockets" of broken noses and black eyes. (McGrath 1984:185–186)

Such rowdy, violent habits resulted in a high overall homicide rate in Bodie. Many of these fighters were willing participants who fought at the least provocation to prove who was the better man, to defend themselves against careless insults, or to reestablish the pecking order in the saloon. It was considered normative to brandish a pistol; shots were most often fired into the air, but wounding was common. In the small town of Bodie, Roger McGrath (1984:191) found newspaper mentions of over fifty nonfatal shootings and shootouts from 1877 to 1883, and there is no reason to believe that every discharge of a firearm was reported in the papers. Thirty-one citizens of Bodie were killed in those years, which gave Bodie an annual homicide rate of 116 per 100,000 residents, somewhere between what the Ju/' Hoansi and Ache experienced (McGrath 1984:254). This rate is also well above the modern US rate of 5 to 10 per 100,000. Indeed, it is even substantially higher than the notoriously violent 15- to 19-year-olds of 1990–1994, whose homicide arrest rate was 35.24 per 100,000.[9] In short, Bodie was an exceptionally violent place.

A number of ecological factors contributed to the high rates of violence and homicide in Bodie. Liberal amounts of alcohol were of course elemental to the bar scene. There was a high proportion of males in Bodie, many of them in their twenties. The presence of unattached women in the bars, many of whom were prostitutes, presented the potential for disputes over manly honor. Most Bodieites were also armed with handguns, bars had no closing hours, and bartenders would sell as much alcohol as patrons could pay for.

Law enforcement in Bodie was also different than it is today. The law permitted violent challenges (including those involving firearms), even if there was a nonlethal way to exit the confrontation. The sheriff would not arrest, nor would a jury convict, someone who responded to a challenge, no matter how grievous the death or injury that resulted. In this ecological context, a culture of honor emerged in which verbal slights, or even looks, were easily (mis)interpreted. The ensuing fights, lethal or not, were not judged to be worthy of intervention from any third party.

As ecological theories would predict, much of the violence in Bodie was generated by impulsive individuals with low self-control, or what McGrath (and others) call "badmen." McGrath points out that the toughs of the town were responsible for over half of the violent deaths he identified. These badmen enjoyed fighting and dominated barroom culture. Much bravado resulted when a drunken badman would announce to the barroom that he would take on all comers. In the following story about Harry Dugan, death is not an immediate result—although this is not due to any lack of intention or foresight on Dugan's part (McGrath 1984:199–201). But it is an excellent example of the violent chaos such a badman could bring to situations such as those found in the barrooms of Bodie.

Harry Dugan arrived in Bodie in 1878 and was described by one of the town's newspapers as a "man of good impulses, but reckless and quarrelsome when under the influence of whiskey." Already by January 1879 he was known for his violence. Joseph Muirhead was a miner who had lost a hand in a mining accident and had a hook as a prosthesis. At a saloon one day, Muirhead attempted to join a group of miners who were entertaining a prostitute. Rebuffed, he nevertheless moved toward the woman, or so Dugan later claimed. Dugan hit him on the head with his revolver and sent Muirhead reeling out of the bar.

Returning to the bar at two o'clock in the morning, Muirhead asked for the man who had hit him. Dugan indicated that he was the one. Muirhead immediately fired at least four shots, all of which missed Dugan, including one that tapped a barrel of ale and another that shot the cigar out of a patron's mouth. Dugan returned fire, wounding Muirhead in the scalp, and Muirhead escaped down the street. Dugan generously replaced the cigar of the bar patron and remained in the bar. Both Dugan and Muirhead were arrested and released later because neither they nor the patrons in the saloon could be persuaded by the police to testify about the incident, which most people in Bodie regarded as legitimate combat.

Just two months later, in March 1879, Dugan was involved in another barroom gunfight. In this fight, Dugan and Frank Black began with a "friendly talk" that escalated to a gun battle in which both men, as well as a bystander, were hit, and Dugan's lung was punctured. Despite the seriousness of his wound and before a court case could be made, Dugan left town. It was reported a year later that Dugan was shot through the stomach in a gunfight in Silver Cliff, Colorado, and that his chances of survival were not good. The paper wrote after the incident that "it was a foregone conclusion that he would die 'with his boots on'" (McGrath 1984:201). Obviously the editor, like Hirschi and Gottfredson, had a good sense of how the presence of an impulsive drunk badman contributed to the lethality of a situation.

Bars in the modern United States may be violent, but they are not as violent as those in Bodie. This is in large part due to modern regulations that remove the more volatile elements from the ecology of bars. Most obviously, there are now restrictions on the carrying of weapons, especially guns. But other regulations reduce the potential for violence in bars. Among these are requirements that bars close at a particular time (typically 1 A.M. or earlier), the banning of juveniles from such establishments, the discouragement of prostitution in most bars, and laws that require bartenders to restrict the sale of excessive amounts of alcohol to any one patron. Today, in the event of even a small verbal altercation, a bouncer—a third party—will intervene quickly, and bar owners are quick to call 911 for official assistance.

Finally, today, the discharge of a gun in a bar leads to the police being summoned quickly, and they are usually respected when they arrive.

Witnesses are likely to come forward because they find the use of violence abhorrent and not a matter of honor. What all this means is that a battle like that between Dugan and Muirhead no longer occurs because elements necessary to the incident are no longer present. First, if an unarmed Dugan were to hit someone over the head even with a beer mug (much less a pistol), a 911 call would summon the police quickly. Also, no one would be at a bar at two in the morning (when Muirhead returned), due to mandatory closure laws. Additionally, Dugan might well have been jailed and may have been awaiting trial during the two months between the fight with Dugan and that with Frank Black. In short, the modern ecology of the situation would make the more serious parts of these incidents unlikely. A Dugan of today might find a way to maintain his tough-guy reputation, but his options in a modern bar are much more limited.

Dead on the Street: The Social Ecology of Modern Street Gangs

Youth gangs proliferate in the social spaces of the modern world, where poor young males who are unsuccessful in conventional society gather. Despite stereotypes to the contrary, few youth gangs have centralized leadership or firm business goals in mind, in contrast to some drug-dealing gangs. Youth gangs are small groups in which marginalized youth hang out together and establish tough-guy reputations that are in opposition to their more conventional brothers (see Klein 1995, 2004; Waters 1999; Vigil 2002). Gang members typically emerge from among those who have done poorly in school in terms of academics and socialization. As outsiders, they seek the company of others like themselves who are itinerantly employed and have poor school records and limited conventional goals. The abuse of alcohol and drugs is common. And in the absence of status rewards from conventional sources, the honor of the gang (or neighborhood) is often very

Table 3.1   Gang Members Reporting Violence in the Last Six Months (percentage)

	Gang	Non-Gang
Set fire to building or car	5	1
Attack with weapons	29	3
Throw objects or rocks at people	42	25
Gang fights	56	9
Hit someone	45	28
Use weapon or force	15	5
Had sex with someone against his/her will	2	3

Source: Klein 2004:129.

important. Gangs often attract the attention of the police, which in turn results in further distrust of conventional authorities. As described in Chapter 2, third-party theories are an effective way to understand the conflicts that emerge when gangs seek to seize control of "turf" from the police or other gangs. But a lack of a legitimated third party is also an element in the social ecology of a neighborhood. Statistics collected by Malcolm Klein indicate that gang members are much more likely than nonmembers to be engaged in a violent incident as perpetrators or victims (see Table 3.1).

Just as in Bodie's bars or with Ju/' Hoansi hunting-and-gathering groups, most incidents of street violence are not lethal, though inevitably a small portion do result in death. But an assault does often provide a pretext for the next assault. This is because attacks, whether lethal or not, are seen as an assault on group identity. Kody Scott, a gang leader from a Los Angeles Crips gang, wrote the following account in his memoir:

> Who fired the first shot? Who knows? But, too, who cares, when one . . . is lying in a pool of blood with his brains blown out. This question becomes weightless in the aftermath of a shooting where someone has died. Thus the goal becomes the elimination of the shooter or as many of his comrades as possible. This inevitably leads to war—a full scale mobilization of as many troops as needed to achieve the desired effect: funerals. (quoted in Yablonsky 1997:101)

Again, the criminological and social focus on the homicides that occur in such situations obscures the fact that most gang violence is not lethal. Rather, the lethal incident, which is of course perceived as the most important, is the result of an ongoing ecology of violence focused by the establishment and maintenance of the reputation of the group. A story by the gang member "Puppet" told to gang researcher Diego Vigil (2002:61) is representative of the type of violence associated with gangs:

> On Thursday afternoon we were just driving. Sometimes we liked to cruise through a neighborhood that we didn't like. This time some guys saw us and went after us. They got us hard and smashed our car with rocks and bricks. One of the vatos [guys] was real messed up and needed stitches. The rest of us just got beat up a little. I got a bump on my head and a scratch across my nose.

Puppet and his friends ultimately responded by "busting in" on parties in the rival gang's neighborhood. From their perspective, Puppet and his gang members needed to protect their own honor, even though there was little meaning and no financial profit in the fighting. Rather, the focus was on the thrill of cruising through a neighborhood in order to provoke a challenge. Aimlessly seeking such a challenge is similar to the sort of poorly coordinated responses of the bad men of Bodie, like Harry Dugan. Or, for that matter, it is similar to the badman of the Ju/' Hoansi, Gau, who pro-voked arrow fights, and to the Ache, who enthusiastically shaped their clubs to inflict the most serious wounds possible in club fights. Ecological theory emphasizes that any deaths that occur are the result of the general violence; they do not necessarily contain the rational premeditated intent assumed in legal statutes.

Malcolm Klein (2004:73–75) points out that modern increases in street gang homicides are primarily a product of a broader pattern of violence, availability of weapons, and the increasing numbers of marginalized young males found in America's inner cities in the 1980s and 1990s. In essence, he says that the ecology of the situation changed to make confrontations more likely to be lethal in the past thirty years. To make his point, Klein com-pares 800 gang members he studied in the early 1960s with data he collect-ed in the 1990s. Only one of the 800 eventually died violently in the three-year period of his study, even though this death occurred in a population that logged over 2,000 arrests and myriad unreported violent incidents. Gang lethality, Klein writes, increased in the 1980s and 1990s when gangs dealing in drugs, particularly crack cocaine, emerged alongside less orga-nized street gangs (Klein 2004:73–75). This change coincided with an increasing availability of firearms, including increased numbers of military-style assault weapons. In this study a gang of about 100 logged two violent deaths in the year he studied them (one in the gang he studied, and the other caused by that gang). Six more of the 100 gang members were dead of vio-lence within two years after the project was completed (Klein 2004:74).[10]

A series of events in Washington, DC, in the mid-1990s provides an illustration of how the ecology of gangs contributes to an upsurge in lethal gang violence. In this case, the presence of young impulsive males seeking to preserve honor collides with a thriving drug market, a lack of impulse control, and the ready availability of firearms.

Jim Myers wrote "Notes on the Murder of Thirty of My Neighbors" for *The Atlantic Monthly* in 2000. Myers's article focused on the suspiciousness and fear that permeated his neighborhood near the US Capitol building fol-lowing thirty murders in the early 1990s. The full story told by this article is described in a case study following this chapter, but here I would like to highlight the ecology of one set of related incidents.

Most of the murders Myers described were attributed to drug-related violence, an ecological category. An illegal drug market plays a crucial role in attracting young males intent on protecting their honor and creates a social area where police have limited access, or, in other words, the area is "virtually stateless." So, when two District of Columbia police officers crept up on a well-financed (and illegal) craps game in 1992, Coy Donae Mason, one of the jittery players, reacted by drawing a gun and firing a shot in the direction of the police. Mason dropped the gun and ran away, apparently after realizing that he had fired upon police officers and not the robbers he probably assumed they were. The equally jittery police, in response to this potentially lethal assault, shot Coy Mason in the back as he fled. This shooting led to a legal assessment of the death, wherein prosecutors evaluated Mason's and the officer's states of mind at the time of the shooting. The assessment concluded that the police officer had reasonable fear of lethal violence, and that the shooting was therefore justified under the law.

But note that this legal assessment only dealt with personal culpability of the officers as required by law; it did not address the social ecological context of such a shooting, such as the availability of firearms in the neighborhood, the drug trade, distrust of police, and other elements of the social environment. As important is the issue of legitimacy of the police—and how it contributes to the ecology of the situation. The problem is that whether legally justified or not, Mason's shooting increased the level of fear of police within the community, as neighbors conducted a running conversation about whether the death of Coy Mason was "fair" or not. And they concluded that since Mason was shot in the back, the killing was dishonorable irrespective of the formal finding of justifiable homicide by the police department and the prosecuting attorney. As Myers points out, because of distrust of the police, there are no residents of the neighborhood or friends of Mason who believe the police account of the incident.

In this context, confrontations between the police department and the largely black and poor urban community raised the level of distrust further. Young men began carrying guns regularly; a sign at the laundromat even asked customers to empty bullets from their pockets before doing their wash. Myers (2000:76) pointed to the mundane nature of the epidemic of violence when he wrote, "There were so many killings that they were like community socials. Neighbors shook hands and shook their heads. I remember hearing one say to another 'Hey, I didn't see you at last night's shooting.'"

As for the police, the confrontations between young men resulting in woundings or even death were not aggressively pursued by the police because they viewed the victims as being a by-product of the illegal drug trade, and therefore not as worthy of investigation as more high-profile shootings. Less than half of the thirty murders in the neighborhood were ever solved. This led to the perception that if you did not take care of your own honor, there would be no justice, because the legitimated third party—the police—would not. The result was a neighborhood filled with suspicion, fear, and armed young males seeking protection in the informal "gangs."

In this context, some of the young black men began to wear black hoods and silver shoes as a show of solidarity against the police, whom they openly mocked. This environment led to, among other things, a heightened level of anxiety among both the police and the citizenry that resulted in the death of Officer James White. On a December night in 1993, White approached Donzell McCauley from behind as he sat on the doorstep of a row house. McCauley responded by firing shots from a pistol that was loaded with lethal "Black Talon" bullets, which expand on impact. The first bullet hit Officer White in his bulletproof vest and knocked him to the ground. McCauley then stood over White and shot him four times in the head, killing him. This killing became the first—the only—death of the thirty to be brought to national attention; President Bill Clinton mentioned it in his 1994 State of the Union message because he wanted to frame it as a uniquely cold-blooded act. But, while it may well have been cold-blooded, such a categorization does not provide an ecological lens through which policies could be adopted to lessen the violence in Myers's neighborhood, reestablish the police as a legitimate authority, or lower the overall homicide rate in the long run. Indeed, from his jail cell, McCauley wrote a letter to Coy Mason's brother explaining that he had shot Officer White so that what had happened to Coy would not happen to him. In McCauley's mind, he believed that the two killings were connected and that Mason's brother would sympathize with this view.

Myers certainly does not excuse the murderer of Officer White. But he does make an important point about the ecology of fear, and law enforcement, when he points to the social implications of singling out just one homicide in preference to others: "Other homicides don't make the news at all, and our young people notice that, too. . . . It wasn't unique at all. Hey, that's how people kill one another in my neighborhood—with point-blank shots to the head" (Myers 2000:75–76).

The point an ecological theorist would make about the ecological term *drug related* is that it can be disassembled into a number of familiar subelements. These include a context of mutual distrust between police and residents, a well-armed population, and the presence of intoxicants, as well as impulsive young males. If guns were less accessible, the craps game had been for lower stakes, or the police were perceived as potential allies, these deaths might never have occurred. The youth would still have been impulsive, perhaps, but the lashing out would have been less likely to be lethal.

The role of challenges, fear, youthful bravado, and luck in gang violence is also illustrated in a courtroom description of what happened outside a pool hall in Sacramento, California, in 1998. This courtroom account naturally focuses on the incident leading to the violation of the law, and not on the underlying ecology of the situation. But much about the role of youthful impulsiveness, guns, and male honor can be inferred.

> The evidence showed that on the evening of April 10, 1998, defendants and two or three companions were shooting pool at Hot Shots Billiards. . . . Both [defendants were] members of Insane Viet Boys (IVB), an Asian street gang. As they were preparing to leave, defendants were involved in a

confrontation with members of a rival gang, El Camino Crips (ECC), at the poolhall counter. When someone in defendants' group identified themselves as IVB, someone in the other group said "fuck IVB," which would have been perceived by a gang member as disrespectful and a challenge. An off-duty reserve sheriff's deputy, Don Ralls, who was working security at the poolhall, intervened and escorted [the] defendants' group to their car, which belonged to Tran. . . . Tran and his group then drove away. Moments later, Tran returned, pulling into the parking lot. As Tran drove slowly past the poolhall with the headlights of his car off, [defendent Ro Van] Vo fired several shots at the people standing outside. Southalay Vongsedon, an ECC gang member known as "Nippy," who was standing by one of the doors to the poolhall, was killed when he was struck in the back of the head by a bullet fragment. Deputy Ralls, who was still outside when the shooting occurred, ran after the car as it left and fired one shot but missed. Defendants and a third suspect, Tuan Huynh, also an IVB member, were eventually arrested and charged with the first degree murder of Nippy . . . and assault with a firearm on Deputy Ralls. (*People v. Ro Van Vo et al.*, Court of Appeal, State of California, 3rd District, Filed August 14, 2003, http://www.courtinfo.ca.gov/opinions/revpub/C034960.PDF)

From a social ecology perspective, much of what happened at Hot Shots Billiards was unplanned and impulsive. It is not even clear that the victim, "Nippy," was targeted; after all, he was killed by a bullet fragment fired by someone from a moving car in the dark. Nippy was also not clearly involved in the previous altercation. Rather, he was a victim of the ecology of a violent situation that included impulsive young males, weapons, wild shots, an honor culture, and an uneasy and distrustful view of the police and the security guard on duty.

Killing at Home: Domestic Violence

Tough neighborhoods in virtually stateless areas are an ecology in which gang activity thrives. By the same token, the virtually stateless areas that are individual households are also a site for violence, and domestic homicide is an occasional result. As discussed in Chapter 2, this is in part because the home is one of the more difficult "virtually stateless" areas for the police to become involved in.

However, as Gottfredson and Hirschi (1990) point out, domestic violence crimes also illustrate the consequences of low impulse control on homicide rates. Provocatively, they note that the actual event resulting in a domestic homicide is not that different from previous violent confrontations that resulted in only insults, bruises, or woundings. Just as with the event that killed Nippy, or led to the violence in Bodie's bars, the final event begins in the context of anger, frustration, and often alcohol. The only reason that the fatal event in a domestic homicide ends differently than a previous confrontation or fight is that a more lethal weapon is present or is used more precisely. A way to think about this type of impulsive domestic violence is that each time an individual (or couple) loses his (their) temper and a confrontation escalates to violence, there is a small chance that the situation will result in a death. Most of the time, of course, even among the most violent domestic situations, death does not result. Nevertheless, the more times the dice of violence are rolled, the more likely it is that a spouse, boyfriend, girlfriend, parent, or child will be killed. In short, homes in which there is intense domestic violence are more likely to experience a domestic homicide.

A good illustration of the randomness of domestic homicide is a "negative case" in which no one died. The case of Buck and Tracey Thurman of Torrington, Connecticut, attracted the attention of the press and in 1989 was made into a television docudrama that focused on police reluctance to arrest Buck despite the chronic nature of his attacks on Tracey. In 1983 these attacks resulted in Tracey being stabbed thirteen times and partially paralyzed. This assault was so serious that Buck was sentenced to twenty years in prison (although he eventually only served nine years). This final assault occurred in the context of multiple assaults and calls to the police during the previous six months. A social ecology theorist would point out that the problem was not simply the response of the police but the fact that Buck and Tracey lived in an environment where weapons were available, alcohol was present, and violence was habitual. A social ecology theorist would also note that Buck's failure to kill Tracey Thurman was not due to any lack of intent on his part one way or the other. Presumably, any one of Tracey's thirteen stab wounds might have been fatal if the knife had severed a major artery or damaged a major organ. That Tracey lived had little to do with Buck's psychological state.

But is death inevitable in chronically violent households such as the Thurmans'? Are frequent calls to police for domestic violence an early warning system for homicide? In the popular press, and even in police circles, this case is sometimes made. But as Lawrence Sherman (1992:232–236) points out, such generalizations lead to what he calls the "hindsight fallacy" in domestic homicide. This hindsight fallacy focuses on the assertion that violent relationships are likely to end in death. Most often, this connection is made when a particularly violent person kills his or her domestic partner after repeated violent incidents: police and others assert that in hindsight, this result was to be expected given the history of violence in that household. And in part, as will become apparent in the following discussion, they are right. But what is actually more interesting is what statistics tell us about the relationship between chronic violence and domestic homicide. What those statistics show should sound familiar to anyone who has studied logic. Lethal incidents are most likely to occur in households that are violent. However, most violent households do not experience a domestic homicide.

A way of thinking about the "hindsight fallacy" is to think about domestic homicide rates. From 1985 to 1989 a study of domestic violence (and homicide) was conducted in Minneapolis, Minnesota.[11] As might be expected, the police never visited most Minneapolis households on a domestic violence complaint; in fact, there were an average of 105,424 households to which the police did not make any domestic violence calls at all, as opposed to 9,586 households that had one or more complaints per year. This means that 8.3 percent of Minneapolis households were visited by the police on a domestic violence complaint, while 91.7 percent were not. What is more, there are a small number of households in which there are "chronic" calls each year. These were the 416 households (less than 0.5 percent of all households) that had nine or more domestic violence calls. In these households fights are frequent, and as a result neighbors and the family itself call the police repeatedly. Presumably, this is the category that Buck and Tracey Thurman's household was in during the months before Buck's final knife assault. In other words, someone responded to screaming, fighting, and tears by calling police at a rate of almost once a month in a particular year. Domestic homicides are most likely to occur in these households because the people living there roll the proverbial dice most frequently and are as a result the most likely to have an incident end in a fatality. Nevertheless, most of these "super-violent" households will not experience a domestic homicide.

During Sherman's five-year study, there were a total of fifty-two domestic homicides in Minneapolis. This is certainly a large number, but it is very small compared with the more than 20,000 domestic violence complaints police responded to during the period studied. Thirty out of those fifty-two homicide cases (57.5 percent of the total) occurred in the 91.7 percent of houses that had never registered a domestic violence complaint. In terms of a percentage, it means that 0.003 percent (i.e., 30 out of 105,424) of the households that did not have any calls had a domestic homicide. In addition, the group with the most calls for domestic violence also had the highest rate of domestic homicide. Seven out of the fifty-two domestic homicides occurred in households that logged nine or more calls to the police. This means that 1.68 percent (7 out of 416) of these chronically violent households had a domestic homicide. Note that this is *fifty-five times* (i.e., 1.68 percent vs. 0.003 percent) the rate of households that did not have a domestic violence call. But still, even nine or more calls to the police are a poor predictor that a domestic homicide will occur. This is because 98.32 percent of the households that were chronically violent did not have a domestic homicide; they were like the Thurmans' house: simply just criminally violent.

But when viewed from a social ecology perspective emphasizing the propensity toward impulsive violence (as opposed to a legalistic intent to kill), these statistics make a great deal of sense. There was not a qualitative difference between the violent individual in the type of household where there was an incident of domestic homicide and the one in which there was not. Both were very violent. Rather, it means that the individuals were probably pretty much the same, only the "luck of the draw," or more precisely put, the ecology of the final lethal confrontation was slightly different.

Lethal Weapons

Weapons are part of the ecological mix that makes otherwise trivial altercations more likely to be lethal.[12] If a loaded handgun is available during a confrontation, there is more likely to be a serious wounding or fatality. It is simply easier to kill someone with a loaded handgun than with your own hands, a knife, or a frying pan. Statistics from emergency rooms in the United States back up this common-sense conclusion. About 17 percent of all gunshot wounds treated are fatal, while only 2 percent of all knife wounds are (Beeghley 2003:109).

But this is not a principle that can only be applied to handguns; it can also be applied to poisoned arrows among the Ju/' Hoansi and to clubs among the Ache of Paraguay. The lethality of the weapon matters, but it does not explain everything. When lethal weapons are available, killing does becomes easier. By the same token, there are places where the easy availability of weapons—the bars of Bodie and American street gangs come to mind—make lethal events more likely.

In most modern countries, guns are the weapon most likely to increase the lethality of an event. Most notoriously, in the United States there is a high correlation between the presence of 200 million privately owned guns and the elevated US homicide rate. Indeed, about two-thirds of all homicides are committed with handguns, and the proportion of suicides committed with handguns is similarly high. Each year in the United States about 10,000 homicides are committed with firearms, which means that about one gun out of each 20,000 guns is used in a homicide every year. These guns are designed for "self-protection" rather than hunting or target sports.

Reliable studies indicate that a 10 percent decline in gun ownership in a city correlates with an approximately 5 percent decrease in robbery rates and a 4 percent drop in robbery-homicide rates (Beeghley 2003:124–125; Sloan et al. 1988). A close correlation between gun ownership and homicide rates is also illustrated clearly by the ecological differences in two neighboring cities: Seattle, Washington, and Vancouver, British Columbia. These two cities have similar non-gun homicide rates, but the gun ownership rate is higher in Seattle than it is in Vancouver. Twelve percent of households in Vancouver have guns, as compared with 41 percent of households in Seattle—and Seattle's gun homicide rate is five times higher than Vancouver's.[13]

But these proportions do not occur in every country where firearms are widely available. For example, in Switzerland, where most men between the ages of twenty and forty are involved in periodic militia training, some 500,000 automatic military weapons are kept in their homes. But gun homicide rates are low—about 1.32 per 100,000. Why don't these Swiss firearms lead to an elevated homicide rate? Ecologically, we can presume that it is because these guns are not easily concealed, unlikely to be in bars or other places where male honor is important, and therefore not available in the contexts where confrontations are most likely to occur.

As the example of Switzerland indicates, the availability of firearms is only one element of a high homicide rate. Guns, for example, are far more lethal than poison arrows and war clubs. Nevertheless, even with the extraordinary problems the modern United States has with gun violence, US rates of violent death are still much lower than rates seen in societies like the Ache of Paraguay, in medieval England, or even among the presumably peaceful Ju/' Hoansi of South Africa.[14] In none of these societies were firearms available. In the broader picture, homicide rates drop because other elements of the social ecology change, particularly in regard to the civility that comes with the legitimacy of an effective legal system, as described in Chapter 2. When an effective third party is in place, the slights, insults, and disagreements that lead to confrontations (with or without weapons) are less likely to result in deadly violence, whether guns are available or not. In the broader picture, this vaguely defined variable is as much a factor as gun ownership. But legitimacy as a quality is difficult to measure, regulate, and monitor. Gun ownership and licensing are something that governments can effectively undertake.

Badmen: Family and Socialization in Social Ecology Theory

An important element in Gottfredson and Hirschi's view of the ecology of a lethal event is the individual—people like "badman" Harry Dugan, the hot-headed Buck Thurman, the aggressive Ju/' Hoansi fighter Gau, duel-loving Andrew Jackson, or even the fictional Muff Potter and Injun Jim are important variables. What these individuals have in common is that they "roll the dice" frequently by impetuously responding to what they perceive as challenges to their honor. We cannot know what kind of socialization these individuals received as children, but ecological theorists do step out on a limb to claim that it is the ecology of home environments and parenting styles that lead to the creation of impulsive individuals. This is called social control theory.

Gottfredson and Hirschi's (1990) reasoning is that since most crime is about lack of impulse control, it is not surprising that many more criminals come out of homes where youth are not socialized to defer their immediate wants. This correlates well with data showing that people raised by parents who are alcoholic, incarcerated, poor, single, or for other reasons have an unstable home, or have poor employment histories, are likely to have lower levels of self-control, resulting in more frequent use of impulsive violence.[15] Psychology actually shows that poorer and less stable households often have more authoritarian parenting styles than wealthy and stable parents do. Still, it is not completely clear whether it is parenting that leads to impulsiveness (a psychological condition), or poverty itself (a socioeconomic condition).

Nevertheless, there is a hesitation to accept this core precept of social control theory by sociologists, because it implies that only parents are responsible for the socialization of young boys rather than a broader social system that tolerates poverty and racism, generates few good jobs for young or undereducated parents, and does not provide affordable housing or funding for good schools. Nevertheless, Gottfredson and Hirschi's central point—that how well boys (in particular) are socialized (whether by parents or society) to exercise self-control plays a role in later self-restraint—does explain the ecological conditions creating more or fewer impulsive "badmen."

Most important, social control theory explains how badmen are created by their social environment; in short, they are not born that way. But this raises thorny policy questions. Changing the conditions in which badmen are created is possible. But it implies fundamental changes in the way families are supported by the larger economic system. In the absence of policies to redistribute income to families with children, finance schools more liberally, and support parents, the creation of violent and impulsive teenage males is likely to remain high.

A Final Note on the Ecology of Righteousness and Social Control

Ultimately, as with the third-party theories described in Chapter 2, issues of righteousness and assertions of rights and wrongs are at the heart of impulsive acts of conflict and violence. At the root of most interpersonal violence is a demand that a wrong be righted, no matter how incoherent it may seem to outsiders. Often, this demand is intensified in the context of anger and other emotions that distort the sense of grievousness, which in turn becomes part of a confrontation.

More so than many other approaches, social ecology theory focuses on the dynamics of the altercation rather than on the psycholegal criterion of intent so important in courtrooms. Ecological theorists assert that altercations do not proceed due to the seriousness of intent, but because the impulsive person takes offense and as a result more readily participates in a cascade of events that most people would avoid. Social ecology theories provide a good framework for thinking about how a slight, insult, or injury raises the chance of an altercation escalating from a simple assault to a death. Such a context is particularly important when thinking about modern societies where violence is by and large restricted to young males and is in large part disapproved of.

But this ecology does not occur in a cultural vacuum. Violent individuals are treated differently in different contexts. Their reputation is particularly ambiguous in small isolated societies, where defense of the group is important. Tough-guy reputations may be honored among groups like the Ache, who value fighting skills, or even among small intimate groups like street gangs, where such reputations are a source of increased status. But there are limits to the value of a reputation for impulsivity and violence in modern mass society. Such reputations in a larger society become dysfunctional, and change the individual from being a protector to being a badman.

What this implies about the rest of us, who generally control our impulses, is that we usually find ways to defer our needs for instant compensation and righteousness. The presence of legitimate institutions, as Chapter 2 points out, helps us control these impulses. And indeed, this deference to the wishes and rights of the larger group—that is, the third party—is at the heart of why society has become more peaceful; the quick and impulsive resort to the club, the knife, or the gun, while perhaps necessary in the anarchic world of stateless societies, is no longer relevant.

Social Ecology Theory and the Criminalization of Killing

Social ecology theory assumes that the intent of the person wielding the weapon is not very important in most killings; in this respect it is very different from the reasoning found in the modern legal system. Social control theorists understand that a fit of anger or lashing out that results in an insult or injury is often the same as the fit of anger or lashing out that results in a death. Conversely, violence that was not intended to kill, but does, can often be attributed to carelessness, impetuousness, or bad luck. This reasoning is contrary to popular conceptions of what differentiates killing and murder, but it is consistent with a wealth of data about situations that tend to result in killings.

Social ecology theory explains observations that violence in modern societies is most often undertaken by young males who are poorly integrated into society, and it also explains why many crimes, but especially violent crimes, are so mundane. This is consistent with the mass of homicide data that indicate that most deaths are the result of fights, brawls, and confrontations—often over trivial matters.[16] Because of this, social control theory explains why one is more likely to observe incidents of violence in bars and other places where young males congregate rather than at church socials, where the majority of people are women over fifty years old.

This social ecological focus suggests that the cascade of events leading to potentially lethal confrontation can be disrupted before violent events escalate beyond the immediate intentions of the participants. This is why there is a shared logic to understanding such diverse events like the behavior of drunks in Bodie bars, how witness inaction led to the death of Kitty Genovese, the violence found among street gangs, the relationships between domestic violence and homicide, and how gun control does (and doesn't) work. Not every drunk or self-righteous badman seeking status is equal and causes the same amount of damage. The ecology of the situation does matter, too.

Notes

1. Donald Black also made the point that violence and conflict are closely related in his book *Crime as Social Control*. He and students have developed a school exploring this relationship by developing anthropological and sociological data. See, for example, Baumgartner 1988; Black 1976, 1993; and Cooney 1997a, 1997b, 1998, and 2003.

2. Statistics about where and how murders occur in the United States can be found in Appendix 1.

3. Jim Rastenburger (2006) has questioned the sequence of events reported in the original March 23, 1964, *New York Times* article that captured worldwide attention. Still, though, I think that Rosenthal's ([1964]1999) point is valid. If any one of the witnesses had correctly interpreted the events they heard or saw, the police would have responded quickly, and Genovese probably would have survived. That they did not interpret what they saw or heard correctly is established fact. Why they did not do so is the source of much discussion since. Was it because it was not possible to do so? Or is there something in the human psyche of us all that makes it difficult to recognize horrific events that might put ourselves at risk?

4. See Appendix 1 for statistics about age, race, and gender of murder victims and perpetrators.

5. See Appendix 1 for O'Brien, Stockard, and Isaacson's data about age and homicide in the United States during the twentieth century.

6. For statistics describing the rise in homicide among young people in the 1990s, see Appendix 1.

7. Summary statistics about the role of gender, age, weapons, homicide circumstances, use of weapons, etc., are found in Appendix 1.

8. For a breakdown in regional rates of homicide in the United States, see Appendix 1.

9. See Appendix 1 for a description of the age statistics of murderers from the 1990s.

10. The inability of these drug gangs to use law enforcement to enforce con-

tracts meant that as many as one in four "soldiers" died during a four-year study conducted in Chicago by Levitt and Venkatesh (2000). This study has since been made widely known in Levitt's best-seller, *Freakanomics*.

11. The data described here are found in Appendix 1.

12. See Appendix 1 for a description of what types of weapons are involved in fatal incidents.

13. The studies he cites are those by Cook (1979) and McDowell (1986). These studies used statistical techniques to understand (among other things) the relationships between gun ownership, robbery rates, and homicide rates. Other studies (e.g., Sloan et al. 1988) compare the "twin cities" of Vancouver, BC, and Seattle, Washington. The two cities have similar rates of non-gun-related homicide. But in Seattle, where 41 percent of households have guns, the gun homicide rate is five times that of Vancouver, where only 12 percent of households own guns (see Beeghley 2003:124–125).

14. See Appendix 1 for descriptions of Ju/' Hoansi feuds. See also Table 2.1 for a description of fatalities among the Ju/' Hoansi and Ache.

15. O'Brien, Stockard, and Isaacson (1999) use the "nonmarital birth" rates as a proxy for parental socialization. Their reasoning is that such boys are more likely to be socialized by one rather than two parents, with low impulse control a consequence. As they note, this in turn correlates with rises and falls in the homicide rate when the boys enter the age for high risk of criminal activity. They claim that this is one explanation for the rise of homicide rates by the young in the 1990s: this correlated with a higher rate of nonmarital births in the 1970s.

16. Cooney (1998) describes this type of killing as "moralistic" as opposed to "predatory."

Notes on the Murders of Thirty of My Neighbors

Writer Jim Myers wondered why thirty of his neighbors were murdered just one mile east of the United States Capitol building during the 1990s. In an investigation of the conditions that led to such a high toll, he found that there was a wide range of circumstances, including "drive-by killings, run-by killings, sneak up killings, gunfights and battles, car chases . . . drug killings, vengeance killings, the killing of witnesses to other crimes, accidental killings, and killings that enforce values we can only vaguely fathom" (Myers 2000:73). The killings occurred in a context in which handguns were common and an illegal drug economy thrived.

By personalizing the victims and perpetrators in his article, Myers provides a nuanced picture of a community where fear, youthful bravado, and distrust of law enforcement lead to confrontations, fighting, woundings, and killings. Notably, the characteristics he describes are not only the people holding the guns or peddling the drugs. Rather, there is a generalized fear in the community, the anticipation of violence by large numbers of people, that provides the context for the killing.

The epidemic of killings Myers wrote about occurred in Police Service Area 109 of Washington, DC, an area only eleven blocks wide, from 1992 to 1998. Twenty-six of the thirty victims were black, and one of the whites was a police officer. Three of the killings were by police officers. Many of the victims and shooters had attended Payne Elementary School, which despite its proximity to the Capitol was one of the most segregated schools in the country. Out of 332 students in 1999, 330 were black, and none were white. Over two-thirds of the killings occurred within 1,000 feet of the school. Four of the victims had been members of the same basketball team (see Figure 3.2).

Myers begins his story by drawing a contrast between the highly publicized killing spree by two teenagers at Columbine High School in Colorado in 1999 and what happened in his Washington, DC, neighborhood. In the case of Columbine, thirteen middle-class students were killed in a single day. The incident received international publicity, and politicians from the president of the United States on down publicly bemoaned the cultural situation leading to the deaths. In contrast, eighteen of the thirty deaths Myers tracked were unsolved at the time he wrote his article. Whereas several had not even merited an article in the local newspaper, the murder of the white

Figure 3.2 Map of Washington, DC, and Thirty Murders

This map shows the locations of the thirty murders Jim Myers describes in his *Atlantic* article. Many of them were centered at Payne Elementary School, which is only a few blocks from the US Capitol building.

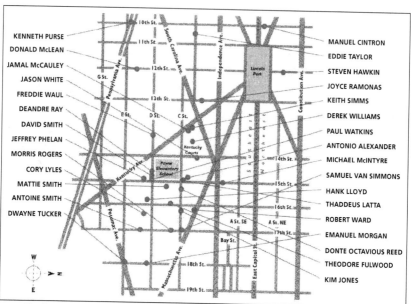

Reprinted by permission of Jim Myers.

police officer received widespread publicity, including a mention in one of President Clinton's speeches bemoaning street violence.

On the micro level, Myers's descriptions of killing in Washington illustrate well the role of youth, impulsiveness, gangs, bravado, guns, and alcohol in setting the context for killing. Most of the killings were of young males by other young males, and most took place on the street. The killings often involved dares and affronts to male honor; one assault would lead to a dare, which would in turn lead to another assault. The injured or insulted person might or might not have been the cause of the initial assault, thus creating a further grievance, and a widening circle of potential enemies. For example, police "solved administratively" the 1992 death of Theodore Fulwood—they stopped their investigation without officially identifying his killers because the police believed the killers themselves had been murdered. Because Fulwood was the brother of a former police chief, the *Washington Post* pursued the story. The newspaper found out that Rowmann

Dildy and his cousin Thaddeus Latta were believed to be the gunmen and had killed Fulwood after an "altercation . . . over a drug transaction." Dildy was killed in April 1993. Latta was murdered in 1995 in the same neighborhood, and his murder is also unsolved. Without an arrest, what is left in the neighborhood is a sense of fear, suspicion, and distrust. No one knows who has killed, and who might kill next.

So, in addition to the issues of youth and impulsiveness, Myers's story was about a neighborhood, or a portion of a neighborhood, where people sought a sense of both safety and justice. Around the area of Payne School, the police could not deliver this sense, because they were perceived as being both untrustworthy and ineffective. Young males in the neighborhood believed that police contact resulted in harassment and did not view them as all-powerful allies in the settlement of legitimate grievances. Potential witnesses were afraid to speak to the police and become witnesses, either because they might have had something to hide or simply because they feared retaliation. Street lore had it that the unsolved death of one fifty-four-year-old woman was attributed to the fact that she herself witnessed a killing; the power and legitimacy of the law become tattered in such a context, when potential witnesses come forward but are themselves murdered. Such killings reinforced fears of retaliation, making even the appearance of cooperation with the police difficult.

Myers was particularly critical of the high number of "administratively closed" cases in which the police abandoned investigations without telling the aggrieved families. This "solving" of crimes without public disclosure protected the rights of the potentially innocent but also raised a separate question for the victim's family about the legitimacy of police decisionmaking. And herein lies a lesson about the tension among privacy rights, the need to know, to "find closure," and justice. Justice, in part, is the need for not only the family but also the neighborhood and larger community to know and understand that blame was assigned. But it is also about protecting the reputations of deceased people who themselves have been victims.

For the community, assigning blame is called *justice;* in pop psychology it is called *closure.* In the Columbine massacre, the killers (who committed suicide) had blame clearly and effectively assigned to them. But, somehow, in the more amorphous world of an impoverished District of Columbia neighborhood, such an assignment of blame did not occur, and the cause of justice suffered as a consequence. Families of Columbine's victims, traumatized as they were, were at least able to achieve "closure." As Myers notes (as does Emile Durkheim), this is an important part in reconstructing society after the trauma of such a crime. But closure never happened in Washington, where the privacy rights of the dead "killers" were respected.

Was one result that, with a lack of closure, angry people took justice into their own hands and killed again?

Further Reading

Myers, Jim (2000). "Notes on the Murder of Thirty of My Neighbors." *Atlantic Monthly*, March, pp. 72–86.

The Trials of
W.T.C. "Rough" Elliott

W.T.C. "Rough" Elliott had a number of serious brushes with the law while living from 1850 to 1900 in California's rapidly civilizing frontier. To a large extent, he was very lucky. At a time when lynch mobs and vigilante groups dished out judgments, he was placing necks in the noose. By the time he himself was put on trial for murder, the rule of law extended into the hinterlands of California, and potential lynch mobs deferred to the local sheriff and even the Supreme Court in distant Sacramento. In the end Elliott walked, ultimately dying of old age.

Besides its relevance as an example of how murder was evaluated on California's rural frontier, Elliott's story also provides an interesting window on the sociology of justice. Wrapped up in this story are the economics of the frontier, issues of social status, the administration of justice in general, and even medical forensics.

William Thomas Cowan Elliott was born in Tennessee in September 1829. In 1850 he headed for the goldfields of California. By 1856 he was living in Lassen County in the northeastern part of the state. There he took a position of leadership in the pioneer society. Most notoriously, he was heavily involved as "the detective" in the notorious lynching of "Lucky Bill" Thorington, a popular gambler from neighboring Nevada, whom locals regarded as a Robin Hood character. Lassen County settlers like Elliott thought it more important that Lucky Bill had been involved in the murder of Harry Gordier.

Michael Makley's book *The Hanging of Lucy Bill* gives an extensive account from the perspective of the settlers. It is relevant to the present discussion because it also tells us about Elliott, who was a key prosecution witness in Lucky Bill's trial by the vigilantes from Lassen County. After the hanging of Thorington, a second man, named "Edwards," was brought forward and accused of assisting Thorington. He, too, met his demise at the end of the lynch mob's noose, all on the basis of Elliott's detective work. Makley (1993:110) recounts the tale from the viewpoint of another settler, R. W. Young:

> Young's version of Edward's hanging offers further insight into Rough Elliott's character: "Edwards pulled off a ring from his pocket and $480.00 (as I understood at the time) from his pocket. And handed them to Rough

Elliott and requested him to send them to his mother which Elliott promised to do. . . . I have been credibly informed that Elliott never sent the things as he promised the dying man."

By 1868 Elliott had moved a few miles east, to Reno, Nevada. He was politically active in community affairs and operated the Capitol Lodging House and Saloon. His wife, the daughter of a locally prominent family, divorced him in about 1879. Elliott appeared frequently in the Reno press, often involved in violent and near-violent altercations of various kinds. About 1880, he left Reno for neighboring Mono County, California. There he apparently lived in Bodie and Sweetwater, finally settling in Inyo County, a few miles further south. He married a widow, Mrs. Fannie Baker, who belonged to a well-respected Inyo County family. This marriage turned sour, but only after they had a daughter. In 1888, when Elliott was 59, Fannie was granted a divorce and custody of the child. She went to live with her uncle John White. Elliott was granted visitation rights to the toddler.

It was two months later, in April 1888, that Elliott stabbed John White to death. Elliott had come to White's house, presumably to see his child. Not finding them at the home, he searched the property. Eventually, he said, he found White in an underground cellar, cutting bacon from a slab of meat. White turned, Elliott said, and lunged at Elliott. Elliott responded by lunging at White with his own knife, stabbing him in the chest and puncturing White's heart. Medical experts called as witnesses at Elliott's trial later testified that it was the kind of wound that killed instantly. Elliott had a slight wound on his head, which he claimed that White had inflicted. He immediately left for town to report the stabbing. When the sheriff arrived at the cellar, he found White's body some 100 feet from the cellar door, clutching a piece of willow cane.

Even though there were no witnesses, newspaper accounts in Inyo County were unanimously convinced that the murder was a premeditated and vicious crime, disbelieving Elliott's claims of self-defense. There were no witnesses, but Elliott was by then an unpopular figure in the town, and he was indicted for murder, quickly tried, and convicted. The jury took an afternoon to reach a verdict of guilty and a sentence of death by hanging. The Inyo *Independent* (July 27[?], 1888) reported:

The people of Inyo County express full satisfaction with the result of the trial. All things in this connection have been done decently and in order. The majesty of the law has been established; there has been no unseemly clamor for violence, nothing of which good citizens need be ashamed, and a solemn warning has been given to all who may be disposed to commit crime that stern justice will be surely and speedily dealt out to the evil doer in Inyo County. Now that Elliott has been sentenced to death there is not a tongue in Inyo that would refrain from uttering a prayer for the salvation of his soul. It was not vengeance but justice that was asked.

But the people of Inyo County were to be disappointed. The conviction made its way through the courts of appeal, all the way to the California State Supreme Court in Sacramento, which ordered a new trial because the publicity given the case was prejudicial against Elliott. In modern terms, the jury pool had been tainted by pretrial publicity, and as a result a retrial was ordered with a new venue. The Inyo *Register* responded in the following manner:

> In a case like this, base a decision on some technical quibble which, in the popular estimate of justice, or as affecting any ordinary transaction, would be too insignificant for a moment's consideration. . . . The people of Inyo county are not imperturbable clams, and certainly did feel, and do feel, that here was a deliberately planned, deliberately executed, and finally a perfectly proved capital crime—murder in the first degree or nothing—deserving the highest punishment. (September 5, 1889)

Elliott was tried a second time in 1890, but with a change of venue to Bakersfield in Kern County. The Inyo *Register*'s article "On a Change of Venue" reported:

> Whatever of good there might have been in Elliott's nature had been effectually drowned out by whisky, the real cause of the whole trouble . . .
> All [White] did was to tap Elliott over the head with a small stick or cane, inflicting an insignificant scalp wound. In popular estimation, he should have kept on pounding him as long as he remained on the premises
> . . .
> Every circumstance goes to prove beyond even a reasonable doubt that every syllable of Elliott's story of the cellar scene is a lie out of whole cloth . . .
> To suppose that John White would go down into such a place with nothing but a willow stick to attempt to drive a man whom he knew to be his deadly enemy, desperate and with that big knife in his hand, is to suppose that John White had suddenly become a fool, without mitigation. (November 7, 1889)

The Kern County trial resulted in a hung jury; four jurors called for murder in the first degree, one for murder in the second degree, and the remaining seven for a verdict of manslaughter. Newspaper reports in Inyo County grew more aggressive in their response to the court's actions. The Inyo *Register* stated that

> to allow such a criminal as this man Elliott to go free because it may cost a few dollars to bring him to justice, or the case to a definite conclusion, would be simply contemptible parsimony, and place crime at a premium. That he is a criminal, and unfit to be at large is established by the unanimous verdict of two juries, each after a full hearing of the charges, even though the last of these juries could not determine the exact degree of his crime. (May 22, 1890)

A May 24, 1890, letter to the editor regarding the Elliott case claimed, "To let a murderer loose is no less than to give license for refuge to scoundrels in Inyo County," urging that the pursuit of another trial for Elliott was necessary. Despite demands for lynch mob action, the writer nevertheless insisted that this only be done within the context of the law.

The Inyo *Register*'s editor, though, was less reticent, warning that Elliott wanted to return to Inyo County to purchase cattle:

> Certainly, Mister Elliott, come right along. You have no idea what a change has occurred in this climate since you left us some nine months ago, a fact that every man in the county will take pleasure in calling to your attention. THE REGISTER may take an early opportunity to set out certain facts relating this "old gentleman," his past history, etc., etc., but for the present will suggest that it will be best for all parties concerned if he should never again set foot in Inyo county. Owing to the change above alluded to, the climate will surely prove very insalubrious for such a "feeble old gentleman," it will for a fact. You seem to have found a congenial climate and congenial people right where you are, and right there you had better stay, Mister Elliott. (June 12, 1890)

A third trial later that year also resulted in a hung jury, this time with eight jurors for acquittal and four for conviction. The Inyo *Register* responded by calling the trial "sickening" but nevertheless was resigned to accepting the rule of law: "as a money-saving proposition (a result being unattainable) [we] believe the wisest thing now to do would be to turn the murderous wretch loose, 'unwept of justice,' simply because it is too expensive for our limited resources to further prosecute" (Inyo *Register*, December 25, 1890). The rule of law had arrived in frontier California. It was apparent that it was not going to be possible to convict Elliott, and the Inyo district attorney recommended dropping the case. Most surprisingly, there were no more emotional calls for lynch mobs. For some unspoken reason, the law had become legitimate on California's frontier. As a result, Elliott lived out his life in Bakersfield, California, dying there of pneumonia at the age of seventy-one.

Further Reading

Makley, Michael (1993). *The Hanging of Lucky Bill.* Woodfords, CA: Eastern Sierra Press.

Deadly "Cafeteria Crime"
Among the Mien of Sacramento

The Polk Street Apartments in Sacramento County, California, are home to a concentration of Mien refugees from Laos. The Mien are a refugee group whose leaders assisted the United States during the Vietnam War. As a result, several thousand were resettled in the United States in the early 1980s.

Local citizens sometimes portrayed the apartment complex as being an idyllic throwback to a rural Laotian village. However, the reputation of the Polk Street Apartments among Mien in the early 1990s was of violence and fear—and with good reason. A survey of court records and my own interviews during the summer of 1991 illustrate how the reputation of the apartment complex changed from being a "rural Laotian village" to being a gang-infested hotbed. The cause was what Malcolm Klein (1996) calls "cafeteria crime," meaning a little of this and a little of that, but no specialization. People were hurt badly, and the authority of police and elders deteriorated. The Polk Street apartment complex helps us understand how waves of violence emerge and accelerate in a context where it is difficult for the state to assert authority. As is apparent from this description, who dies or is hurt is actually somewhat arbitrary. It could have been anyone, depending on how a bat was swung, a gun aimed, an arrest made, or a knife thrust. The following timeline shows how and why this fear was generated in the summer of 1991.

May 1991: A federal sting operation results in the arrest of two people for opium trafficking.

May 1991: As a result of a dispute between members of the "Polk Street Boys" over a girl, a thirty-nine-year-old Mien man, Ee Choy Saelee, is fatally stabbed in the groin. The actual fight was between supporters of the Polk Street Boys leader, who while in juvenile hall had "lost" his girlfriend to another member. The victim was the uncle of the boy whom the girl had "gone out" with while her boyfriend was in jail; he was not involved in the initial melee. Complex residents ask that the leader of the gang be arrested because he was the one who they believe initiated the fatal confrontation. The police do not do this because the leader was not present at the time of the attack. Residents decline to give evidence about who was present due to fears that if they point out the perpetrators, the leader of the gang will seek revenge.

June 1991: The landlord of the Polk Street Apartments begins evictions, apparently with the aim of controlling gang activity. In retaliation, the windows of the manager's apartment are shot out. No one is hurt or arrested.

June 1991: Four Mien juveniles and an adult from another refugee group are arrested for possession of a pipe bomb and an assault rifle. Authorities have no idea why the boys possessed a pipe bomb, which the police find disconcerting.

July 1991: The management of the complex hires a security company to control violence in the apartments and posts a nineteen-year-old Caucasian guard. On his second night, the man is hit on the head with a baseball bat, an assault reported by anonymous 911 calls. The calls indicate that four young men were involved. Despite the fact that the callers refuse to talk to the police, four arrests are made, including three Mien, along with one other youth. A broken and bloodied bat is found in the bushes. After the victim recovers, he indicates that he saw one of the four arrested men shortly before being hit on the head, but otherwise remembers nothing. Mien who are interviewed say that the people who are arrested are "bad people" and should be kept in jail a long time, even though they are not convinced that they did the actual assault. Word on the street is that one of the attackers is still free.

July 1991: One Lao juvenile is arrested for the June murder. Lack of willing witnesses does not permit the investigation to go further, and the youth is released.

August 1991: Charges are dismissed against three of the four defendants in the baseball bat case due to lack of evidence. The fourth is released on $3,000 bail after a pretrial hearing. The defense attorney tells me that he will drag the case out as long as possible, and points out that the only legally admissible evidence is from the victim, who himself did not see the assault, did not see the defendant with the baseball bat, and had a questionable capacity to remember much given the nature of the vicious assault. The individuals who made the original 911 reports refuse to testify out of fear for the Polk Street Boys.

August 1991: After a neighborhood watch program is conducted by the Sacramento County Sheriff's Department and a new security agency is hired—Freedom Security, which is owned and operated by ethnic Lao—the complex calms down, or so the sheriff's department claims. For the month of August, the complex is "quiet" from a law enforcement perspective.

September 1991: After securing an introduction, I visit the Polk Street

Apartments. Polk Street Boys graffiti is present in one corner of the complex. However, when I talk to one of the elderly leaders, he indicates that the complex is calm and claims not to know what the graffiti means. He and his friend credit Freedom Security, which they say is more effective because the company uses older men as guards and not "children" like the man who was beaten earlier. Otherwise they speak in generalities.

September 1991: A thirty-nine-year-old Caucasian woman is shot in the shoulder while sitting in her car after a dispute involving Mien members of the Polk Street Boys.

The point here is that much of the violence—including the death—was random and chaotic. Many of the same individuals may have been involved, but there is no identifiable purpose connecting the incidents. Indeed, all they really had in common was the apartment complex in which the police were unable to gain the trust of the community.

As for a solution to the murder? When I called the Sacramento County Sheriff's homicide division in 2005, all they could tell me was that an arrest had been made and that from their perspective the case was closed. The fact that the accused had been released within a few days was not recorded in their files—and the case was still closed. My phone calls to the district attorney were never returned. There is apparently little interest in resolving a case that, though enormously disruptive among the impoverished refugee community, was of little interest to mainstream society.

Further Reading

Waters, Tony (1999). *Crime and Immigrant Youth.* Thousand Oaks, CA: Sage.
Waters, Tony, and Lawrence E. Cohen (1993). *Laotians in the Criminal Justice System.* Berkeley, CA: California Policy Group.

CHAPTER 4

Societies Respond to Killers: The Need for Catharsis and Outrage

To illustrate how the concept of crime and punishment changes, the sociologist Michel Foucault begins his book *Discipline and Punishment* with a description of the 1757 execution of Robert-François Damiens, a man sentenced to death as a "regicide" (monarch killing) for stabbing King Louis XV. Latter-day analysis indicates that Damiens himself was probably insane. However, insanity was not a mitigating factor for sentencing in 1757. Damiens's execution took place in a public square, where all could observe the ferocity of the king's men and the sufferings of Damiens. The court felt it important to sentence Damiens to make the *amende honorable* in the following manner. He was to be taken

> wearing nothing but a shirt, holding a torch of burning wax weighing two pounds then, "in the said cart to the Place de Greve, where, on a scaffold that will be erected there, the flesh will be torn from his breasts, arms, thighs and calves with red-hot pincers, his right hand, holding the knife with which he committed the said parricide, burnt with sulphur, and, on those places where the flesh will be torn away, poured molten lead, boiling oil, burning resin, wax and sulphur melted together and then his body drawn and quartered by four horses and his limbs and body consumed by fire, reduced to ashes and his ashes thrown to the winds." (Foucault 1976:3)

An officer of the watch named Bouton left the following description of Damiens's actual execution:

> The sulphur was lit . . . then the executioner, his sleeves rolled up, took the steel pincers, which had been especially made for the execution . . . and pulled first at the calf of the right leg, then at the thigh, and from there at the two fleshy parts of the right arm; then at the breasts. Though a strong sturdy fellow, the executioner [found it] so difficult to tear away the pieces of flesh that he set about the same spot two or three times, twisting the pincers as he did so. . . . After these tearings with the pincers, Damiens, who cried out profusely though without swearing, raised his head and looked at

himself; the same executioner dipped an iron spoon in the pot containing the boiling potion, which he poured liberally over each wound. . . . The horses tugged hard, each pulling straight on a limb, each horse held by an executioner. After a quarter of an hour, the same ceremony was repeated and finally after several attempts, the direction of the horses had to be changed, thus: those at the arms were made to pull towards the head, those at the thighs towards the arms, which broke the arms at the joints. . . . Two more horses had to be made to those harnessed to the thighs, which made six horses in all. Without success . . . finally, the executioner drew out a knife from his pocket and cut the boy at the thighs instead of severing the legs at the joints; the . . . horses gave a tug and carried off the two thighs after them. . . . When the four limbs had been pulled away, the confessors came to speak to him; but his executioner told them that he was dead, though the truth was that I saw the man move, his lower jaw moving from side to side as if he were talking. (Foucault 1976:3–5)

The execution of Robert-François Damiens is barbaric by modern standards. In fact, it was barbaric by eighteenth-century standards, which of course is the reason it was done in the first place. Why did the French authorities go to so much trouble—and expense—to torture and kill Damiens for assaulting the king? It would have been simpler and cheaper to simply hang him, impale him, behead him, or burn him at the stake. Why did the court think that this demonstration of barbarity was necessary to protect the king? For that matter, why do we go to such great extremes to avoid such pain in the modern United States, where the rare execution is carried out in secret using an intravenous injection designed to minimize the suffering of the condemned and the discomfort of squeamish modern witnesses? What special catharsis did the brutality of this earlier execution bring to eighteenth-century French society, and why do we no longer need such a catharsis?

Contrast the reaction to the assault on Louis XV to the punishment meted out to John Hinckley, the man who shot US president Ronald Reagan in 1981. Hinckley (who *was* clinically insane) was simply assigned to a mental hospital; despite the similar assault on a head of state, there was no execution, pincers, potions, or horses. Finding the answer to this question is clearly not just about the severity of the crime; Damiens's crime was not noticeably more or less serious than Hinckley's assault on President Reagan. Rather, the answer is to be found in investigating *the nature of the society* exacting the punishment. It is the society that punishment is necessary for, not only the condemned.

Crime Is Necessary

The classical French sociologist Emile Durkheim provides a way to start thinking about such questions. He points out that executions, punishments, and the reaction to crime often have little to do with the needs of the prisoner, or a rational calculation of the damage the criminal has caused a society; likewise, it is not simply about righting a wrong, rough reciprocity, or a more abstract sense of "justice." Rather, Durkheim claims that the reaction to crimes is important because society needs punishment to illuminate what is considered moral. Durkheim writes that such a reaction is necessary for the "normal evolution" of law as social conditions change. The conclusion from this type of thinking is that the amount and type of punishment undertaken by a government reflect not only law and justice for victims (see Chapter 2) but also a need of a particular society to maintain a moral order that is the underlying "social fabric" holding society together.

For an act to be viewed as wrong, immoral, or illegal by the broader society, there must be a reaction when the law is violated. This reaction, which is the expression of revulsion for a particular killing, needs to be communicated in a clear and effective fashion that emphasizes the scandalous nature of the act about which the public is excited. This reaction is why even in a society of "saints," it is necessary to have crime. Durkheim wrote:

> Imagine a society of saints, a perfect cloister of exemplary individuals. Crimes properly so called, will there be unknown; but faults which appear venal to the layman will create there the same scandal. . . . If, then, this society has the power to judge and punish, it will define [therefore] these acts as criminal and treat them as such. . . .
> Crime is, then, necessary; it is bound up with the fundamental conditions of all social life, and by that very fact it is useful, because these conditions of which it is a part are themselves indispensable in the normal evolution of morality and law. (Durkheim 1938[1895]:68–69)

Durkheim's theoretical approach highlights that there are values underlying a society's power structure; after all, it takes power, rooted in a monopoly over the use of coercive violence, to judge and punish. It is not a question if someone will be punished, but who. In effect, it is a game of musical chairs in which the loser becomes the example used to describe a moral or legal boundary. In the case of Damiens, the fact that he had wounded France's king made the state's response particularly ferocious. A similar attack in an eighteenth-century French tavern between two travelers would not have merited the six horses, much less the specially made pincers and potions. Indeed, given the poverty of rural France at that time, the state may easily have ignored the death altogether—as indeed the US legal system sometimes effectively does when one drug dealer kills another drug dealer.

But in the case of Damiens, the powers in France used his execution to excite the public about the assault on the king, emphasizing that Louis XV was a "father figure" and that Damiens had committed not just assault but "parricide." The underlying issue was the role of the king in society, and Damiens's execution was used to emphasize that the king was elemental and "bound up with the fundamental conditions of all social life" in France. Durkheim would speculate that the response to Damiens was so ferocious because there was anxiety in the society about whether the role of the king and staging a brutal execution were a way to defend the legitimacy of the crown. And indeed perhaps there was such a threat: events during the French Revolution in 1789, only thirty-two years after Damiens's execution, did indicate that the French aristocracy was vulnerable to challenges.[1]

The Catharsis of Reaction:
From Damiens to the Supermarket Checkout Line

Central to the point I want to make here is that the public is excited about some murders and not others. And indeed, an entire school focused on "the sociology of deviance" emerged to explain how some deviants become the focus for revulsion and punishment while others committing similar acts are ignored. In the modern United States, you can observe this in a place as normal as the supermarket checkout line. There, magazines such as the *National Enquirer* and *People* highlight a few murders on their covers while ignoring the vast majority of mundane killings. On the surface, the public shaming focused on cases like that of O.J. Simpson, Charles Manson, John Hinckley, or other celebrated criminal cases has little to do with what French society experienced as a result of Damiens's execution. But I think Durkheim would point out that what Damiens's execution and the *National Enquirer* have in common is that both reflect on matters that are of concern to the general society. The question is, what is the underlying issue that makes the crime so much more interesting than other killings? For Damiens, it was the stability of the French state. By this reasoning, it might be inferred that the Simpson and Manson cases threatened underlying values that the American middle classes held sacred, perhaps with respect to the safety of women. The Hinckley case of course involved a direct assault on President Reagan, and as such threatened the stability of the government.[2]

So, from Durkheim's perspective (and that of the sociology of deviance), the *definition* of and *reaction* to venality are the point, and not the actual crime or the ecology of the situation. The punishment—that is, the *amende honorable*—is interesting, and not only because of who the perpetrator is, the cost to the victim, or demands for justice by the victim's family. Just how seriously the society is affected by a particular act is best understood by watching the reaction of the public to a particular crime as the morality play of gossip, press coverage, investigation, trial, and punishment unfolds. From Durkheim's perspective it is how a society responds that is interesting, not just the characteristics of the criminals themselves. This is why when evaluating when a particular killing becomes a crime, it is important to watch not only what the killers do but also how the society reacts.[3] Which people are blamed for a killing, whether they are guilty in a legal sense or not? What do justifications for an act indicate about a society's values? What does the selection of prosecutable cases tell us about the same society? What are considered to be mitigating circumstances of killing? What is considered to be an appropriate reaction? From this perspective, crime is necessary because the state needs to "shout out" that it is in charge by punishing enthusiastically on behalf of those who hold power. Or, to consider the issue in the same fashion as sociologist Robert Nisbet wrote, "Until a catharsis has been effected through trial, through the finding of guilt, and then punishment, the community is anxious, fearful, apprehensive, and above all contaminated" (see Gelernter 1998:21).

Legal and Illegal Killing: The Evolution of Law

A number of examples from well-known and lesser-known cases can help us think about how human societies define when it is appropriate to kill, when it is not, and what is the appropriate response. That all of these examples are now illegal despite having once been a subject of fascination by the public is an indication of what Durkheim called a "normal evolution of morality and law." Consider these examples of killing that were legal in the past, and illegal and worthy of a strong reaction today:

- In the wild West of Bodie, California, a challenge to a fair fight was considered a good enough reason to use lethal violence, and the resulting wounding or death was excused as justifiable irrespective of who "started it."
- The use of lethal violence was even ritualized in the event of a duel, and powerful gentlemen like Andrew Jackson engaged in this violent practice.
- Feuds between elite families were considered legitimate combat and not worthy of a legal response.
- Summary execution by lynch mob was long considered to be unworthy of investigation.
- In Cameroon, a man was arrested and imprisoned for witchcraft after "his" python ate a woman, a criminal act. But when he died in police custody, the situation was not considered necessary for comment (Fisiy 1998).
- Until the 1970s in Texas, it was justifiable to kill one's wife and her

lover if they were caught *in flagrante delicto*. Such cases were routinely dismissed.[4]

And now briefly consider the relative ferocity of reaction in three well-known American cases that have galvanized American interest. Note that none of these cases are representative of the vast majority of killings that occur in the United States, as described in Chapter 3.

- The murder of Polly Klaas, an eleven-year-old child kidnapped and murdered by a paroled ex-con, was used as the exemplary case to persuade California voters to approve "three strikes and you're out" legislation to imprison offenders with life sentences who were convicted of three serious crimes, whether they were violent or not.
- In my criminology class, I routinely ask students if they have ever heard of Charles Manson, the leader of a cultish hippie family that killed seven people in 1969. Though the murders took place long before most of my students were born, they all have heard of the case as a result of books, articles, television, and other dramatizations (see, e.g., Bugliosi 1994). And yet few have heard of the killer Juan Corona, who was convicted of killing twenty-five itinerant farmworkers and vagrants in 1971 near my university in Chico, California.
- The rape and killing of seven-year-old Megan Kanka in 1994 by a sex offender, a relatively rare crime, excited the public to demand registration of released sex offenders under "Megan's Law." Such sex registries both stigmatize the individual concerned and excite the public. By 2005, approximately 500,000 individuals were required to register under this law.

Individuals, including newspaper reporters, television producers, police, prosecutors, and criminal investigators, routinely make decisions about which cases are worthy of thorough (and expensive) investigations and which are not. In many respects, this is the modern context of killing. Even in the case of modern massacres are similar judgments routinely made. Genocide cases in the former Yugoslavia, Kurdistan, and Rwanda are exhaustively investigated by international tribunals, while those in the Democratic Republic of Congo, Sudan, Chechnya, and Colombia are not. And on a more local level, the death of a drug dealer in Washington, DC, is likely to result in a cursory investigation whereas the case of a missing (and eventually murdered) twenty-four-year-old intern like Chandra Levy, Congressman Gary Condit's lover, resulted in sustained examination in the press and Condit's defeat at the next primary election, even though someone else was eventually accused of the crime. Clearly, some murders attract more attention than others.

Durkheim's approach introduces a way of looking at killing and murder that is different from the approach discussed in previous chapters.[5] The focus is not on the use of coercive power, or on how individuals deal with self-defense, feuds, duels, honor, or violent confrontations. Rather, the focus is on the society that creates laws and the means to enforce them. To help describe the process by which morality evolves, sociologists following in Durkheim's tradition have developed a number of useful concepts to understand how the enforcement of law changes.

• *Moral entrepreneurs* are advocates who persuade others to change the boundaries of a law, moral, or norm. This term comes from symbolic interactionism and labeling theory, which assumes that law enforcement emerges from a shared understanding of what is right or wrong. To change this consensus, a social movement articulates a new definition (and solution) for a particular social problem. Moral entrepreneurs, many of whom are prestige bearers, emerge and with a single-mindedness seek to change the law. Anecdotal examples—parables—are important in framing such views, whether or not they are important from a social scientific point of view. Moral entrepreneurs quite often include law enforcement officials, reformers, the press, politicians, and others who disseminate information (see Becker 1963:147–163).

• *Moral panic* is a movement based on a perception that some group is a special threat to society. Moral panics emerge from a culture in the form of gossip, urban legends, or rumors that are in turn amplified by the press or other institutions that spread fear and outrage. Moral panics typically trade on outrage at a particular deviant group, which may be a subculture, ethnic group, religious group, or other group considered particularly menacing to the social order. Moral entrepreneurs sometimes try to create a moral panic. The spreading of rumors, press attention, and even mass hysteria are symptoms of moral panic.

• *Morality tales* are the stories that moral entrepreneurs tell to excite a moral panic. The stories excite outrage about the behavior of someone who is regarded as exemplary of either a deviant group or a type of action that is a particular threat and must be controlled. Morality tales often take the form of awkward parables that reflect preconceived opinions or views about how a social problem is addressed.

• *Running conversation* is the process of definition that occurs through complex interaction and communication between members of a privileged group. Prestige bearers, including political leaders, dominant individuals, and ordinary laypeople, generate this through talk, stories, gossip, anecdotes, messages, pronouncements, news accounts, orations, sermons, and the like. Note that such communication may be formal or informal, official or unofficial (Blumer 1956).

Emphasized in these concepts is that interaction between the powerful and society involves a symbolic give-and-take. Policing and a "monopoly on the use of coercive power" are important. But it is not the whole story. From Durkheim's viewpoint, it must include how people think and talk about the monopoly over the use of coercive force. This in turn shapes when and how this coercive force is used, or not, and whether a moral panic occurs.

A Brief Example: The Columbine and Red Lake High School Shootings

A good way to illustrate why we need to evaluate the nature of the social response to a criminal incident is to compare the school shootings at Columbine High School in Littleton, Colorado, in 1999 and at Red Lake High School in 2005 in Minnesota. At Columbine, fifteen individuals died, including the two shooters, who committed suicide. At Red Lake, nine people died, including the shooter, who also committed suicide. What is interesting about the events is not the fact that the killings occurred at school, but the different reaction of the public to the tragic deaths. In the case of the Columbine shootings, there was a great deal of what Durkheim called *agitation*. A moral panic ensued as policy advocates sought to use the Columbine killings to make political claims about preferred policies for social change. Despite the fact that the body counts and methods at Red Lake were similarly horrific, such a widespread moral panic did not ensue in 2005. A comparison with the circumstances surrounding the two cases provides an answer for why this may be so.

The shootings at Columbine High School involved two boys who were part of a subculture at Columbine High School that liked certain types of heavy metal music, wore trench coats, and were on the bowling team. Middling students, the two boys showed up with weapons and a plan to kill 500 students on April 20, 1999, and then commit suicide. They planted a bomb in the school cafeteria at about 11 A.M. When the bomb did not go off as planned, they attacked the school with guns, killing thirteen students and teachers and wounding twenty-four others before committing suicide within minutes of the attack. The attack was the subject of television coverage the day it happened, and it became a focus of fascination to the American public. As such, the killings became the touch point for a wide range of social issues, including gun control, school morality, heavy metal music, and parenting. Analysis of the shootings dominated press coverage for weeks afterward. References by moral entrepreneurs to Columbine became a staple of editorial writers and political campaigns as the school became shorthand for youth gone awry and any other social ill that could be plausibly connected. The massacre was used as the pretext for at least three *Time* magazine cover stories in the two years after the killings. A popular documentary movie,

Bowling for Columbine, by filmmaker Michael Moore, used the high school's name to make its point about violence and gun control in the United States. The film was successful enough to win the 2002 Academy Award for "Best Documentary." Coverage of the shootings, funerals, and aftermath dominated press coverage for weeks in a manner few other news events do.

Interestingly, the issues highlighted by the activists and moral entrepreneurs reflected the anxieties of the culture rather than a sociological or criminological assessment of the actual event. Durkheim's point would be that the Columbine killings were only a rhetorical device for illustrating preexisting ideas. Depending on who was making a claim, the killings were blamed on bullying jocks, heavy metal music, inattentive parents, poor school security, or failure to monitor the shooters' web page postings. Evangelical Christians used it to heroize victims who professed a belief in God before being shot, and blacks were concerned that one victim was shot because of his skin color. Gun-control advocates and opponents both used the incident to advocate for preexisting positions. Law enforcement took advantage of the tragedy to reassess its role in the prevention of school shootings, and then requested funding for special programs. Schools developed practice drills to deal with "intruders on campus," and the FBI in July 1999 convened a meeting of administrators from eighteen schools that had experienced school violence. This meeting resulted in the report "The School Shooter: A Threat Assessment Perspective." With little evidence other than the anecdote of Columbine, money was appropriated to improve security in high schools across the country, and strict "zero tolerance" policies for weapons and verbal threats were adopted by school boards in the name of preventing another Columbine. The problem of school shootings in general, and Columbine in particular, was injected into congressional debates, where it was used to advocate for laws promising school safety.

Retrospective looks at Columbine show that many of the demands for social change created by the incident were based on faulty data. For example, the two shooters did not apparently go bowling with their team the day of the shooting, as asserted in the title of the Michael Moore film; the two were not core members of the "trench coat mafia"; and the student murdered after affirming her belief in God may not have actually done so. In terms of a systematic approach to "risk assessment," a school that has had the misfortune of a school shooting will not be any more likely to provide expertise about violence prevention than one that has not experienced a shooting. To argue that this would be the case is, as with cases of domestic homicide, a "hindsight fallacy." Or, to borrow a logical example from ecological theory, interviewing only school principals from schools that had a shooting, and excluding those who did not, makes about as much sense as interviewing the next-of-kin of those killed with cast-iron skillets while ignoring the cases in which people were only assaulted with aluminum skillets. But from the Durkheimian perspective, most relevant was the reaction—the catharsis, if you will; the *belief* that the school victimized by a shooter knew more about "risk" than those that had not.

In contrast to the Columbine shootings of 1999, similar cultural undercurrents were not apparent in 2005 at the time of the school shootings at Red Lake High School, located on an Indian reservation in northern Minnesota. Writing in the *Columbia Journalism Review*, Brian Montopoli (2005) actually noted that the lack of focus on the sensational resulted in higher-quality reporting about the facts of the Red Lake killings. Montopoli wasn't sure whether this was because journalists had improved their reporting skills since Columbine or because the lack of fascination with these killings gave reporters more time to be careful. I think Durkheim would claim that Montopoli missed the main point, which is that the *reaction* to any shooting reflects underlying anxieties, not the actual "facts" of a particular incident. I think Montopoli's mistake is assuming that the reporters were telling only a factual story. What Durkheim might say is that the Columbine-focused journalists were moral entrepreneurs participating in a running conversation emerging from a broader public, as much as from the skills of professional reporters. For whatever reasons, the Red Lake incident did not resonate with the running conversation in the same manner that Columbine did. In part this could be the arbitrary whim of a fickle public. As likely, though, is the fact that the larger public identified more clearly with the middle-class culture of Columbine than with the remote Native American population on the Red Lake reservation.

Certainly, the media are powerful in such circumstances, but they are not alone in setting the agenda. Again, I think that Durkheim would say that the point is that at different times and places, anxiety about the underlying social fabric is discussed in a different way. The body count itself is not the point; it is how elites—the moral entrepreneurs—talk about the crime, and how the public responds. The evolution of policy, law, and rule is the result of this discussion.

Wayward Puritans, the NAACP, and a Burning Bed

Durkheim's point is that there is an interaction between how law evolves and the underlying issues that make society anxious. To illustrate this point further, I will tell three stories. The first is of the rise and fall of the Puritan state in colonial Massachusetts. The story as told here will focus on the moral panic about venal crimes that today are considered imaginary: antinomianism, Quakerism, and witchcraft. The second tale is about how white elites in the defeated post–Civil War South used dramatic lynchings in an attempt to sustain their authority despite the crushing defeat by federal military forces in the Civil War. This technique, of course, was eventually used against the same white elites by twentieth-century civil rights activists seeking to reassert federal authority over civil rights issues. The third is about the movement to criminalize domestic violence from the 1970s to 1990s in the United States. What these three very different social movements have in common is that, as Durkheim described, the actual crimes themselves are almost tangential to the underlying social change, which was about rule by the church (colonial Massachusetts), civil rights and federal control (lynching), and the women's movement (domestic violence). What emerges from these examples are the following points with respect to Durkheim's approach:

- Crime and drama are necessary in shaping normal change.
- Moral entrepreneurs—individuals and groups—emerge and shape the discussion about change using anecdotes, case studies, emotion, and, in the modern world, dramatic magazine stories and movies.
- Despite claims to the contrary, there are limits to how far and fast law changes.
- In any crisis, the deviant and marginalized are the most vulnerable to the scapegoating that often accompanies the change Durkheim wrote about.

Criminal Puritans

The classic description of why crime is necessary to social order was written by sociologist Kai Erikson about seventeenth-century Puritan Massachusetts, a society that saw itself literally as being one of saints ruled by the church's most learned ministers. Erikson's study did not directly involve murderers, although there is plenty of violent death. But all killing is done in the form of capital punishment in response to what Puritan leaders believed were crime waves. As a sideshow of sorts, it also involves the extremely lethal "King Philip's War" (1675–1676) between the Puritan settlers and the Native Americans who initially welcomed them.[6] In describing Durkheim's "crime is necessary" approach, Erikson makes the point that the crime waves were, as Durkheim wrote, an agitated response; that is, a moral panic by a public to underlying political issues, which may have little to do with an actual increase (or decrease) in the number of crimes.

The Puritan colony established in the Massachusetts Bay by John Winthrop in 1630 was a poor remote society. Establishing fields and farms was difficult, and in the first winters many colonists died from hunger-related causes. But the survivors pulled together and adapted their crops and farming systems to the new environment. New recruits screened by the church in England also arrived, ready to replace the casualties. High death rates and tragedy only seemed to confirm for the survivors that God had blessed them as a special and unique community.

But this impression was not to last. Erikson writes that the first breakdown in the theocratic formula for Puritan Massachusetts occurred in 1636–1637 when there was a leadership crisis within the ruling church. Ironically, this was at a time when conditions had finally improved. Wintertime death rates had declined as settlers both adapted food production activities to the harsh winters and established trading relationships with the local Indians (see, e.g., Cronon 1983). And so in this time of relative plenty, John Winthrop's leadership was challenged. The colony, which numbered about 8,000, quickly split into two factions, one consisting of the rural conservative clergy rallying around Winthrop, and a second one of more urban secular interests organized around colonists who had arrived more recently and had never known the hardships of the first settlers.

The issue that became the flashpoint for this first political division was an obscure point of Puritan theology called *antinomianism*. This concept involved Puritan interpretations about which ministers would have the power to determine who was a church member and who was not. While the conversation was rooted in tedious debates about church doctrine, in fact, as Durkheim would say, the underlying (and unstated) issue was about who would rule the colony. Would the "old-timers" like Winthrop remain in charge, or would the newer immigrants rule?

Antinomianism was not a source of strife before 1636, nor would it be in the future. But, during the morality plays of court trials in 1637, the crime was the focus of widespread agitated discussion. Eventually, accusations were made particularly against a newly arrived woman, Anne Hutchinson, and her supporters. Besides being a newcomer, Mrs. Hutchinson was an articulate proponent of Boston's urban elite, who believed that newly arrived preachers were the best judge of who was theologically qualified to be a minister. In response to the challenge to Massachusetts's established church, Mrs. Hutchinson was arrested by Winthrop's magistrates, examined for skin blemishes (which could have identified her as a practitioner of witchcraft), and put on trial. Her prosecution involved classic morality tales in which Hutchinson was used as an example of the threat that the newly arrived posed to the stability of the colony. And despite the fact that everyone agreed Anne Hutchinson argued very effectively, she, her family, and her supporters were nevertheless convicted. As punishment, they lost the right to bear arms, and Anne Hutchinson and her large family (she had fifteen children) were banished[7] and sent into the wilderness of Rhode Island.[8]

Although few of the colonists understood the theological points of antinomianism, a fact even acknowledged by Winthrop, all agreed that the trial was a defining point in 1630s Puritan politics. Cotton Mather, who became a historian of the incident sixty years later, wrote, "'Tis believed that multitudes of persons, who took with both parties did never to their dying hour understand what their difference was." So why did the issue become so important? Erikson writes that the issue was important because it "marked a shift of boundaries which the settlers of Massachusetts could not articulate in any other way" (see Erikson 1967:74). Change had come to the colony with the arrival of newcomers, and it was necessary for the rules to evolve. The trial of Anne Hutchinson provided the means—the morality play—by which the group reorganized itself.

Following the Antinomian Controversy of 1636–1637, Winthrop reasserted his control of the colony. There followed a relatively peaceful period in which the courts dealt only with mundane deviance, particularly crimes against the church, contempt of authority, and fornication (Erikson 1967:175). But in the 1650s, political changes began to occur again: Winthrop and the other founders had died, and perhaps more important, in England there was a civil war between Puritans, led by Oliver Cromwell, that successfully challenged the power of King Charles II of England and his Church of England. The colonists in Massachusetts of course supported the Puritans, who they believed would create a theocracy in England modeled after their own experiment in the New World. Erikson considers this political transition to be the second "boundary controversy" searching for a crime to prosecute. And so, after a relatively uneventful twenty-year period following the Antinomian Controversy, a new scourge emerged: Quakers. And it emerged at a time when the colony became more authoritarian and could exact more severe punishment.

Seventeenth-century Quakerism was a new Protestant sect similar theologically to that of the Puritans. Both groups emerged from the religious ferment of seventeenth-century England, in opposition to the Church of England, and both emphasized the role of a personal relationship between the individual and God. It was said that there were only two ways laypeople could tell Puritans and Quakers apart: Quakers refused to wear a hat while in front of a magistrate (as required under Puritan law), and they used the pronouns "thee" and "thou" whereas Puritans did not. The differences were trivial in England, where until 1649 the sects were allied against the royal state church headed by King Charles II. But in 1649, Charles II was beheaded and succeeded by the Puritan leader Oliver Cromwell, who pushed religious tolerance to the center of English politics. Despite the victory of their coreligionist, Puritan ministers in Massachusetts felt threatened by the emergence of a regime supporting a tolerance that was contrary to their own theocratic leanings. But, the question was, how to express this difference? According to Erikson, Quakers provided the means to express the underlying ferment.

The Puritan campaign against the Quakers began in 1656 with the arrival of two Quaker housewives by ship. The women were the first Quakers in the colony, and their presence created both a conundrum and an opportunity for the Puritan theocracy. There was no law against Quakerism in Massachusetts (as presumably there was with respect to antinomianism), but the authorities believed that such a group was a threat. As a result, the two "heretics" were immediately banished, and in October 1656 a law banning "the cursed sect of heretics . . . commonly called Quakers" was announced that permitted banishing, whipping, and using corporal punishment (cutting off ears, boring holes in tongues). In addition,

> [the] master or commander of any ship, barke, pinnace, catch, or any other vessel that shall henceforth bring into any harbor, creeks, or cove without jurisdiction any known Quaker or Quakers, or any other blasphemous heretics shall pay . . . the fine of 100 pounds . . . [and] they must be brought back from where they came or go to prison. (http://www.rootsweb.com/~nwa/dyer.html)

However, this law was not to prove adequate to eliminate the scourge of Quakerism from Puritan Massachusetts. The Quakers kept coming. To control the future arrival of Quakers and, more important, the conversion of Puritans to Quakerism, moral entrepreneurs demanded harsher penalties. In 1659–1660, the Puritan state decided that more punishment was appropriate, and the penalties for Quakerism were upped. Ear amputations were introduced for returnees, and hanging was added to punish Quakers who persisted. But the repeat offenders nevertheless came, some carrying their own burial shrouds, determined that peaceful disobedience was the will of God. The most prominent was Mary Dyer, a friend of Anne Hutchinson who was exiled to Rhode Island in 1637 and there converted to Quakerism. In early 1660, Mary Dyer was marched to the gallows with two men, fellow Quakers. At the last minute she was reprieved, but the two men were hanged.

Curiously, something unsuspected by the moral entrepreneurs and their ever-harsher penalties happened: the Quakers still did not obey. And so arrests, particularly "Crimes against the Church," soared in Massachusetts. Erikson's research in colonial archives shows that hangings were only the tip of the iceberg, as an increasingly autocratic church sought to protect its power. Arrests for crimes against the church rose from a rate of 0.36 offenses per 100 people in 1651–1655, to 1.85 offenses per 100 people in 1656–1660, and to 3.15 per 100 people in 1661–1665 (Erikson 1966:175). This pushed up the overall conviction rate in places like Essex County (see Table 4.1). Mary Dyer even managed to get herself hanged for Quakerism after returning in June 1660. But then an odd thing happened: the crime rate declined. But this wasn't just because the acts of disobedience stopped.

Erikson notes that such a high rate of prosecution must have pushed beyond the capacity of the state to exact punishment. In short, every time a

Table 4.1   Convictions in Essex County Court, Puritan Massachusetts, 1651–1680

	1651–1655	1656–1660	1661–1665	1666–1670	1671–1675	1676–1680
Convictions	190	275	394	393	391	311
Population	4,500	5,200	6,100	7,300	8,900	7,500
Convictions per 100 population	4.22	5.29	6.46	5.38	4.38	4.15

Source: Erikson 1967:173.

member of the community was hanged, whipped, mutilated, or banished, the underlying fabric of society was either reinforced or torn. In the case of the Quaker crisis, Erikson claims that punishment by an increasingly isolated state began to tear more, and reinforce less, thereby threatening to destroy the legitimacy of the Puritan state from within. The determined civil disobedience of the Quakers became too much to bear, and so the state simply stopped enforcing this law. Cromwell died, England moved back into the control of the monarchy, and the Puritans were again an out-of-power minority. Quakerism was legalized in the late 1660s at the order of the new king (which was accepted), and the moral panic over the presence of Quakers disappeared.

The next period of political upheaval Erikson writes about coincided with a war between the Puritans and the Algonquian nation that came to be known as King Philip's War (1675–1676) in reference to a Wampanoag chief named Metacom whom the colonists called Philip. This was the most violent war in American history in terms of fatality rates. The English colony, which had experienced robust population growth, actually declined 16 percent as a result of war-related fatalities. The Indian casualties were higher, and native life in the region was effectively exterminated. Indeed, the war was not concluded until the Puritans had destroyed the Wampanoag villages, killing as many as 700 Wampanoag in one attack. As for Philip himself, after he was betrayed and killed by one of his own men, the Puritans had his body drawn and quartered and his head paraded throughout the English villages. The head itself remained on a pole outside Plymouth Village for some twenty years afterward, a symbol of the ferocious resolve of the Puritan state to maintain its monopoly over the use of coercive powers against all opponents.

But the final death throes of the Puritan theocracy came fifteen years later, when the British monarchy revoked the Puritans' status as a self-governing colony and appointed a royal governor to replace the Puritan ministers. Erikson describes this political upheaval as a violent morality play undertaken in opposition to the witches in the village of Salem. The hysteria began when a small group of girls aged 9–20 went into violent convulsive trances and accused three women of witchcraft. As Erikson notes, the first three accused could not have made better "witches" for the purposes of a morality play. Tituba was a West Indian slave known to practice voodoo. The second was Sarah Good, a woman whom Erikson (1967:143) describes as a "proper hag of a witch if Salem Village had ever seen one." She wandered about the countryside smoking a pipe, begging for a living, and uttering threats against people who displeased her. Sarah Osbourne was of higher status but had in the previous year permitted a man to move into her house without becoming her husband.

This nineteenth-century illustration by Howard Pyle depicts the arrest of an older woman for witchcraft by the Puritan state. Such arrests were particularly common at the time of the Salem witch trials in 1691, which were described in an article for which this illustration was prepared.
Harper's New Monthly Magazine, 1883.

At the trial, Tituba confessed with enthusiasm. She even provided elaborate testimony about how she and the two other women had conducted the dark rituals that bound them to Satan. This confession trumped the otherwise weak evidence of witchcraft and convinced the court that the problem was far worse than they had thought. The young accusers were emboldened by their new status as moral entrepreneurs and presented themselves as seers, able to divine the presence of witchcraft in the community. Laws and rules of evidence (even those regarding body blemishes) were quickly relaxed to permit easier prosecution and harsher punishment. The excesses of the girls are of course well-known today, made famous by the Arthur Miller play "The Crucible." During the second half of 1692, hundreds were accused, and ultimately nineteen people were executed following hysterical accusations (see Erikson 1967:141–150).

Then, just as with the hysteria over Quakerism, the crisis of witches ended. Indeed, it ended even more quickly. But the human cost of the moral panic was high; virtually everyone in a colony of 50,000 would have known a person who was accused, jailed, or executed. Thousands more were among the accusers or were accomplices of the prosecutors. In Erikson's view, what happened was that as with the Quakers, the capacity of the colony to punish was exceeded. The only plausible response was to simply legalize what had so recently been considered venal.

There are academic controversies about Erikson's choice of cases to illustrate the "crime as necessary" argument. Particularly historians specializing in New England believe that his "three crises" formula is too neat. Less controversial, though, is the robust idea he championed, which is that when a society undergoes rapid political change, it seeks out scapegoats that may have little to do with the underlying political dilemma. Through his discussion of antinomianism, Quakerism, and witchcraft in Puritan Massachusetts, Erikson makes the point well that crime waves are not only the consequence of criminals performing venal acts but also the need of the state to assert its authority.

The story of Quakerism in Massachusetts has its parallels in familiar tales of social changes even in the twentieth century. Alcohol was criminalized in the United States in the 1920s. But the wave of arrests that resulted constituted too great of an assault on the underlying social fabric, and the law (and its enforcement) were discarded in 1933. Southern segregation laws in the 1950s and 1960s were challenged by peaceful protestors submitting to mass arrests that in turn tore at the underlying social fabric, and as a result the powerful segregationist states were unable to enforce their own laws and eventually reversed themselves.

A relevant point about the nature of how the state uses deviance to reinforce its power can be drawn from Erikson's examples. First is the fact that in some poor, remote societies like Puritan Massachusetts, penalties are harsh. In part this is because the society cannot afford long-term imprisonment in jails and prisons with its attendant costs for nonproducing guards and prisoners. But harshness is also necessary because public whippings, hangings, and stonings are "necessary" to communicate by word of mouth to the near and far that the power of the state is not to be challenged.

Today, of course, such statements are made more subtly. Indeed, my own favorite place to observe the work of modern moral entrepreneurs is in the aforementioned supermarket checkout line, reading the headlines in the *National Enquirer* and *People* magazine. Another place is on television programs like *CSI, 20/20,* and even *60 Minutes,* which serve the same purpose of broadcasting the latest morality plays as they make celebrities and even a few common people into moral examples. No longer is word of mouth necessary, as it was in the days of the Puritans. What is the same is the need of the moral entrepreneurs to stimulate a running conversation on behalf of the established order.

The Rise and Fall of the American Lynch Mob

Lynching involves the achievement of "justice" by an extralegal group. It is by definition a challenge to a state, and as such it occurs in areas where the state is weakly legitimated. In his book *Lynching in the South: Virginia and Georgia 1880–1930,* Fitzhugh Brundage (1993) claims that there are in fact five forms of American lynching: posses, terrorist mobs, private mobs, mass mobs, and a category of unknown mobs. What they share are their extralegal character and a belief that the people as represented by a large group deliver righteous justice in a manner that the state cannot. In such cases the anonymity of a large group is important; such killings are not undertaken by an individual but by a "mob" or at best a posse delegated by a sheriff.[9]

The United States is perhaps the country best studied with respect to lynching; indeed, lynching has been called a "national tradition, and a southern obsession," although the United States is not the only place in the world where extralegal violence is practiced. Indeed, such killing was reported (and celebrated) in newspapers regularly when I lived in Dar es Salaam, Tanzania, in 2003–2004.[10]

Three stories about lynching follow. They are told in order to illustrate the different reactions—and how those reactions have changed—across time. The first account is from the 1890s, when in terms of political strength, the segregationist states were very powerful. Allen D. Candler, a candidate for governor of Georgia, was even elected on a prolynching platform in 1898. The second account is told from the perspective of the 1920s. Lynching was still used as a means to instill fear within African American communities not only in the South but in the North as well. That is when an organized campaign—a moral crusade—emerged to challenge the rule of the lynch mob. Lynching became an embarrassment for the United States as a result of agitation by the National Association for the Advancement of Colored People (NAACP) and other antiracist groups that used lynching to make their case about the importance of legal protection under the law. The third account is of a more recent lynching, during the civil rights movement that began in the late 1950s. These cases have been a prominent part of the national discussion, particularly as the national press became more far-reaching

On the surface, of course, lynching seems to be very different from the legal prosecutions of the Puritan state in seventeenth-century Massachusetts. And on the surface it is. But the process by which extralegal killing was used by the moral entrepreneurs organizing the lynch mob, as well as the opposition to lynching, was rooted in the language of moral panics, just as were the "legal lynchings" of witches in Salem, or for that matter Quakers in the 1660s or antinomians in the 1630s.

This photograph is a reproduction of a postcard made after the lynching of Jesse Washington in 1916. Washington was tortured before he was burned alive in front of a large crowd in Waco, Texas. The postcard was published by the NAACP's *Crisis* magazine in an attempt to demonstrate to the larger US public the barbarity of mob justice in the American South.

From "The Waco Horror," *Crisis* 12, no. 3 (supplement July 1916). Reprinted by permission of Crisis Publishing Company.

The Lynching of Sam Hose

The torture and burning of an African American laborer named Sam Hose occurred in 1899 in a decade when lynching became more and more frequent in the American South (see Table 4.2). Typically, lynching was used

Table 4.2   Lynchings in the United States by Year and Race, 1882–1968

Year	Whites	Blacks	Total
1882	64	49	113
1883	77	53	130
1884	160	51	211
1885	110	74	184
1886	64	74	138
1887	50	70	120
1888	68	69	137
1889	76	94	170
1890	11	85	96
1891	71	113	184
1892	69	161	230
1893	34	118	152
1894	58	134	192
1895	66	113	179
1896	45	78	123
1897	35	123	158
1898	19	101	120
1899	21	85	106
1900	9	106	115
1901	25	105	130
1902	7	85	92
1903	15	84	99
1904	7	76	83
1905	5	57	62
1906	3	62	65
1907	3	58	61
1908	8	89	97
1909	13	69	82
1910	9	67	76
1911	7	60	67
1912	2	62	64
1913	1	51	52
1914	4	51	55
1915	13	56	69
1916	4	50	54
1917	2	36	38
1918	4	60	64
1919	7	76	83
1920	8	53	61
1921	5	59	64
1922	6	51	57

(continues)

Table 4.2 continued

Year	Whites	Blacks	Total
1923	4	29	33
1924	0	16	16
1925	0	17	17
1926	7	23	30
1927	0	16	16
1928	1	10	11
1929	3	7	10
1930	1	20	21
1931	1	12	13
1932	2	6	8
1933	2	24	28
1934	0	15	15
1935	2	18	20
1936	0	8	8
1937	0	8	8
1938	0	6	6
1939	1	2	3
1940	1	4	5
1941	0	4	4
1942	0	6	6
1943	0	3	3
1944	0	2	2
1945	0	1	1
1946	0	6	6
1947	0	1	1
1948	1	1	2
1949	0	3	3
1950	1	1	2
1951	0	1	1
1952	0	0	0
1953	0	0	0
1954	0	0	0
1955	0	3	3
1956	0	0	0
1957	1	0	1
1958	0	0	0
1959	0	1	1
1960	0	0	0
1961	0	1	1
1962	0	0	0
1963	0	1	1
1964	2	1	3
1965	0	0	0
1966	0	0	0
1967	0	0	0
1968	0	0	0
Total	1,297	3,445	4,742

Source: Statistics provided by the Archives at Tuskegee Institute, February 1979, http://faculty.berea.edu/browners/chesnutt/classroom/lynching_table_year.html.

Note: The data do not specify victims by ethnicity or by race other than black and white. The slight discrepancy in the yearly totals compared with totals by race is not a typographical error; it derives from the complexities of recording mob action.

against rural African Americans who had for some reason offended the white establishment. In turn, this establishment was dealing with the stresses of an emerging world economy in cotton and an African American population seeking the broader rights promised by the Union victory in the Civil War. In this context, lynching was typically justified by asserting that it was necessary for the protection of white women from aggressive black men.

At the time, Hose's lynching was widely celebrated, and just as with the Columbine killings, it was used as an example by advocates interested in making a political point about a favored policy. As with the Columbine killing, the excitement often led to a predictable exaggeration of the facts concerned. Also as with the Columbine shootings, advocates on both side of the lynching debate—pro and con—used the Hose lynching as a rhetorical device to support preexisting positions. The following are the facts that have been established by scholars in the years since the lynching. Notably, the story told here is different from what an excited public believed at the time Sam Hose was arrested, and in the immediate aftermath of his lynching.

Sam Hose was a twenty-one-year-old laborer on the Cranford farm in Palmetto, Georgia, a town that already in March 1899 had removed nine black men from the jail and lynched them. A month later, Hose and his employer, Alfred Cranford, had a dispute over wages, and an argument ensued on April 12, 1899. The argument continued near where Hose was chopping firewood. Cranford was armed with a pistol, with which he threatened Hose. Hose threw his ax at Cranford. The ax struck Cranford in the head, and he died instantly (Brundage 1993:82–83). Hose immediately fled, headed for his mother's home some seventy-five miles away. Note how this incident was very similar to the typical and mundane type of homicide described by Hirschi and Gottfredson: two young men had a dispute, weapons were nearby, and in the course of the fight one of them died.

But there was a broader issue, which was to be broadcast far and wide by newspapers like the Atlanta *Constitution* and by Georgia's new governor, Allen D. Candler. Lynching was an important political issue in 1899 Georgia. As mentioned earlier, Candler himself had run on a "prolynching" platform in the 1898 election, which emphasized the role that lynching played in delivering quick justice where courts were ineffective. Candler immediately declared the Palmetto murder "the most diabolical in the annals of crime," calling its details "too horrible for publication." Others were less shy about the details. Georgia congressman James M. Griggs created (or repeated) a story that went like this:

[Sam Hose] crept into that happy little home . . . [and] with an ax knocked out the brains of that father, snatched the child from its mother, threw it across the room out of his way, and then by force accomplished his foul purpose. [He] carried her helpless body to another room, and there stripped her person of every thread and vestige of clothing, there keeping her till time enough had elapsed to permit him to accomplish his fiendish offense twice more and again! (Dray 2002:4)

Rumors and gossip spread quickly. It was widely reported that Cranford had been eating dinner when attacked, that his eight-month-old child was near death, and that Mrs. Cranford had been raped twice despite having earlier provided medicine to treat Hose's assumed case of syphilis (Brundage 1993:83).

The Atlanta *Constitution* was particularly aggressive in stressing the importance of arresting and lynching Sam Hose, announcing in a front-page headline the next day, "Determined Mob After Hose; He Will Be Lynched If Caught." The subhead recommended an appropriate punishment: "Assailant of Mrs. Cranford May Be Brought to Palmetto and Burned at the Stake." Thus, what had started out as a mundane dispute over wages was framed by the press as a threat to the safety of white women throughout the South. The Newnan *Herald and Advertiser* wrote, "The black brute, whose carnival of blood and lust has brought death and desolation to the home of one of our best and most worthy citizens, [must be] run down and made to suffer the torments of the damned in expiation of his hellish crime" (quoted in Dray 2002:5). Despite the demand for summary lynch justice, the Atlanta *Constitution*, private citizens, and the governor announced monetary awards for anyone handing Hose over to the authorities.

Hose was captured near his mother's house on April 22, some ten days after Cranford died, by two men eager to collect the reward. They attempted to smuggle Hose back to Atlanta on April 23 in order to collect the reward but were recognized en route by people eager to commence the lynching. Following some negotiations, a special railcar was detailed to take Hose and 150 "escorts" back to the county seat of Newnan, near the scene of the crime. In Newnan, Hose was then briefly handed over to the sheriff's deputies in order that his captors could collect the bounty. He was then unceremoniously released to the mob, which took him to the home of Mrs. Cranford's parents for the positive identification of the prisoner. After a perfunctory identification by Mrs. Cranford's mother and sister (Mrs. Cranford never did confront the prisoner and was variously reported as being "crazed" or "demented" as a result of the crime), the mob proceeded toward the site of the lynching.

Additional trains were detailed so that the citizens of Atlanta, some thirty-five miles away, could participate in the Newnan lynching. The excitement of getting on the train was so intense that the railway was unable to collect fares from the people hanging on to the sides. By that time as many as 4,000 people had arrived to observe the event. Haste was viewed as important due to unsubstantiated rumors that soldiers would arrive to stop the lynching. Sam Hose was tied to a pine tree, and a number of men carried out prearranged duties such as collecting wood for the bonfire and obtaining a supply of kerosene. A heavy chain was wrapped around Hose and his clothing stripped from him. The Atlanta *Constitution* in a special edition on April 23, 1899, proudly reported:

> First he was made to remove his clothing. . . . Before the fire was lighted his left ear was severed from his body. Then his right ear was cut away. During this proceeding he uttered not a groan. Other portions of his body were mutilated by the knives of those who gathered about him, but he was not wounded to such an extent that he was not fully conscious and could feel the excruciating pain. Oil was poured over the wood that was placed about him and this was ignited.
>
> The scene that followed is one that never will be forgotten by those who saw it, and while Sam Hose writhed and performed contortions in his agony, many of those present turned away from the sickening sight, and others could hardly look at it. Not a sound but the crackling of the flames broke the stillness of the place, and the situation grew more sickening as it proceeded.
>
> The stake bent under the strains of the Negro in his agony and his sufferings cannot be described, although he uttered not a sound. After his ears had been cut off he was asked about the crime, and then it was he made a full confession. At one juncture, before the flames had begun to get in their work well, the fastenings that held him to the stake broke and he fell forward partially out of the fire.
>
> He writhed in agony and his sufferings can be imagined when it is said that several blood vessels burst during the contortions of his body. . . .
>
> One of the most sickening sights of the day was the eagerness with which the people grabbed after souvenirs, and they almost fought over the ashes of the dead criminal. Large pieces of his flesh were carried away, and persons were seen walking through the streets carrying bones in their hands.
>
> When all the larger bones, together with the flesh, had been carried away by the early comers, others scraped in the ashes. . . . Not even the stake to which the Negro was tied when burned was left, but it was promptly chopped down and carried away as the largest souvenir of the burning. (Wells 1899:chapter 2)

The "other mutilations" of the body referred to by the newspaper were similar to what Damiens had suffered 142 years earlier, including the cutting off of his fingers and genitals. His knuckles were reportedly put on display in urban Atlanta within a few days. The torture and burning of Sam Hose were quickly followed the next day by the hanging of a sixty-year-old preacher named Elijah Strickland because the lynch mob believed he had somehow assisted Hose in the murder of Cranford. This brought the number of extrajudicial executions in the small area to eleven in March and April 1899.

The terror created by the lynching worked. Blacks disappeared into the forests, fearing white mobs and the outriders who dominated rural Georgia.

Mob justice became implicit even in minor disputes over wages, such as that which led to the death of Alfred Cranford. It was clear to blacks that they had little recourse before the law, which, rough though it was in practice, was still a final recourse for whites not only for disputes between themselves but in reinforcing the racial hierarchy. Investigator Louis P. LeVin, who was hired by antilynching crusader Ida Wells-Barnett to investigate the racial climate in Palmetto, concluded:

> No one . . . thought much about the matter [of the eleven lynchings]. The Negroes were dead, and while they did not know whether they were guilty or not, it was plain that nothing could be done about it. And so the matter ended. With these facts I made my way home, thoroughly convinced that a Negro's life is a very cheap thing in Georgia. (Wells-Barnett 1899, chapter 4)

The pride felt by much of white Georgia by Sam Hose's lynching continued. The display of power was something to be proud of, a statement that "the people" were in command and that those who brought offense were criminals subject to summary justice.

But there was also an underlying current, even in Georgia. Former Georgia governor William Yates Atkinson (1894–1898), who lived in Newnan and supported an antilynching law passed in 1893, pleaded with Hose's lynch mob, "Do not stain the honor of this state with a crime such as you are about to perform." More important in the long run was to be the role that Hose's lynching played in galvanizing black activists to challenge the role of "Judge Lynch" in the subjugation of southern blacks. Ida Wells-Barnett, the reporter based in Chicago who had almost single-handedly led the antilynching movement up to that time, was joined following the horrific Hose lynching by prominent black intellectuals, particularly W.E.B. DuBois. They argued that the "negro problem" of the South was not just one of schooling for uneducated blacks but also the result of white racism that created the lynch mobs.

It was true, advocates like DuBois and Wells-Barnett asserted, that the white power structure in the South could use the ferocity of lynch justice to reinforce the existing power structure, but it was also true that the same events could be used to appeal to the sensibilities of more moderate southerners and northerners. The issue of such lynching was a major impetus when the NAACP was founded in 1909. And it was to be through the outrages of the same cases in which the South took such pride—such as the lynching of Sam Hose—that the NAACP would appeal to a national audience.

The NAACP Nationalizes the Antilynching Issue: A Moral Crusade

The NAACP was founded in 1909 to address issues of racial inequality. Legal segregation was spreading rapidly with the implementation of Jim

Crow laws restricting where blacks could live, what jobs they could hold, access to schooling, segregation of public transportation, restrictions on voting, and exclusion from courts. The racial hierarchy was even beginning to move out of the South and into the northern cities to which blacks were migrating. Of the many possible issues that the NAACP and other civil rights groups could highlight, lynching with its brutal violence was perhaps the most dramatic. Brutal cases of public mobs like that which lynched Sam Hose may have thrilled southern audiences, but they appalled the northern public and were an embarrassment in Europe. Lynching also presented a uniquely brutal way to highlight the racial hierarchy and provided raw material for a dramatic moral crusade that persisted throughout much of the twentieth century. The public knew that any mundane argument in the South could lead to the terror of mob justice. What is more, the inflammatory methods and language used by proponents to justify lynching were already part of the running conversation; the rhetorical excesses of newspapers like the Atlanta *Constitution* could be used against them.[11]

The strategy of the NAACP was to reframe lynching as a national civil rights problem. For example, when the dismemberment, hanging, and immolation of seventeen-year-old Jesse Washington in 1916 by a lynch mob in Waco, Texas, resulted in gruesome photographs from a postcard maker, W.E.B. DuBois, acting as the editor of *Crisis*, the NAACP's newspaper, published the cards on the front cover (Dray 2002:315–319). Sensitive to national opinion, Waco's boosters suppressed further distribution of the cards, a backhanded acknowledgment that lynching had gained the attention of the wider national audience.

Brutality provided the frame for the NAACP to push the issue of lynching into the political arena. Instead of focusing its campaign on the reform of rural white Georgians (and Mississippians, Arkansans, Indianans, etc.), the NAACP nationalized the issue. Leading this charge was a Republican congressman from St. Louis, Leonidas Dyer. Dyer represented a largely black district and, beginning in 1911, sought to federalize lynching by making it a crime for a sheriff to release prisoners to mobs, and fining counties in which this happened (Dray 2002:259–260).

Following World War I, a war fought to defend the rule of law, the Republican Party joined with the NAACP to make lynching a federal crime. The proposed Dyer Act provoked opposition by southern members of both the House and Senate but passed in the House of Representatives by 231–119 votes in early 1922, largely with Republican support, including that of President Warren Harding. The 119 representatives who voted against the act were southern sympathizers who offered defenses of states' rights over criminal law and spoke of "racial instincts," which still resonated particularly well in the South. They claimed that making lynching a federal crime would encourage rape and be interpreted as a "federal license to commit the foulest of outrages" (Dray 2002:264–265). It was typically pointed out, too, that existing laws in the states were adequate for the prosecution of what they perceived as being simple murders.

But, James Weldon Johnson, secretary of the NAACP, framed the issue as being "more than murder," arguing that lynching was anarchic violence that challenged the state's monopoly on the administration of justice:

> The analogy between murder and lynching is not a true one. Lynching is murder, but it is also more than murder. In murder, one or more individuals take life, generally for some personal reason. In lynching, a mob sets itself up in place of the state and acts in place of due process of law to mete out death as a punishment to a person accused of crime. It is not only against the act of killing that the federal government seeks to exercise its power . . . but against the act of the mob in arrogating to itself the functions of the state. . . . The Dyer Anti-Lynching Bill is aimed against lynching not only as murder, but as anarchy—anarchy which the states have proven themselves powerless to cope with. (quoted in Dray 2002:267–268)

Weldon frequently pointed out that lynching was a source of national embarrassment: "The veil of self-satisfaction has got be torn away from the face of this nation, and it must be made to look at itself as it is. . . . The raw, naked brutal facts of lynching must be held up before the eyes of this country until the heart of this nation becomes sick, until we get a reaction of righteous indignation that will not stop until we have swept away lynching as a national crime" (Dray 2002:258). Weldon's use of the word *anarchy* was particularly strategic in the 1920s, explicitly comparing lynch violence to the much-feared bomb throwers and others who had attempted to disrupt American and European society during the previous fifty years.

Dyer's bill passed the Senate Judiciary Committee on an 8–6 vote. Weldon then sent a letter on June 1, 1922, to all the US senators dramatizing the fact that twelve individuals had been killed in lynchings the previous month. Indeed, May 1922 was particularly gruesome for black Americans; a lynch mob in Kirvin, Texas, provided the most dramatic tale, with three dead following a castration and burning. The publicity led to major fundraising successes by the NAACP as they sought to influence the Senate vote. An ad was even taken out in four major newspapers, including the Atlanta *Constitution* on November 22–23, 1920, pointing out in bold type, "Do you know that the United States is the Only Land on Earth where human beings are BURNED AT THE STAKE?" (see Dray 2002:269–270). Nevertheless, the Dyer bill never came to a vote in the full Senate. Instead, it died before action could be taken. Procedural tactics included a filibuster that continued until December 1922, when the Senate was adjourned.

The NAACP's legislative strategy was, in fact, not to actually succeed until the 1960s, when the federal government finally began prosecuting cases under federal civil rights laws passed at that time. Although the defeat of the Dyer Act was, in historian Philip Dray's words, a "decided setback" (2002:273), Dray notes that the debate—that is, the running conversation—itself shifted as a result of the unsuccessful political challenge. Dray writes that the defeat of the act made it robustly clear that lynching was a subject of fierce condemnation, and that claims that lynching was "necessary" became a point of ridicule in the national discussion. He notes that in some southern states where lynching had once been done freely, "sentiment had turned against the practice" (p. 273). Indeed, Table 4.2 indicates that the number of lynchings in the United States had declined in the years between Sam Hose's 1899 lynching and the early 1920s (Zangrando 1980:214–215). By the time the Dyer Act was defeated in 1922, despite the lack of federal sanctions, incidents had declined.

Emmett Till, Mississippi Burning, and Edgar Ray Killen: Lynching 1955–2005

Mass public lynchings slowed by the 1930s. But secretive extralegal disappearances and other killings continued until at least the 1960s. Mississippi was the state most affected by the persistence of lynching. Lynching there and elsewhere by organized "posses" or "private mobs" continued until the 1960s, albeit with slowly declining chances for impunity. Particularly notorious was the 1955 lynching of a fourteen-year-old boy from Chicago named Emmett Till, who apparently teasingly propositioned a twenty-one-year-old married white woman, Carolyn Bryant, at a small country store. Till was abducted and killed in 1955 by Ray Bryant, the woman's husband, and his half-brother, J. W. Milam. This case, which normally would not have attracted attention beyond the backwoods of Mississippi, was brought to the attention of the national media by Till's mother, who arranged for a public funeral in Chicago in which 10,000 mourners showed up for an open-casket funeral featuring Emmett's battered body dressed in a tuxedo. Pictures of the funeral were published in *Jet*, a national African American magazine, in a manner that brought the incident to national attention. The governor of Mississippi, who called the case "straight out murder," was among those demanding a trial of Bryant and Milam. But even though the men were tried for the murder, they were quickly acquitted by the all-white jury; only later did they confess, in an article published by *Look* magazine.[12] The facts were publicized widely by the NAACP and other advocates for the rights of African Americans because of both the arbitrariness and brutality of the murder, and the refusal of the jury to convict despite abundant evidence.

In 1964 another case of lynching entered into the nation's running conversation. Three civil rights workers—two whites and one black—were arrested and then released. As they left town, they were stopped by a private mob organized by the local Ku Klux Klan, killed, and their bodies buried in a dam. A subsequent trial before another Mississippi jury resulted in an acquittal in 1966. Seven of the eighteen defendants were then tried in a federal courtroom. They were convicted in 1967 of civil rights violations and given sentences ranging from three to ten years. Such killings and trials—morality plays—were eventually dramatized in a book and the 1980s movie *Mississippi Burning,* which embarrassed both the federal government and the state of Mississippi for their inaction. One of the acquitted defendants, Edgar Ray Killen, who had been the leader of the local Ku Klux Klan, was retried and convicted by local Mississippi courts in 2005. At the age of seventy-nine, he was sentenced to twenty years in prison for manslaughter.

The End of Lynch Law in the United States?

Philip Dray wrestles with the consequences of twentieth-century American antilynching campaigns, well aware that there were few clear-cut explicit victories, even though the practice has effectively disappeared. Why, indeed, was the "war" against lynching won, even though the battles in the war were a series of legislative defeats, acquittals, witness intimidation, racist editorials, and charred bodies? In tracing this success, Dray asks, what were the "lasts" when it came to lynching? When did it stop? Trying to answer this question, he came up with the following list:

> *1930s:* Annual lynching of blacks dropped below ten per year.
> *1934:* Claude Neal lynching (Florida)—last lynching in which there was advance publicity.
> *1937:* Duck Hill, Florida, blowtorch lynching. Last "spectacle lynching." The two victims were tortured with a blowtorch, before one was killed with a shotgun blast, and the other set afire.
> *1964:* Civil rights workers—last time a mob acted in collaboration with official law enforcement to intercept prisoners leaving jail. (Dray 2002:457–463)

I believe that opposition to lynching is ultimately rooted in how the expansion of a monopoly over the use of coercive power expands. This expansion is facilitated by moral panics, whether created by the people protecting the preexisting social order or by those advocating protection from a more distant central government. In the case of the lynching, this pitted proponents of the local white elites against proponents of civil rights, such as the NAACP, that operated on a national scale. A similar example occurred with the case of the Quakers and witches of Puritan Massachusetts. There, appeal was made to the king in England. In each case the normal changes Durkheim wrote about came about in the context of sustained challenges to established authority in which subordinated groups—be they the small group of Quakers or the millions of African Americans—challenged the legitimacy of the continued rule of an oligarchic local authority. To do this, moral entre-preneurs pushed themselves into a wider consciousness. As Durkheim and Erikson predicted, changes in the fundamental conditions of social life occurred in a context where the power to judge and punish was critical.

Creating a Modern Morality Tale:
The Criminalization of Domestic Violence

> A woman met us at the door. She was crying and very upset. She had some bruises on her face and her lip was swollen and bleeding. She said that her husband had hit her, that she was not going to take it any more, and that she wanted him arrested. The officer had her sign a complaint form. At this point the man upstairs began yelling and cursing at the woman. It turned out that the man and the woman are not married but have been living together for some time and have a small baby. The woman thought that they were married, but the man is in the process of getting a divorce from his wife. The officer went upstairs [with the woman] to try to talk to the man who was very angry and yelled at the woman and the officer. The officer threatened him with arrest. Finally the officer shut the door to keep out the woman. She got very upset and felt that the officer was taking the side of the man. The back-up officer arrived and found the woman in the corner of the small room, still crying. She told the second officer that she thought she was legally married to the man [even though he was still legal-ly married to another woman] . . . When the man came downstairs with the first officer, he said he was going to his mother's house. The officer asked if everything would be okay. The man said yes. The woman remained sit-ting in the corner crying. The officers left. (Sherman 1992:50, after Oppenlanter 1982)

Written by an observer in 1977, this account illustrates the long and ambivalent history that the United Sates has had with two developments in the nature of the law. First is the increased capacity of officers to respond to domestic disturbances as a result of telephones, vehicles, and radios. Second are concerns about when and how it is appropriate for officers to intervene in squabbles in the virtually stateless area represented by family and romantic relationships. What happened in the incident described above was consistent with policing policies of the 1970s emphasizing that the best action for officers responding to a domestic violence call was to provide counseling and a cooling-off period. This may be surprising for most stu-dents in the first decade of the 2000s because the above situation would have resulted in an immediate arrest today.

What follows are accounts of some of the moral crises that emerged since 1970 as domestic violence changed from being viewed as a matter best dealt with in the home to one in which police intervention and arrest became required. Shaping this change is a running conversation about domestic violence that is ongoing both in the supermarket checkout line and in popular entertainment. Important foci for this conversation were a number of celebrated cases in which women were denied assistance from the police and then turned around and killed their abusers. Unlike the cases of witchcraft and lynching, though, attempts to control domestic violence are still contested.

The case of Roxanne Gay was among the earlier and more important and high-profile cases. Roxanne Gay had repeatedly requested police intervention when her husband, Philadelphia Eagles defensive lineman Blenda Gay, beat her. Indeed, she requested police intervention more than twenty times in their three-and-a-half-year marriage; neighbors reported that he had "bounced his wife off the walls" whenever the Eagles lost a game (Jones 1980:287). In December 1976, Roxanne stabbed Blenda in the throat as he slept, killing him. The Ms. Foundation and other advocates raised money for her defense, and she was eventually found not guilty by reason of insanity. This was not the clear-cut result that feminist advocates wanted, but from a Durkheimian perspective, it was the type of case that shifted the nature of the running conversation, making new ways of looking at the issue of spousal abuse possible.

The best-known opportunity to test the laws came with the case of Francine Hughes in 1979. Francine had married her high-school sweetheart, James Hughes, at age sixteen in 1963. After four children and eight years of marriage and beatings, she divorced him in 1971 and moved away. Six months later, after visiting the children and having a fight with Francine, James had an automobile accident. In his convalescence, he moved into a home next door to Francine, where he was cared for by Francine and his mother. Permanently unemployed, he began beating Francine again. On March 9, 1977, he tore up Francine's books from the business classes she was taking at a local college and told her that he was going to kill her that night. Twelve-year-old Christy Hughes called the police, who arrived quickly but then left because they believed James's threat to be idle. James in the meantime fell asleep. Francine snuck into his room, poured gasoline over the bed and James, and lit him on fire. She then drove straight to the sheriff's office and turned herself in for homicide.

The Francine Hughes case grabbed the public's attention in ways that the Blenda Gay case had not. It was a tough case to present as a killing that occurred during the heat of a battle between two squabbling spouses. After all, James had been sleeping. But more important for advocates, it gave the legal defense fund the opportunity to establish "battered woman syndrome" as a psychological condition justifying even homicide. The legal argument was that a history of battering, which in Hughes's case lasted thirteen years, meant that killing a man, even in his sleep, was justifiable particularly when the police did not respond. As with Roxanne Gay, Hughes was acquitted due to "temporary insanity." Feminists were pleased that after routine psychiatric tests she was quickly freed, but they again viewed the case as only a partial victory because she had had to demonstrate insanity rather than simply demonstrate the righteousness of her act.

The court cases were not enough, though, and feminists began to suffer setbacks in the supermarket checkout line where the broader running conversation was taking place. Initial reactions to Francine Hughes's acquittal were negative because some believed that this meant "open season" on men. Influential publications like *Time* and *Newsweek* reflected a public consensus that the law had been stretched too far. Convictions of women who killed their spouses began resulting in second-degree murder convictions. Sentences of 15–25 years were handed down by judges to women who killed their husbands, irrespective of a history of spousal abuse. However, this concern was not shared by all, and in fact by 1979, jury verdicts again began to shift, and women who had killed their husbands were acquitted. Cases were grabbed by advocates of both sides to illustrate preconceived political positions, as the debate about battered women continued (see Jones 1980:291–292).

In the 1980s, perceptions of domestic violence changed further as movies were made to dramatize the deaths. *The Burning Bed* (1984), starring Farrah Fawcett and dramatizing the Francine Hughes case, was perhaps the most well-known, attracting a great deal of sympathetic publicity for battered wives. This was followed by a number of Hollywood productions dealing with domestic violence, such as *The Color Purple* (1985); *Mesmerized* (1988); *A Cry for Help: The Tracey Thurman Story* (1989); *Love and Hate: A Marriage Made in Hell, Part 1* (1989); *Sleeping with the Enemy* (1991); *Bed of Lies* (1992); *Silent Victim* (1992); and *Breaking the Silence* (1992). Such films from a Durkheimian perspective are important because they are the product of an attentive movie industry responding to (and creating) an excited public. They are good indicators that what Durkheim called the "normal evolution of law" was being discussed, and a new consensus reached.

The consequence of this discussion about domestic violence and homicide was to nationalize the problem. Most notable was the federal Violence Against Women Act, which was passed in 1994, renewed in 1998 and 2005, and is a subject of an ongoing discussion. The act includes federal funding for domestic violence prevention programs, training for police likely to encounter domestic violence situations, and incentives to make "quick arrests" when police have evidence of domestic violence. Like the campaign against lynching, this is an attempt to nationalize something that is a private or local issue under existing law. The ultimate effects of the Violence Against Women Act are not known, but it is certain that advocates will continue to use dramatic events to demand federal action.

The story of Francine Hughes, who burned her abusive husband to death in 1977, was dramatized in the 1984 film *The Burning Bed* starring Farrah Fawcett.
Licensed by MGM Products. Use kindly authorized by Farrah Fawcett.

The Normal Evolution of Law

Ultimately, this chapter is about what Durkheim called "the normal evolution of law," that is, how law and morality slowly change. From the diverse examples of social change described herein, a few general principles about how this happens can be identified:

- Governments generate morality crises to shape normal change to preserve their own power, but the consequences of such incidents are not always predictable.
- Crime and drama are necessary in shaping normal change.
- Moral entrepreneurs—individuals and groups—emerge to shape the discussion about change using anecdotes, case studies, emotion, and in the modern world dramatic magazine stories and movies.
- Despite claims to the contrary, there are limits to how far and fast law changes.
- In any crisis, the deviant and marginalized are the most vulnerable to the scapegoating that often accompanies the change Durkheim wrote about.

- Social change, changes in the law, and changes in behavior do not always proceed together.

The conclusion that crime is necessary for the perpetuation of state power is in many ways cynical. On the surface, such a view leads to a conclusion that the criminal justice system is a game of musical chairs in which losers become the focus of prosecution. Change demands a loser who is labeled *deviant,* and as a result the status quo adjusts itself until the next moral panic sets the music in motion again. The losers described here include people like Robert-François Damiens, Mary Dyer, Tituba, Sam Hose, Francine Hughes, and even Edgar Ray Killen. Each at the time of conviction was marginal to mainstream society. This assumption is also a powerful social scientific tool because it leads to the conclusion that there are patterns in how the state goes about preserving itself while adjusting to change. It also illustrates that powerful states can be effectively challenged by moral entrepreneurs persistently pointing to the moral inconsistencies that always underlie state power.

The common thread of the diverse examples in this chapter is that *the nature of the reaction to crime varies according to the needs of a larger social unit* and is not solely dependent on the actions of the perpetrator. In other words, the fact that the French state under Louis XV reacted so harshly to Damiens tells us more about the nature of the French state than it does about Damiens. And the fact that Francine Hughes was not convicted of murder for burning her husband to death tells us at least as much about the concerns of the American people in the 1970s as it does about Francine Hughes.

Morality Plays: Strong Status Quo or Weak Status Quo?

Residents of modern Massachusetts prefer to think of their predecessors as honored pioneers, which they were. Indeed, Plymouth village has been re-re-created as a monument to the hard work, dangers, and successes of a people who took great risks for their religious beliefs. This is, of course, an accurate picture, and one particularly suited to a commemorative project in twenty-first-century Massachusetts.

Less honored but more dramatic are remembrances about how a small Puritan society went about protecting power relations by exiling antinomians, hanging Quakers, beheading dead Indian chiefs, and dealing with the witchcraft crisis of 1691. The difference between the seventeenth century, when violent death was perceived as a necessary catharsis for preservation of the status quo, and today, when the state of Massachusetts rarely if ever uses lethal force, is dramatic. And yet both times have a status quo that is widely accepted as "normal." This same metric can be applied to any number of other practices that have moved from being normal to criminal. Dueling comes quickly to mind, as do lethal barroom brawls, combat between spouses, Ache club fights, Ju/' Hoansi arrow fights, and lynching. What must have happened between the time when such acts were normative or even rewarded and today, when they are criminalized, is the normal source of change that Durkheim describes. Individual cases seized upon by moral entrepreneurs changed the running conversation, and a change in behavior followed.

But today change is generated across a much wider world than Puritan Massachusetts, as theatrical films and other forms of mass media engage in an interactive process—a running conversation—as society evolves. Millions of people now are vicariously involved in conversations about the justice of Francine Hughes's acquittal or the drama of a Columbine, thanks to modern mass media. In the process, millions seek to identify how laws should change and adapt to meet new circumstances. As Durkheim (and Erikson) implied, the people engaged in the conversation are not necessarily themselves aware of the significance of their conversations. For that matter, it is doubtful that the prosecutors of Quakers or witches knew that they were facilitating normal and needed political changes. Nor do the people talking about Michael Jackson's 2005 trial for sexual deviance, or consumers of stories about Natalee Holloway, the eighteen-year-old who disappeared on the Caribbean island of Aruba in 2005. But ultimately they are creating new norms regarding sexuality, roles of youth, and fears about international travel.

The Vulnerability of the Deviant and Unpopular

If crime is necessary, or at least the reaction to crime is useful for the fundamental conditions of social life, then who is held up as exemplary of what is wrong and evil? Whenever a great deal of punishment is "necessary" to assert a new morality, who will be held up as exemplary? Whose role in society will be defended most aggressively, and who will be stigmatized as venal? When the question is framed in this fashion, the answer is logical and parsimonious: it is those who lack the power to themselves label who will become deviant—that is, the powerless. And it is those who are conventional and normative—that is, tied to the established order—who are defended most vigorously. At its heart, Durkheim's definition of law, law enforcement, and deviance is about the consequences of the inequalities in power always found in modern government.

Both the powerful and weak can use the same principles to create a moral panic, but they use it in different ways. Thus *The Burning Bed*'s James Hughes in death became the poster child for domestic violence foes. Notably, Hughes was an unemployed drunk, not a high-status person like the director of enforcement for the Securities and Exchange Commission, John Fedders, who was fired by President Reagan after Fedders's wife filed for divorce, citing eighteen years of domestic violence as grounds (Sherman 1992:6–7). Like the many, many people with a similar record of domestic violence, Fedders never had a movie made about his case, and he resumed his life after dealing with his legal troubles. My point: that Hughes's and Fedders's crimes may have been similar under the law, but the reaction of the public was not. This was due to the fact that Hughes's life fit the needs of the public to demonize the marginalized, and Fedders's did not. In many respects, this is also why it was so difficult to prosecute the Ford Motor Company in the manslaughter deaths caused by defective gas tanks. If they had thought the case through, the Ford executives undoubtedly could have known that their actions would lead to a higher fatality rate. Indeed, *Mother Jones* had bluntly and publicly told them so only a few months earlier. But the Ford Motor Company is a large and powerful corporation that produces products much needed by consumers.

The same principle applied in Puritan Massachusetts, where odd women like Anne Hutchinson, Mary Dyer, Tituba, Sarah Good, and Sarah Osbourne were readily labeled as deviant rather than the many powerful citizens responsible for the unjust hanging and jailing of so many fellow citizens. But just pointing at the powerless and deviant is not enough. After all, there is a question of what the broader society needs, not just the venality of the crime or the presence of outcasts.[13]

There are, however, also unexpected consequences as social change movements unfold. Social change movements organized by the powerless can also take advantage of Durkheim's insights as they influence the evolution of law and morality. Successful social movements push existing law until it is no longer enforceable because to do so rips at the underlying fabric holding society together. When too many opt out of the game of musical chairs at the same time, the game becomes confused. To a large extent, this is what the Puritan Quakers did by continuing to violate the law of the Puritan state. It is also what Martin Luther King Jr. did when he and his nonviolent followers agreed to be arrested for violating segregation laws in the 1960s. As Erikson wrote, ultimately the capacity of society to punish is limited; failure to recognize this fact can be used to slowly and painfully tear at the moral glue that holds society together.

Notes

1. Cooney (1997a) emphasizes that absolutist states like France in the 1700s tend to be more violent than more democratic states. This point will be returned to in the conclusion.

2. Many times, the cases celebrated by popular magazines like *National Enquirer* and *People* are much more ephemeral than cases like those of Manson, Simpson, and Hinckley. For example, in 2005 the *National Enquirer* and *People* magazine focused on the disappearance of an Alabama high school student, Natalee Holloway, who vanished while on a high school trip to the Caribbean island of Aruba. Before that, the most important case in the supermarket checkout line was that of singer Michael Jackson, who was tried for child molestation in 2005. And before that, an important case was that of Scott Peterson, a middle-class man who had an affair, and killed his wife on Christmas Eve 2003 when she was nine months pregnant. Now, in the annals of American crime, none of these cases are any more tragic or strange than the thousands of other killings, disappearances, and molestations that did not receive widespread attention. Why they are important, Durkheim would say, is that as with Damiens's assault on Louis XV, they highlight issues that are important to the underlying social fabric of American society in 2005. In a good Durkheimian tradition, pundits and armchair analysts point out why these particular cases attracted the attention of the American public. For example, the Holloway case illustrates anxieties about traveling outside the United States, and a wished-for innocence for middle-class high school students. The Jackson case reflected fascination with celebrity, race, and sexuality. The Peterson case perhaps reflects the anxieties of the middle class about adultery, marriage, and childbearing. These are all the types of conclusions Durkheim would have approved of. Just as the execution of Damiens was a catharsis for French society, so too are the discussions of these cases in American society as the boundaries for what is right and wrong are discussed and renegotiated.

3. See Appendix 1 for a description of how US homicide rates have varied depending on what and who is doing the counting. Particularly in earlier years of the twentieth century there is a great deal of variation. See Appendix 1 also for historical examples from England.

4. See Appendix 1 for data about how cases in Houston, Texas, in 1969 were dealt with by the authorities.

5. See Appendix 2 for actual examples of laws against murder. Included there are statutes from California and Texas. For an understanding of how rare justifiable homicide has become, see Appendix 1.

6. King Philip's War occurred in 1675–1676 and in terms of soldiers and civilians wounded and killed had one of the highest rates of casualties in US history. However, this occurred at a time when population density was much lower than it was to be in the future.

7. Hutchinson and her large family eventually settled in Long Island, where she and five of her children were killed by Indians in 1643.

8. This is a relatively mild punishment compared with the executions that were to come in response to the Salem witch trials in 1691, perhaps reflecting the relatively high level of openness in the governmental structure as opposed to the more authoritarian structure that was to emerge in coming years (see Cooney 1997b).

9. See Appendix 1 for a description of why mobs justified lynching as well as rates of murder by race across time. Data are presented for both victims and perpetrators.

10. Typically such lynching involved offenders being identified by the call of "thief" in a marketplace. The crowd would form an instant mob, chasing the accused. If he was caught by the mob, he would be beaten, often fatally. His goal was to reach a police station, where he would at least be protected from the uncontrolled wrath of the mob.

11. The fact that I quote such inflammatory words from the Atlanta *Constitution* reflects NAACP's efforts to turn the running conversation around, using the words of segregationists themselves.

12. See http://www.pbs.org/wgbh/amex/till/sfeature/sf_look.html.

13. And today, the mass murderer Charles Manson, who charmed middle-class hippie teenagers into killing minor Hollywood celebrities for him in the 1960s, remains a focus of middle-class fascination. But Juan Corona, whose body count was much higher than Manson's, has disappeared from the public's consciousness, despite the fact that he was convicted of killing twenty-five itinerant farmworkers and vagrants. Again, it is not abstract assessment of threat to public safety, but what the public needs to be part of the running conversation, that determines who will be left out of the game of musical chairs Durkheim described.

CASE STUDY
Vigilantism in a Tanzanian Village

By Essau Magugudi in Kigoma
NOVEMBER 27, 1997, is deeply etched in the memories of Shunga villagers. It was on this day that they took law into their own hands and hacked to death three bandits who they suspected of carrying out acts of robbery in villages surrounding refugee settlements of Mutabira and Muyovozi.
Such retribution was unprecedented. . . .

I found the above article while cruising the Internet in 1999, after typing in the key word "Shunga" on a lark. Shunga is a remote village in western Tanzania where my sister-in-law lived for sixteen years, and also where my wife and I were married. I had also spent six weeks there writing an article about Shunga itself, which was later published in *African Studies Review*. The article struck me as odd because lynch law was not unprecedented in that part of Tanzania, as is asserted in Essau Magugudi's article. Rather, it is fairly typical of remote Tanzanian villages. Indeed, during the three years I lived in the nearby town of Kasulu (1984–1987), typically once or twice per year, some kid would be caught in the market stealing something trivial. Someone would yell "thief," and he would run toward the police station as fast as he could, with an angry mob chasing after him. The unspoken arrangement was that if he made it to the police station he would be arrested, and a legal case would be made against him. Thus, the police station was "safe," so to speak, even though he would be prosecuted. But, if the crowd caught him, he would be beaten to death. Similar rules of summary justice were applied to Shunga. The big talk in Shunga in previous years had been of rumored poisonings, the attempted murder of a former ward councilor (someone set his grass roof on fire in the middle of the night), and the execution by a burning tire "necklace" of a thief caught in a neighboring village. Vigilante justice and summary execution are not that unusual in this part of Africa, where the courts and police find it difficult to find transportation to the remote villages even if they are called. Without access to a vehicle, police officers must walk for at least half a day even to ask the first question. What has changed is that because of the refugee crisis, journalists now come to the area looking for stories, some of which might end up on the Internet, where I can find them. Essau Magagudi's account continues:

> The three slain bandits had on that day ambushed a peasant along the main road. . . . As luck would have it, the peasant escaped narrowly from his custody of his captors who had tried to seize his bicycle. He then reported the incident to the villagers who were bathing at a nearby stream. As the bandits emerged from their hideouts and descended towards the stream, they were stopped by villagers for questioning. It was discovered that the bandits were refugees at Muyovozi [refugee] camp. Upon searching them, the villagers found them with three locally made guns secured in an old sack. The bandits were handcuffed and taken to the ward office where a mob of angry youths hacked them to death.

Not much of a criminal investigation here. Probably most relevant is the fact that the dead youths represented the threat that the refugee camp provided to the village. Since 1994, Shunga, which has a population of about 4,000, has had a United Nations–supported refugee camp built on its boundary. In 1997, there were 50,000 refugees from Burundi living there. This camp has changed the social order in unexpected ways. If I look for an analogous reaction in sociology, I think that it would be seventeenth-century Puritan Massachusetts, which Kai Erikson wrote about. Political and social change resulted in the legal execution of Quakers in the early 1660s and of witches in 1691. Again, Essau Magagudi's account:

> The hacking of the bandits did arouse mixed feelings among villagers, especially when the councillor of the ward was taken by the police at Kasulu for questioning, but residents of Shunga and other neighbouring villages believed the killing of the bandits would minimise, if not stop altogether, acts of banditry which had been increasing in the villages.

"Mixed feelings" is usually an indication that there are doubts about "legitimacy," particularly in the context of the removal of the ward councilor. Did the villagers ask themselves whether they should have killed the refugees or not? How does it feel to live next door to people who have killed publicly in this fashion? What can the central authorities, whose authority was usurped, actually do? Should they have presented the thieves to the ward councilor while still alive? There are doubts among the villagers about whether the right thing was done, and whether they had legitimate authority to do what they did. Notably, though, the doubts were about who should have responded, not whether the punishment for theft was just. Rather, it was about who is the legitimate third party: the central government, ward councilor, or village mob? There is also fear that "two party" justice exposes the villagers to retaliation by the dead refugees' friends.

I pity government officials assigned to rural areas of Tanzania, like the ward councilor. He was sent to a remote village with the idealistic assumption that he could persuade villagers to develop and pay for a modern state, even though they will never receive things like police investigations. And from the villager perspective, the most prominent duty of the ward councilor is to collect the annual head tax, a job that confers little status, and for which councilors receive a miniscule salary (which is typically late). In fact, the salary is so small and irregular that as with virtually every other person living in Shunga, the ward councilor had a subsistence farm in order to raise enough food to eat.

Not surprisingly, in many parts of Tanzania the situation often leads to corruption. Technically, of course, the Shunga ward councilor had the Kasulu police force to back him up, but then so does each of the forty or fifty ward councilors in the district. When I lived in Kasulu, the police had only one or two vehicles, and were unlikely to respond to a remote robbery case. A consequence is that the problem escalates into the type of lynching described here. This is a classic case of a weak state that has little legitimacy built up, and as a result has difficulty asserting the monopoly over the use of coercive force.

In fact, the central government is aware that Shunga has had a history of problems with ward councilors. One of the previous ward councilors, who pushed projects of school construction and tax collections too hard (he was known as a modernizer), had the grass roof of his house burned late one night, in an attempt to kill him. He eventually was given a transfer by the central government. No one ever prosecuted (or lynched) those responsible for the torching: "Four months after that incident, several more incidents of banditry and robbery have been reported from villages near refugee settlements in Kasulu district."

So much for the hope that lynching controls stealing. Banditry was a chronic problem before and after the incident in Shunga. Lynching was perhaps less so, but the point that Essau Magugudi makes here is a good one. Lynching is not necessarily an effective means of crime control. Nor were the footraces out of the Kasulu marketplaces. Stealing was present both before and after "executions"; so much for theories equating severity of punishment with deterrence. This is a stark reminder that capital punishment of the most horrific sort did not control theft in the area. In such a context, other explanations for the brutal lynchings need to be sought, and Erikson's (and Durkheim's) point that such violence is important at times when social boundaries are realigned becomes relevant.

What happened in Shunga was consistent with what Cooney, Weber, and Durkheim write about homicide, the state, and the nature of social control. In countries where the state is weak and the representatives of the government have low status, there is much social change of the sort found in the remote Puritan Massachusetts described by Erikson.[1] I suspect that explanations of what happened in Shunga are probably more rooted in such experiences than the hoped-for control of crime that the villagers and perpetrators articulate. I am also sure that without even the rudimentary guarantees of a functioning justice system, the innocent are also likely victims.

Further Reading

Waters, Tony (1997). "Beyond Structural Adjustment: State and Market in a Rural Tanzanian Village." *African Studies Review* 40, no. 2: 59–89.

Note

1. In the small country of Guatemala, it was recently claimed by that country's presidential spokesman that there were 278 victims of lynch mobs in 1997. The lynch mobs use stones and gasoline (among other means) to kill, with such imprecision that in 2000, Japanese tourists were also victims of the violence. See "Lynchmord auf Verdacht: Weil die Justiz korrupt und untaetig ist, greifen Buerger zur Selbsthilfe. Die blutige Rache trifft oft Unschuldige" [Lynch killing on suspicion: Because justice is corrupt and inactive, the people seize on self-help, and bloody revenge hits the innocent], *Focus* 30 (July 24, 2000): 188.

Massacre in a
Chinese Labor Camp

The 1928 massacre in "Big Camp" occurred in a Chinese agricultural community in northern California. The camp had been established fifty years previously and in 1928 was composed of about 200 persons, all Chinese, most of whom were middle-aged or elderly men. The massacre is of interest here because it illustrates well the role that criminal investigation and law play in assuaging fears in the context of an extremely violent incident.

This case is also appropriate for illustrating the context that a well-legitimated third party plays in criminal investigations, and the tenuous relationships among police, courts, and a community isolated by segregation. The police and community worked awkwardly through their mutual suspicions to deal with fear and horror. Theirs is a story of action and reaction, in which events were interpreted through veils of distrust that may seem anachronistic today. For example, prisoners are no longer routinely presented to the community to demonstrate that a case has been solved (although this practice was still routine even at the time of President John Kennedy's assassination; Lee Harvey Oswald was shot in 1963 during such a show). Likewise, today no community would be searched and its weapons seized due to fears of a "tong war." Modern communications would have permitted a quicker response and arrest. Finally, it is unlikely that an entire community would hide the two most obvious victims (i.e., the surviving girls) from the police.

But though the actual methods are anachronistic, the sociology of the situation is not. Irrespective of the logic of a particular situation, communities do feel better when a notorious killer is caught. Communities are also reassured by a quick response by police. Particularly in isolated minority communities, concerns remain today about how well the justice system serves their needs and, especially in violent cases, assuages their fears. Such enduring concerns were at the root of the response in Big Camp.

Situated on an isolated Suisun Valley slough in California's Delta region, Big Camp came to an abrupt end as a result of the murder of ten people on August 22, 1928, by an itinerant Chinese laborer. At the time, the Sacramento *Bee* claimed that the massacre established a California record as the "most killed by one man in [a] single day." Behind the record was a sad story in which seven members of ranch foreman Wong Gee's family were fatally shot or stabbed and three others were murdered.

145

According to accounts, fortified with opium,[1] Leung Ying attacked the ranch foreman, Wong Gee, while he was in an underground room playing a card game. Wong Gee was a powerful figure in the small community. Indeed, he had killed another Chinese man the previous year. This killing had been ruled self-defense by the court, a ruling that was supported by the Chinese community that turned out in force at the courthouse to demand Wong Gee's release. On that August day in 1928, Leung Ying blocked the main entrance and shot Wong Gee and his card-playing partner before they could escape through the concealed exit that led onto the banks of Suisun Slough. He then ran to the house of Wong's brother, shooting both the brother and a cook. Next he ran to Wong Gee's house, where he murdered Wong's wife and four of their children, as well as another cook. Two of Wong Gee's daughters escaped death in an upper room of the house. The murderer then left the scene in his Dodge touring car.

Upon learning of the deaths, residents of the camp immediately sent a runner to the nearest telephone, located at the Rockville cemetery some two miles away. Because they did not know why the brutal attack had taken place, they hid the two surviving girls from the sheriff, fearing that they could be the targets of a conspiracy.

In response to the report, Solano County sheriff George R. Carter immediately ordered a roadblock on the road to Sacramento. Leung Ying, however, managed to slip past the roadblock and made his way to Grass Valley, some eighty miles away in the Sierra foothills, by nightfall. Abandoning his own car, Leung Ying then commandeered a car owned by a local Chinese acquaintance of his. After being recognized by others, he took his friend hostage and spent the night hiding in a chicken coop near the Empire Mine, an industrial complex that was the biggest employer in the area. The next morning, Sheriff Carter arrested him without incident.

When word reached the Chinese community at Big Camp that the murderer was captured, the entire community, still fearful, went to the jail to see if the sheriff had the right man. The sheriff, concerned that a lynching might result, ordered special security during the period when the prisoner was displayed before the crowd of angry Chinese and for photographs by the press. This extra security was due, the sheriff said, to the fact that the murders were part of a "tong war." (Tong were Chinese secret societies or fraternal organizations that were notorious for gang fighting.) As a special precaution, he ordered a search of Big Camp so that all weapons could be confiscated in order to prevent a "Chinese uprising." This cache of seized weapons was later proudly displayed to press photographers.

Leung Ying pled guilty to the murderers at his arraignment on August 30. An examination by the doctors from the nearby Napa State Hospital was ordered for the next day, to test his sanity. The doctors reached the conclusion that the defendant was sane and therefore guilty of first-degree murder.

On August 31, the judge ordered him to hang at San Quentin Prison on November 9. Citing fears on the part of the sheriff that the Chinese community would retaliate before that date, the judge ordered immediate transfer to death row. Leung Ying cheated the hangman by committing suicide on October 22, "saving the state 15 feet of well stretched hemp," reported the Solano *Republican.*

The murders created a sensation in their day, and there was immediate speculation about the motive for the crime. The newspapers and sheriff both leaned toward the "tong war" theory, even though the West Coast tong wars had subsided some twenty years earlier. Other theories pointed to Leung Ying's history as an opium smoker, describing him as a "dope fiend" or, in the slang of the day, a "hophead." Years later, a descendant of Big Camp's pioneers, Christopher Yee, said that he thought that a personal rift led Ying to commit the murders; it was rumored that Wong Gee had refused to re-hire Ying three months earlier because Ying had expressed an interest in his teenage daughter. As for Ying himself, while he was in custody his story changed several times. When arrested in Grass Valley, he showed the sheriff a cake that he claimed the victims had tried to poison him with. Later he said that incessant teasing had been the motive for the crime.

Further Reading

Delaplane Conti, Kris, with Peter Leung and Tony Waters (1997). "Chinese Pioneers Make It Big at Big Camp," and "The Depression Shuts Down Big Camp." *Vacaville Reporter,* February 16 and 23.

Note

1. Chinese at the time were stereotyped as opium addicts, and it was assumed in the larger population that using the drug turned people into "fiends" that made them capable of crimes requiring "fiendish" bursts of energy. This, though, probably had more to do with ethnic stereotypes of the day, which focused on the role of some Chinese in the provision of vice opportunities for whites and Chinese alike. In fact, opium is a depressant that causes users to become drowsy. An excellent review of the role Chinese communities played in the vice trade is found in Ivan Light, "From Vice District to Tourist Attraction: The Moral Career of American Chinatowns, 1880–1944," *Pacific Historical Review* 43 (1974): 367–394.

The Case of the Exploding Pinto

Accidents by companies seeking to create wealth for themselves are a by-product of the industrial age. But who is responsible when a product fails or an accident happens: is it the person who buys the product, or the person who sold it, or perhaps some earlier person who manufactured it? Because many individuals and organizations are involved in the production and sale of modern manufactured goods, this question often does not have an easy answer.

A particularly well-known story of product safety is that of the Ford Pinto. This case became especially famous when in a seven-page cost-benefit analysis done by Ford Motor Company, a human life was valued at $200,000, and as such the analysis concluded that it was cheaper to be sued by the predicted 180 burn fatalities and 180 serious burn victims than make an $11 design modification on a predicted eleven million cars. Indeed, the analysis estimated that lawsuits would cost Ford $49.5 million, which was far less than the $137 million needed to redesign and retrofit the popular low-cost car (Strobel 1980:286).

Local governments wrestled with questions of product liability in the way they administer civil and criminal law. With regard to the Pinto, the best example of this occurred in August 1978, when three Indiana girls died in an accident in which their Pinto was rear-ended by Robert Duggar. Duggar, who had a poor record of driving as well as open alcohol containers in the vehicle, was not charged in the accident. But then the Elkhart County district attorney, Michael Cosentino, took an unusual step. There had already been wide publicity regarding the dangers created by the design of the Pinto's gas tank. Indeed, investigative reporting by *Mother Jones* magazine in 1977 had revealed that a bolt protruding from the axle punctured the gas tank in the event of a rear-end collision. This design flaw meant that many low-impact, low-speed accidents resulted in lethal explosions. Cosentino pointed out that since the Ford Motor Company was well aware of this flaw, it could be tried for manslaughter. And under Indiana law this was possible.

Here are the facts of the case: In August 1978, Judy Ulrich was driving the Pinto she had bought earlier that year with her father as a high school graduation present. On their way to a volleyball game at a church some twenty miles away, she and her two sisters stopped for gas and then apparently drove off with the gas cap still on top of the car. After the gas cap fell off as she pulled onto the highway, Ulrich made a U-turn and slowly drove back, looking for her gas cap. Apparently after spotting it by the side of the highway, she slowed. As she did this, the van driven by twenty-one-year-old Robert Duggar came up behind her at a speed of 50 mph, well within the speed limit, and struck the Pinto. The gas tank was forced into a protruding bolt on the rear axle that punched a two-and-one-half-inch hole in the just-filled eleven-gallon gas tank. Gas splashed into the passenger compartment, and before the vehicles had come to a stop it exploded.

The death of the three Ulrich girls in the Pinto at first mystified Cosentino and his staff. Six months earlier, one of the investigative staff had read about the dangers inherent in the design of the Pinto gas tank in an article published in the September–October 1977 issue of *Mother Jones*. The article "Pinto Madness" detailed how the Ford Motor Company ignored engineers' concerns about the safety of the rear-mounted fuel tank, which had been designed in order to accommodate a corporate goal of producing a 2,000-pound car for less than $2,000. The article indicated further that a follow-up study by the National Highway Traffic Safety Administration (NHTSA) found that thirty-eight cases of rear-end collisions with Pintos had resulted in twenty-seven deaths. Of these deaths, all but one were the result of a damaged gas tank and subsequent fire. Safety tests conducted by the NHTSA revealed that an impact of 35 mph or greater was likely to result in a burst gas tank and the immolation of any occupants in the passenger compartment. In February 1978, a California jury awarded $128 million in civil damages in an accident involving a 1972 Pinto (the verdict was eventually overturned, and Ford paid only $3.5 million). On June 9, 1978, two months before the Ulrich accident, Ford announced a recall of the 1.5 million Pintos then on the road.

The death of the Ulrich girls created a legal conundrum for the conservative Republican prosecutor. He could do nothing and permit the case to go to civil court; judging from past awards, the girls' parents would likely win a judgment against Ford Motor Company. He could prosecute Duggar for manslaughter, on the grounds that his reckless behavior had led to the death of the girls. Or he could try a novel approach, and make a *criminal* charge against the Ford Motor Company and its executives by arguing that in ignoring the obvious faults of the Pinto, Ford had committed "reckless homicide." In other words, without Ford's recklessness and disregard for consumers' lives, the accident would not have been fatal.

The Elkhart County grand jury gave Cosentino what he asked for: an indictment of the Ford Motor Company for reckless homicide. The indictment sent a shiver through corporate America. This happened because while the maximum criminal penalty for Ford was a trivial $30,000, executives could in the future be held criminally liable for financial decisions leading to the deaths of consumers.

At the trial, the expensive legal team for the Ford Motor Company chipped away at the charges. The judge limited the question of recklessness to whether Ford had been too slow in pursuing the recall in the forty-one days between the recall and the Ulrich accident. Ford made the claim that if there was to be criminal liability, it should be on the driver of the van that collided with the Pinto, Robert Duggar.

After days of difficult deliberation, the jury returned a unanimous verdict that declared Ford Motor Company to be not guilty of the criminal charges brought by Cosentino. Members of the jury later indicated that although they thought Ford had been negligent, their decisionmaking did not rise to a level under which a conviction was possible under Indiana's homicide statute.

Despite the acquittal in criminal court, a "Pinto narrative" quickly emerged as being paradigmatic of corporate preference for profits over human life. Like high-profile domestic violence cases, the case changed the nature of the running conversation about who is really responsible for death. Despite the courtroom loss, books, articles, and texts continue to hold up the case as the type of conscious decisionmaking that results in victimization in the pursuit of profit. Provocatively, sociologists Matthew Lee and M. David Ermann (1999) called this assumption into question, noting that "decision makers" working in a corporate environment do not make conscious decisions to market an "unsafe vehicle." Rather, they assert that such amoral calculations emerge not as a result of legal intent, which implies conscious decisionmaking, but in the context of broader institutional forces that emerge from the institutional cultures (in this case Ford) and the automobile industry in general. This means that court proceedings that probe the minds of individual decisionmakers may not be adequate for exploring how decisions leading to a great deal of human suffering occur.

This thesis is important for understanding not only how product safety decisions are made, but how any type of corporate decisionmaking resulting in death is evaluated. Simply put, correcting the decisionmaking of individuals through the application of criminal law does not by itself result in more moral decisions. Attention has to be paid to the context—that is, the ecology—of decisionmaking.

Further Reading

Dowie, Mark (1977). "Pinto Madness." *Mother Jones,* September/October 1977.

Lee, Matthew T., and M. David Ermann (1999). "Pinto 'Madness' as a Flawed Landmark Narrative: An Organizational and Network Analysis." *Social Problems* 46, no 1: 30–47.

Strobel, Lee Patrick (1980). *Reckless Homicide? Ford's Pinto Trial.* South Bend, IN: And Books.

CHAPTER 5

When the State Kills: Execution, War, and Genocide

It is an infinitely tragic fact that the greatest crimes of history are committed with the cooperation or at least with the passive consent of the solid citizens who constitute the stable backbone of the community. The sporadic crimes that soil the front pages, the daily robberies, assaults, rapes, and murders are the work of individuals and small gangs. They are committed by manifest criminals whom the community despises and punishes. But the great evils, the persecutions, the unjust wars of conquest, the mass slaughters of the innocent, the exploitations of whole social classes—these crimes are committed by the organized community under the leadership of respectable citizens. (Furfey 1966:17)

The state—government—was implicitly at the center of the previous three chapters even though I wrote primarily about private killing, that is, individuals who kill other individuals. But the state does more than enforce laws. The state also kills. And because some governments at some times kill so prolifically, the state came up repeatedly. And yet the state is not typically the focus of the moral scorn directed at the faults of the marginalized and poor. Paul Furfey (1966:17–19), reflecting on this phenomenon after World War II, noted that the opinions of the powerful are respected not because of their moral rectitude but because of social criticism emerging from the privileged that ignores the deficiencies of the upper classes and emphasizes the sins of the poor and unfortunate. Or, to borrow from previous chapters, the sins of the Ford Motor Company are evaluated less critically than, say, the drunk driver who ran into a poorly designed Pinto fuel tank.

In part, this is because the capacity to use violence underlies legitimacy, lawmaking, law enforcement, and the power to label wrongdoing. These are all forces that restrict the use of private violence by turning killing into a phenomenon associated with the assertion of a monopoly over the use of coercive force, regulation of social ecology, and morality plays. But this begs a basic issue. Killing in the name of the state is the greatest source of violent death, not private violence. In the twentieth century, 129 million people died from organized state executions and starvation while 34 million died in war (see Cooney 1997a). Governments have been responsible for the deaths of far more people than small stateless tribes like the Ju/' Hoansi or Ache, feuds, dueling, or the range of other killing described so far. Governments do their killing through war, execution, or genocide. By the legalistic definition of the same state, such killing is always "legal." Indeed, the idea that government killing could be illegal murder changed only after war crimes began to be prosecuted following World War II.

Mass killing orchestrated by the state is a current and ongoing issue. Rwanda and the former Yugoslavia came under the control of genocidal governments in the 1990s. Parts of Sudan are, even as I write in early 2007, probably suffering from genocidal attacks that have been recognized as such since 2004. In the Democratic Republic of Congo, it is believed that four million people have died since 1996 as a result of militia attacks, executions, and war-induced famine and disease. In Baghdad, Iraq, there are in 2006–2007 daily reports of bound, tied, and tortured execution victims.

But few of the people who killed in these places, or even orchestrated the killings, will ever be brought before a court for the sort of trial that private killers risk. And who is brought to trial will often depend on the relative power of those who organize the killing. The international criminal justice regime that could potentially bring to trial genocidal governments has no police, no army, and few tools with which to command obedience.

There is also a great deal of variation in whom governments kill, why they kill, how many they kill, and the manner in which they kill, which is why state-sponsored killing is a legitimate subject for a book dealing with the sociology of killing. In part, this is because when it works, state power is so legitimate that all types of violence, whether by the state or private individuals, is exceedingly rare. Thus, between 1900 and 1940 there were only two recorded murders in Iceland, despite an ancient history that had featured violence for many centuries (Daly and Wilson 1988:275). But the opposite of course is also true, particularly when the state undertakes to kill in a frantic attempt to preserve its own power, as happened recently in Rwanda, Cambodia, and toward the end of World War II, when the Nazi government ordered the execution of prisoners in concentration camps. In the case of Rwanda, 5–10 percent of the population died within three months.

By this point, it should be obvious that the monopoly over the use of coercive force is not utilized only to pursue an abstract sense of justice. If it is used for good, it can also be used for evil. If there is too little power, the anarchy described in Chapter 2 results, and complex society, even civilization itself, is not possible. If too much power is concentrated in the state, the elites become socially distant and their position can be maintained only with the use of violence and terror, such as that maintained by absolutist rulers like Louis XV of France or Pol Pot in Cambodia. This brings us back to the right side of Cooney's curve. As Mark Cooney (1997) has pointed out, the most peaceful central government is one with enough power to avoid anarchy but not so much that it resorts to the arbitrary power of a police state. As Cooney's U-shaped curve (see Figure 2.1) illustrates, this means that democratic countries in which citizens participate in governance and those who abuse power can be held accountable will have the lowest rates of violent death as private violence decreases (see also Table 2.1). Governance matters. Here it means that there should not be too much concentration of power (in which case you get totalitarian rule), or too little. Like the Three Bears eating the porridge, the ideal society has only the "just right" amount of state power, not too much and not too little.

But, in fact, getting the "just right" amount of anything is possible only in fairy tales. In real life, there is variation in how much violence and killing a state uses to maintain its power and legitimacy. Because there is this variation, sociologically the types and reasons why state violence varies can be evaluated. Thus, this chapter explores the relationships between killing and the state. It does this in three ways: first is a typology of state violence developed by Randall Collins for a 1973 article that describes the different ways states exercise lethal violence. Included are ferocious killing, bureaucratic killing, and ascetic killing. The second approach is adapted from Mark Cooney and emphasizes how the different types of states kill, including through execution, war, and genocide. The final approach assesses how modern nationalism and psychological techniques are used to persuade humans to kill strangers. This is based on Benedict Anderson's (1991) and Dave Grossman's (1995) descriptions of how governments order citizens to kill on their behalf.

Embedded in each of these approaches are questions about how and why different states use killing to maintain control. How much killing is "necessary" for a state to maintain control? How do you persuade citizens to kill on behalf of a government, and when does too much killing lead to instability? At the opposite extreme, when does state weakness lead to anarchy and more killing? Finally, why do some modern states kill remarkably infrequently while others effectively commit suicide by collapsing into a paroxysm of killing, as the Rwanda government did in 1994?

The Callous State: Ferocity, Bureaucracy, and Asceticism

Drawing on examples that included ancient China, Rome, the Mongol empire, Nazi Germany, Stalin's Soviet Union, and the US bombing of Vietnam, sociologist Randall Collins (1973) categorized state-sponsored violence into three types: ferocious killing, bureaucratic killing, and ascetic killing. In each of these categories, the perpetrators justify to themselves and those around them that what they are doing is normative, legal, and necessary to preserve the existing social order.

Ferocity, Inequality, and Empathy

Ferocious killing is done by a state to emphasize its power over its subjects. Ferocious killing is done publicly in a manner that communicates to all the power of a chief or king. The execution of Robert-François Damiens (discussed in the previous chapter) was certainly of this nature. In describing this type of killing, Collins draws on an example from early modern France that he found in the writings of Alexis de Tocqueville, best known for his descriptions of the United States in the 1830s. Explaining how this example is relevant requires some thought about the world in which de Tocqueville lived.

Alexis de Tocqueville was surprised at the benevolent atmosphere he found in the America he observed in the 1830s. Irrespective of the fact that it was a time of slavery, frontier lynching, dueling, whipping, tarring and feathering, and (compared with today) routine executions, de Tocqueville found the atmosphere to be much more pleasant than what he had seen as an aristocrat in France. Presumably, this was because as an adolescent during the Napoleonic Wars, he observed the excesses of France's highly unequal society of aristocrats and peasants. He lived at a time when conscript peasant armies were brutally demolished, the guillotine used regularly, and cities routinely destroyed.

From such a context, the young United States seemed pretty good, and de Tocqueville wanted to explain why. As a result, he hypothesized that the American emphasis on relative equality between people of different stations created an empathy that was not restricted to members of one's caste. De Tocqueville explained that when "the chroniclers of the Middle Ages who were all by birth aristocrats, relate the tragic end of a noble, there is no end to grief; but they mention all in one breath and without wincing at the massacres and tortures of the common people." He went on to point out that customs "softened," or civilized, as relationships between different castes dissipated.

To illustrate the callousness of Europe's aristocrats toward people of different stations, de Tocqueville quoted from a routine letter from an aristocratic woman, Madame de Sévigné, to the wife of the governor of Rennes.

Do you wish to hear the news of Rennes? A tax of a hundred thousand crowns has been imposed upon the citizens; if this sum is not produced within four and twenty hours, it is to be doubled and collected by the soldiers. They have cleared the houses and sent away the occupants of the great streets and forbidden anybody to receive them on pain of death; so that the poor wretches (old men, women near their confining, and children included) may be seen wandering around and crying on their departure from this city, without knowing where to go, and without food or a place to lie in. Day before yesterday a fiddler was broken on the wheel for getting up a dance and stealing some stamped paper. He was quartered after death, and his limbs exposed at the four corners of the city. . . . Sixty citizens have been thrown in prison, and the business of punishing them is to begin tomorrow. This province sets a fine example to the others, teaching them above all that of respecting the governors and their wives, and of never throwing stones into their gardens.

Yesterday [was] a delightful day [for] Madame de Tarente visited these wilds. (de Tocqueville 1840, vol. 2, part 3, chap. 1)

The brutality of the state toward its citizens is incidental to this letter. As de Tocqueville points out, in Madame de Sévigné's mind, the suffering and pain of a fiddler "broken on the wheel" are a normal part of city life, and there is little empathy for the fiddler or his family. Likewise, the many people wandering the streets (including pregnant women) until a doubled tax is paid, and the sixty people punished for throwing stones into the governor's gardens, are not considered tragic. The cruelty of the methods and the pain suffered by the victims are taken for granted and are not an issue to be sanitized or objected to on humanitarian grounds. Indeed, as Madame de Sévigné writes in the second of the quoted paragraphs, "Yesterday [was] a delightful day."

Like de Tocqueville, Collins (1973) finds this level of brutality typical of states in which there is a pronounced separation between the aristocracy and the common people. He points out that such brutality is incidental to all the large states based on a small urban elite that extracted a surplus from peasant farming areas. The peasant and aristocrat were people between whom there was a wide social gulf—whose paths were unlikely to cross. The aristocrat was so different that Madame de Sévigné could not imagine what it was to be turned out on the street, any more than she would have imagined being a horse beaten into compliance.

Such social distance and callous cruelty were not, of course, limited to nineteenth-century France. In fact, they were routine in the premodern world: in ancient Rome, the government's enemies were fed to the lions for entertainment; in China, punishment by amputation was normal; and in the Aztec empire, beating hearts were routinely removed from victims atop pyramids. In such societies, morality is dependent on caste membership (e.g., as an aristocrat) rather than the shared citizenship de Tocqueville admired in the United States of the 1830s. Cruelty outside the caste is routine, and in the absence of a common citizenship there is no pretense that "there for the grace of God go I."

The evidence that premodern states experienced high rates of callous, ferocious killing is well documented by archaeological and written records. Mass burials at battle sites, ceremonial altars in Aztec Mexico, stories from the Old Testament, mass burials outside Gallic towns (LeBlanc 2003:17), and cities sacked by Genghis Khan are all evidence of the brutality that premodern states routinely practiced. Steven LeBlanc (2003) writes that this occurred because such states were dependent on access to agricultural lands that had to be exploited to feed not only the farmers but also the elites living in distant towns and cities. Chiefs and kings had to induce the peasantry to send surplus crops into the town or city. As discussed in Chapter 2, they did this by maintaining a monopoly over the use of coercive force rooted in a combination of ideology, respect, tribute, and fear. The monopoly was in turn used to subjugate—violently and cruelly when necessary—the common people. For this system to work, social distance must be maintained.

Distancing Techniques and Modern Bureaucratic Killing

Torture, breaking on the wheel, ripping flesh off with red-hot pincers, drawing and quartering, amputations, mutilated bodies, and so forth sound callous to the modern ear. But Collins points out that modern nations have only a different type of callousness. This callousness is not a failure of empathy created by a persistent inequality rooted in a caste system. Rather, it is delivered impersonally by a bureaucratic enterprise in which no one person is responsible for the killing and citizens can plausibly deny that killing was done in their name. This happens when the modern bureaucracy makes killing into a complex task instead of an explicit and overt display of brutality. The mass death sentences handed down to Europe's Jews and others disliked by the German state during World War II are Collins's paradigmatic example of this type of state-sponsored killing. The point of the death sentence was not to cause pain in order to demonstrate the power of the state. Indeed, the German middle-class masses would have objected to daily public hangings or drawing and quartering. Rather, it was to "sanitize" the population of people deemed undesirable. The killing was done in a manner in which the less was known by the populace, the easier it would be to claim a lack of awareness. A large bureaucracy in which responsibility is diffuse was the way to undertake a task of sustained killing, the scope of which had not been seen before.

Ultimately, the problem the German bureaucracy encountered was the potential for empathy between non-Jewish and Jewish citizens. As recently as the 1920s, German populations were mixed, and intermarriage common; therefore, a German might easily imagine that a Jewish victim could have been a mother, father, brother, or sister. The way to organize mass killing in such a context was to create a bureaucracy in which each person understood his or her function and no one person or organization was responsible for the genocide itself. Historian Raul Hilberg describes the bureaucratic origins of the Holocaust in the following fashion:

> The perpetrators were people who played a specific role in the formulation or implementation of anti-Jewish measures. In most cases, a participant understood his function, and he ascribed it to his position and duties. What he did was impersonal. He had been empowered or instructed to carry out his mission. Moreover, no one man and no one organization was solely responsible for the destruction of the Jews. No single budget was allocated for this purpose. The work was diffused in a widespread bureaucracy. . . . For these reasons, an administrator, clerk, or uniformed guard never referred to himself as a perpetrator. He realized, however, that the process of destruction was deliberate, and that once he had stepped into this maelstrom, his deed would be indelible. (Hilberg 1992:ix).

The following account, which was part of the evidence at the Nuremberg war trials, was given by Hermann Graebe, a construction engineer who witnessed portions of the German massacres of 5,000 Jews in Dubno, Ukraine. Compare his empathetic wistfulness about what he observed with the earlier observations of Madame de Sévigné:

> On 5th October, 1942, when I visited the building office at Dubno my foreman told me that in the vicinity of the site, Jews from Dubno had been shot in three large pits, each about 30 meters long and 3 meters deep. About 1,500 persons had been killed daily. All of the 5,000 Jews who had still been living in Dubno before the pogrom were to be liquidated. As the shooting had taken place in his presence, he was still much upset.
>
> Thereupon I drove to the site, accompanied by my foreman and saw near it great mounds of earth, about 30 meters long and 2 meters high. Several trucks stood in front of the mounds. Armed Ukrainian militia drove the people off the trucks under the supervision of an S.S. man. The militia men acted as guards on the trucks and drove them to and from the pit. All these people had the regulation yellow patches on the front and back of their clothes and thus could be recognized as Jews.
>
> My foreman and I went directly to the pits. Nobody bothered us. Now I heard rifle shots in quick succession from behind one of the earth mounds. The people who had got off the trucks—men, women and children of all ages—had to undress upon the orders of an S.S. man, who carried a riding or dog whip. They had to put down their clothes in fixed places, sorted according to shoes, top clothing and underclothing. I saw a heap of shoes of about 800 to 1,000 pairs, great piles of under linen and clothing. Without screaming or weeping these people undressed, stood around in family groups, kissed each other, said farewells, and waited for a sign from another S.S. man, who stood near the pit, also with a whip in his hand. During the 15 minutes that I stood near I heard no complaint or plea for mercy. I watched a family of about eight persons, a man and a woman both about 50 with their children of about one, eight and ten, and two grown-up daughters of about 20 to 24. An old woman with snow-white

hair was holding the one-year-old child in her arms and singing to it and tickling it. The child was cooing with delight. The couple were looking on with tears in their eyes. The father was holding the hand of a boy about 10 years old and speaking to him softly; the boy was fighting his tears. The father pointed to the sky, stroked his head and seemed to explain something to him. At that moment the S.S. man at the pit shouted something to his comrade. The latter counted off about 20 persons and instructed them to go behind the earth mound. Among them was the family which I have mentioned. I well remember a girl, slim and with black hair who, as she passed close to me, pointed to herself and said, "Twenty-three." I walked around the mound and found myself confronted by a tremendous grave. People were closely wedged together and lying on top of each other so that only their heads were visible. Nearly all had blood running over their shoulders from their heads. Some of the people shot were still moving. Some were lifting their arms and turning their heads to show that they were still alive. The pit was already two-thirds full. I estimated that it already contained about 1,000 people. I looked for the man who did the shooting. He was an S.S. man, who sat at the edge of the narrow end of the pit, his feet dangling into the pit. He had a tommy gun on his knees and was smoking a cigarette. The people, completely naked, went down some steps which were cut in the clay wall of the pit and clambered over the heads of the people lying there, to the place to which the S.S. man directed them. They laid down in front of the dead or injured people; some caressed those who were still alive and spoke to them in a low voice. Then I heard a series of shots. I looked into the pit and saw that the bodies were twitching or the heads lying motionless on top of the bodies which lay before them. Blood was running away from their necks. I was surprised that I was not ordered away, but I saw that there were two or three postmen in uniform nearby. The next batch was approaching already. They went down into the pit, lined themselves up against the previous victims and were shot. When I walked back round the mound I noticed another truckload of people which had just arrived. This time it included sick and infirm persons. An old, very thin woman with terribly thin legs was undressed by others who were already naked, while two people held her up. The woman appeared to be paralyzed. The naked people carried the woman around the mound. I left with my foreman and drove in my car back to Dubno.

On the morning of the next day, when I again visited the site, I saw about 30 naked people lying near the pit—about 30 to 50 meters away from it. Some of them were still alive; they looked straight in front of them with a fixed stare and seemed to notice neither the chilliness of the morning nor the workers of my firm who stood around. A girl of about 20 spoke to me and asked me to give her clothes and help her escape. At that moment we heard a fast car approach and I noticed that it was an S.S. detail. I moved away to my site. Ten minutes later we heard shots from the vicinity of the pit. The Jews still alive had been ordered to throw the corpses into the pit; then they had themselves to lie down in this to be shot in the neck. (http://web.jjay.cuny.edu/~jobrien/reference/ob57.html; Shawcross 1985:15–17)

Hermann Graebe personally identified with the victims in a manner that would never have occurred to Madame de Sévigné or, presumably, to an Aztec priest removing a beating heart from his victim. This empathy created a problem for the genocidal German regime, because they knew that if such stories emerged in a plausible fashion, the German middle class, irrespective of the well-cultivated anti-Semitism, could become anxious or even protest (Hilberg 1992:21). This is why the Holocaust was carried out at a social distance from the public supporting the Nazi government. In short, society was different than it had been in Aztec days, or in France in the 1750s when brutality was celebrated. Public torture and ferocity were no longer pertinent for the maintenance of power in the 1930s and 1940s.

But a government like that of Nazi Germany still had the need to kill, and it did so with efficiencies that were previously unknown. Implicit to this was the idea that police, soldiers, and complicit technicians lacked free will and were simply following orders. As a result, a "decision" to commit genocide was not needed; rather, genocide became a routine outcome of organizational subunits, each tasked with a specific job.[1] The bureaucratic nature of the excuse—that soldiers were following orders—is the routine result. And the killing was not undertaken to make a public example that would be talked about far and wide, but as a bureaucratic measure designed to assuage the fears of those in power. What makes it so dangerous and far-reaching is that unlike the ferocious killing of eighteenth-century France, ancient Rome, or even an American lynching, there is no need to appeal to the bloodlust of a crowd. The killing is routine, just like the distribution of pension checks or even the post by the same government.

The bureaucratically organized killing from 1938 to 1945 was more intense and prolonged than that in any of the brutally sustained agricultural kingdoms of the past. It was also more complex, involving a wide range of offices within the German government and economy (Hilberg 1992:21–24). And so millions died in the German death camps in a manner that, while extraordinarily callous, did not share the ferocity displayed by, say, Romans with their hillsides of crucifixions, Aztec pyramids covered in blood, the enthusiastic execution of Robert-François Damiens, the execution of Salem's witches, or even the naked barbarity of an Ache club fight. Violence and torture were no longer part of the ritual of state-sponsored execution; instead, simple bureaucratic efficiency was the goal.

But while the bureaucratic violence of the Nazi regime may be the paradigmatic example of modern state-sponsored violence, Collins cautions readers against being overly confident about other modern countries. States continue to exhibit the callousness of bureaucratic killing in the adoption of military policies, particularly those involving aerial bombing such as that undertaken by the United States in Vietnam at the time Collins was writing. Collins claims that the American bureaucratic technique was similar in organization to the German excesses. No single person was responsible for the immensity of the death created in Vietnam. And in the case of such modern bureaucratized killing, Collins points out that it is the same bureaucratic response. In comparing the Holocaust and the US bombing of

Vietnam, the techniques, scope, and scale are of course different. But in both, bureaucracies were created that allowed civilian populations to deny that they had helped to fund and support the killing. There was also a similar goal—to prevent the general population from becoming anxious in a manner that would induce protest. And so in Vietnam the lethal project was buried in abstract bureaucratic languages meant to obfuscate civilian casualties as "collateral damage." And while it is perhaps easiest to recognize this as salient to aerial bombing, it actually applies anytime bureaucratic rules of engagement are implemented.

And so risk is evaluated in Washington, DC, and orders issued from the Pentagon based on intelligence sources the trigger pullers do not even know. This is what happens when rules of engagement are developed for soldiers, tank drivers, pilots, and infantrymen, whether with the US military in Iraq, the insurgents planting improvised explosive devices on Iraqi roads, the Israeli army patrolling Gaza, or even UN peacekeepers in the Democratic Republic of Congo. There are prescribed rules for when a trigger may be pulled and when it should not. And when the bureaucratic conditions are met, the trigger puller is implicitly absolved from personal responsibility—or rather the organization implicitly accepts responsibility. Rules of engagement are ultimately a bureaucratic formula for identifying who is legitimately killed, and who is not: in other words, what is lawful killing, and what is murder. These regulations can be made more liberal—in which case more mistakes will be made. Or they can be made more conservative—in which case soldiers accept greater risks to their own lives. In neither case, though, is moral responsibility clearly with the individual; rather, it is with a more abstract organization. Moral responsibility is transformed by a faceless bureaucracy.[2]

Asceticism and Purification

Collins calls the third type of modern state violence *ascetic killing*. Such killing is carried out by totalitarian states against their own people. Collins calls it *ascetic* because in terms of motive it involves a "purification" of a master race or special class. Killing is in the interest of protecting the purity of an honored but oppressed group. Examples include Joseph Stalin's purges of his supporters in the 1930s, the Khmer Rouge killings of peasants from among whom they had risen in the 1970s, and the liquidation of millions in the Chinese Cultural Revolution of the 1960s. Millions died in these attempts to "purify" a social movement by expelling traitorous elements. This is, of course, the most deadly of all the forms of twentieth-century state violence.

Denunciations, confessions, and show trials are often part of bureaucratic mechanisms justifying such policies. In the case of the Soviet Union show trials in the 1930s, confessions were rehearsed by the KGB before the defendants were put on trial. Self-criticism in coordination with political indoctrination was an integral part of the Cultural Revolution in China as well as the Khmer Rouge years in Cambodia. At the Khmer prison at Tuol Sleng, where some 15,000 Khmer died, meticulously recorded confessions from victims were collected and signed before the prisoners were executed. Records recovered after the prison was closed by the invading Vietnamese forces demonstrated that many of the victims were former Khmer Rouge members and soldiers.

Such ascetic killing is done in a personal manner using guns or tools, and often with the participation of bystanders. At the center of the idea is the fact that it is not important whether an individual lives but that the revolutionary movement prospers.

The Utility of Collins's Typology of State-Sponsored Killing

The utility of Collins's typology is in how effective it is for evaluating war crimes and genocides committed since his writings were published in the

These skulls are part of a memorial near Tuol Sleng concentration camp in Cambodia, where former allies of the ruling Khmer Rouge government were pressured into providing confessions before being executed.

Photo courtesy of Ron Gluckman.

early 1970s. What is surprising is that when Collins's frame is used, a great deal can be understood about the state-sponsored killing that has occurred since then. After Collins published his typology, the Khmer Rouge killed millions in the ascetic manner described previously. There were show trials to legitimate the killing, and it occurred in the context of a purifying revolution. As for bureaucratic killing, the US military's redefinition of civilian casualties as "collateral damage" during the first Gulf War in 1991, and the bombing of Serbia in 1999, are classic efforts to distance a home population and soldiers from killing in a modern bureaucratic war. For that matter, so are the rhetorical devices used by the Americans to define the people they kill in the Iraq and Afghanistan wars as "terrorists."

Collins's typology also helps in an evaluation of the Rwanda genocide and the brutal Congo Wars (1996–2002) that followed. These wars featured a ferocious brutality similar to that seen in premodern agricultural societies. Bodies were mutilated and displayed in such a way that enemies would see them, and much of the killing during the Rwanda genocide in 1994 was done publicly. Indeed, killers went to great lengths to push mutilated bodies into rivers, where they were sure to float into neighboring countries and be seen (Waters 2001:126–127, 208–209). Broadcasts over the radio boasted of the killing and urged perpetrators to continue "the work"; international journalists were even permitted to videotape killings at roadblocks, at least during the early days of the genocide. Rwandan and Congolese societies are largely agricultural, and clan and ethnic loyalties are very important. In this respect, such public brutality is most similar to older agricultural societies,

This body was one of several thousand discarded in the Akagera River during and after the Rwanda genocide in 1994.
Photo by the author.

such as the Puritans in Massachusetts, where severed heads were placed at the entrance to the village. Seemingly, this type of ferocious killing still resonates well with such populations.

Oddly, the logical extreme of this ferocious brutality was perhaps most evident in the beheadings webcast by Iraqi militants in 2004. Repelled by such executions, Western bureaucratic societies used the webcasts to inflame their publics against the enemy and justify their own wartime acts. Though such webcasting ended in 2005, in early 2006, tortured execution victims continued to be found in public areas of Baghdad, apparently proud displays of brutality created by Sunni or Shiite militia. Again, such a style of killing is a throwback to a prebureaucratic society in which brutality is celebrated and designed to instill a fear most commonly associated with earlier horticultural empires.

Durkheim Revisited:
The Catharsis of State-Sponsored Killing

David Gelernter is a commentator famous for, among other things, having had his hands blown off by the Unabomber, Ted Kaczynski, in 1993. Both as a commentator and a victim, he thinks a great deal about the meaning of punishment and the role that the third party must play in delivering a righteous penalty:

> When a murder takes place, the community is obliged, whether it feels like it or not, to clear its throat and step up to the microphone. Every murder demands a communal response. Among possible responses, the death penalty is uniquely powerful because it is permanent and can never be retracted or overturned. An execution forces the community to assume forever the burden of moral certainty; it is a form of absolute speech that allows no waffling or equivocation. (Gelernter 1998:22, 24)

Gelernter is writing about a cleansing of the body politic, or what sociologist Robert Nisbet called "a catharsis [that] has been effected through trial, through the finding of guilt, and then punishment" (Gelernter 1998:21). Though he is right about the unique clarity of an execution in expressing community values, he only implicitly acknowledges Durkheim's point that such clarity is subject to change, and varies from society to society. So why is it that some powerful governments (e.g., those of Western Europe and several states in the northeastern United States) do not need the death penalty while other powerful governments (e.g., Saudi Arabia, China, and Texas) do? Why is it that some societies (Mexico, Colombia) that long ago abolished the death penalty have high rates of violent death, while others do not? Why is it that some countries still value public displays of ferocity and conduct amputations and executions in public (e.g., Saudi Arabia) while others execute in private and the middle of the night (e.g., the United States)? Sometimes it seems the use of the death penalty correlates with a peaceful society, but at other times it does not (see Table 5.1).

In sorting out these issues, Cooney's typology of execution, war, and genocide is useful. Cooney (1997a) writes that execution is the lawful killing by the state of a particular individual. War is legal killing of a person because he or she is a member of an enemy group that is engaged in active combat. Genocide is the killing of people because they are members of a particular ethnic group that has been declared an enemy of a state. Each category has its own internal dynamics and logic. Legal execution assumes a functioning government and justice system able to evaluate individual cases. Degradation rituals and the trappings of the legal process are part of this. War, in comparison, assumes that the government does not have the capacity to evaluate individual guilt or innocence and is using violence to contest control over who should have the monopoly over the use of coercive force. War is in effect an admission that a government does not have the capacity to conduct trials or the power to assign individual guilt. Finally, genocide assumes a mixture of the two conditions. It assumes a functioning legal infrastructure capable of identifying a particular group as being a threat. Looking at how governments justified or restricted execution, war, and genocide helps us understand how these occur, and how they might be controlled.

The Rise and Decline of Modern Execution

Before World War II, most countries used the death penalty; indeed, the death penalty was long taken for granted as something governments do. Countries that today abhor the death penalty, such as Great Britain, France, Germany, and Italy, executed people for a range of political and civil crimes enthusiastically until World War II, and even afterward. For example, Great Britain, where only fifteen people per year were executed in the early 1950s—and fewer than four per year between 1957 and death penalty abolition in 1965—hanged more than a thousand people in its Kenya Colony for insurrection and other crimes associated with the Mau Mau Rebellion of the 1950s (Anderson 2005). France had a similar history, restricting its use of execution during the 1950s, with the last actual use of the guillotine in 1977 (the death penalty in France was abolished in 1981). But while execution and torture declined in France itself after World War II, they were commonly used during France's colonial war in Algeria, which ended in 1961. Since then, though, there has been a rapid decline in the use of the death penalty across Europe. Indeed, in the social democracies of Western Europe, its use is abhorred (see Table 5.2).

Table 5.1 The Paradox of the Death Penalty

Japan has the lowest murder rate of any major industrial country, with fewer than 1 in 100,000 murders each year, and prisoners only rarely executed (www.nationmaster. com/graph/cri_mur_percap-crime-murders-per-capita).

Between 20 and 50 million Russians died in Stalin's purges beginning in the 1930s and in World War II as a result of government actions (users.erols.com/mwhite28/ warstat1.htm).

The Japanese military was known for its brutal and even lethal discipline of its own soldiers, and for mass killing during the occupation of China and other countries (Bradley 2003:52–62).

Two to 4 million Vietnamese died during the Vietnam War, many as a result of US bombings (www.vietnam-war.info/casualty).

Writing in the 1830s, Alexis de Tocqueville commented on how rarely, compared with Europe, the death penalty was used in the United States (de Tocqueville 1990:166).

In Iceland, there were only two murders in the first forty years of the twentieth century: a woman who poisoned her brother for financial gain in 1913, and a nineteen-year-old burglar who beat to death a man who surprised him at work. This low murder rate occurred in a population noted for its brutality only a few hundred years earlier (Daly and Wilson 1988:275).

Mexico has a high murder rate but has not executed anyone since 1937 (www. nationmaster.com/graph/cri_mur_percap-crime-murders-per-capita; www. infoplease.com/ipa/A077460.html).

Colombia has the highest murder rate in the world (reported as 62 per 100,000 in 2005) but abolished the death penalty in 1910 (www.nationmaster.com/graph/ cri_mur_percap-crime-murders-per-capita; www.infoplease.com/ipa/A077460. html).

During the reign of Henry VIII in England, executions occurred at the rate of 2,000 per year in a population of only about 3–5 million (Tom Hatfield, "The Problem with Modern Capital Punishment, 2005, www.writing.com/main/view/item_id/ item_id/1224734).

The British hanged more than 1,000 Kenyans during the Mau Mau Rebellion in the 1950s at a time when execution in Great Britain was in rapid decline and soon to be abolished (Anderson 2005:353).

When the Americans captured Benedict Arnold's British contact, Major John Andre, in 1780 and determined he was a spy, there was a debate over how he should die. Andre (and his friend Alexander Hamilton) preferred shooting so that he could die like a soldier, while George Washington opted for the disgrace of the scaffold (www.ushistory.org/march/bio/andre.htm).

Data from Texas in the 1960s indicate that it was the harshest of states, executing more defendants than other states, while at the same time releasing others due to very liberal self-defense laws (Lundsgaarde 1977:224–229).

In Kentucky in the 1930s, 11,000 people turned out for what would be the state's last legal execution, indicating the popularity of the sentence. The state legislature, which was elected by the same people who showed up for the execution, was embarrassed, and responded by requiring that all future hangings be done in private and inside the prison (www.geocities.com/lastpublichang/LastPublicExecution.htm).

Table 5.2   **Status of the Death Penalty and Homicide Rates in Twenty Countries, 2004**

Country	Homicides per 100,000	Homicide Rank	Year of Death Penalty Abolition
Colombia	61.8	1	1910
South Africa	49.6	2	1995
Jamaica	32.4	3	
Russia	20.2	5	
Mexico	13.0	6	2005
Thailand	8.0	14	
Poland	5.6	20	1997
Uruguay	4.5	22	1907
Bulgaria	4.5	23	1998
United States	4.3	24	
India	3.4	26	
France	1.7	40	1981
Iceland	1.7	42	1928
Canada	1.5	44	1976
United Kingdom	1.4	46	1973
Spain	1.2	48	1978
Germany	1.1	49	1987
New Zealand	1.1	52	1961
Japan	0.4	60	
Saudi Arabia	0.3	62	

Source: Infoplease.com, 2006.

Notes: Homicide rates should be interpreted with caution because different countries have different reporting criteria. In 2004, there were 3,797 people executed in twenty-five countries. Ninety percent of these executions are believed to have been in China, for which homicide data are not available. In the same year, 7,395 individuals were sentenced to death in sixty-four countries. In the United States, 38 out of 50 states continue to have the death penalty. Twelve states (and the District of Columbia) have discontinued its use.

Even so, countries are capable of callousness whenever political extremists take power and isolate themselves from accountability to a larger public. In the twentieth century, such situations resulted in mass executions of "enemies of the state" both in right-wing regimes like Nazi Germany, Japan, Spain, and Argentina *and* in left-wing regimes in the Soviet Union, China, and Cambodia. In total, 129 *million* people died in the twentieth century from execution ordered by governments. Some of the highest rates of killing were during World War II in Europe, when about 1,008 per 100,000 citizens died, and in Cambodia during the Khmer Rouge years (1975–1979), when 8,160 per 100,000 citizens died (Cooney 1997a). These cases seem to reflect the spasms of violence that the strong centralized state is capable of while in the pursuit of external wars, and the quashing of internal rebellion.

So there is a paradox. Countries that have at times killed enthusiastically have rapidly pulled back from the use of the death penalty. But this happens in unusual ways. Indeed, the modern democratic country that Europeans are most critical of for using the death penalty, the United States, had an ambivalent record of using the death penalty in the second half of the twentieth century.

The Peculiar Decline of the American Death Penalty

The United States is one of the last of the modern Western countries to use the death penalty. But as in the rest of the developed world, the number of judicial executions has declined in the United States. Nevertheless, after a brief national abolition of the death penalty (1971–1976), the number of executions rose to a peak of ninety-eight in 1999, of which thirty-five were in Texas. Although with nearly 300 million people living in the United States this rate of execution is very low, the American uniqueness in using the death penalty is still noteworthy.[3] Public opinion polls in the United States continue to show that the public sentiment is consistent with what Gelernter writes about execution being appropriate as a punishment in the most heinous of cases. Generally, poll respondents qualify this by asserting that there is a certainty regarding the guilt of the condemned. Despite a lack of social scientific evidence, the same surveys typically show that Americans also believe that having the death penalty on the books deters others from killing. Whatever the logic, Americans seem to need, as Gelernter (1998) writes, the unique power and certainty that the catharsis of an execution provides, albeit one tempered by some ambivalence.

One of the great ironies in the enthusiasm of the United States for the death penalty is that there is little political will for actually putting people to death. This is because there is a contradiction—a paradox—inherent to American attitudes toward execution. The certainty of the death penalty may be needed as a catharsis for society in ways no longer demanded in Western Europe. But according to poll results, the same society also asks for a certainty that the person executed actually committed the crime of which he or she is accused. This leads to political support for an elaborate death penalty appeals process, which can last decades. In large part, this is due to an insistence that extensive judicial review be permitted to ensure the fairness of the death sentence. In California, for example, appeal to the state Supreme Court is automatic in any death penalty case.

But even this level of review often proves inadequate in the establishment of an effective death penalty. Twenty to thirty people are sentenced by courts to death each year in California, even though the execution rate since 1990 is less than one per year.[4] The result is that a death row prisoner in California, as well as other states, is far more likely to die of natural causes than from a lethal injection. The result in the case of California is that the state will soon be building new death row cells. Durkheim probably would chuckle about California's predicament. Apparently, the increasing numbers of unexecuted death row inmates are useful and even indispensable as California slowly grapples with the "normal evolution of morality and law."

War: Challenging the Monopoly on the Use of Coercive Force

War is the declaration that military rule trumps the rule of courts and law. In the twentieth century, 34 million people died as a result of war (Cooney 1997a:330), and while this number is dwarfed by the 129 million executed by totalitarian regimes, war is the source of a great deal of violent death. In war, killing enemies does not require a trial that focuses on the acts or evil of the particular individual. Rather, dehumanization is focused on a generalized "enemy." Killing is justified due to membership in a particular group; for example, soldiers of an opposing group, proximity to soldiers of an opposing group, or social proximity to members of an opposing group. Philosopher Glenn Gray describes the route by which states go about making this distinction: "The basic aim of a nation at war is establishing an image of the enemy in order to distinguish as sharply as possible the act of killing from the act of murder" (quoted in Grossman 1995:193).

War between two nations is ultimately an admission that political matters cannot be settled by two-party negotiation, while a civil war is a violent internal challenge to the legitimacy of an established government. In either case, standards for individual justice and fairness are suspended as combatants seek advantage through the use of lethal force. In this sense, war is, like a feud or Ache club fight, a fight between two roughly matched combatants; it is not surprising, then, that lethality in war escalates as both sides seek revenge for offenses.

In war, members of an ethnic group, caste, religious group, or national group are the enemy and therefore do not have legal protections. War is also ultimately about who will have control over the monopoly to use coercive force—that is, who will have the final word when judging the conduct of others. This returns us to Max Weber's original definition of government, which points out that state power is always embedded in at least a plausible threat of violence.[5] His definition assumes that acts committed in the context of war are inherently done on behalf of a government and are therefore legal.

But acts of war are no longer inherently legal. Particularly since the end of World War II, there have been significant efforts to extend the rule of law to address particularly serious cases of state-sponsored killings. Statutes and weak international courts have been established to prosecute genocide and war crimes. The effect has been to criminalize acts by states and their leaders in the hope that the practice will wither away. While the levels of criminalization remain imperfect, it is still worthwhile looking at the sociology of laws against genocide.

Genocide

As a legal category, genocide is modern; it was not written into law until after World War II.[6] Indeed, the word became well-known as a way to describe the horror the world felt at what the Germans did to the Jews during World War II. A term—a crime—needed to be identified that separated what was done to the Jewish civilian population from the type of killing that the Allies did in their conduct of the war, especially the high-altitude bombing of German and Japanese cities and the nuclear attacks on Hiroshima and Nagasaki. In this context, the crime of genocide, which refers to purposeful killing to eliminate an ethnic or religious group, was created. Such a statute applied easily to the case of Nazi Germany, which had explicit laws, courts, and policies requiring the elimination or expulsion of Jews. The law against genocide did not apply to civilian deaths created by firebombing or nuclear bombing because these acts were not directed at a specific "ethnic group." Thus, from the perspective of other World War II combatants, the law against genocide did not apply.

Genocide involves mobilization against all members of an ethnic or national group. Raul Hilberg (1967), author of *The Destruction of the European Jews*, writes that there are in fact four steps that create the prerequisites—that is, a social ecology—for modern bureaucratized genocide. These conditions make the commission of genocide possible:

1. Definition of a target group through scapegoating
2. Expropriation of property
3. Concentration into camps or segregated regions
4. Mass killing

It is of course only the final step that is "illegal" under laws against genocide, but the former conditions create the context—that is, the ecology—that makes more killing possible. There are no laws or restraints on governments that proceed all the way to "concentration," even though from an ecological standpoint, concentration is what makes genocide possible in the first place. Note that by this rubric, the United States policies regarding Japanese and Japanese Americans living in the United States during World War II continued through the first three conditions. Ethnic Japanese were defined as a target group, property was expropriated, and they were moved into camps in remote locations. Although there was no mass killing, the ecological conditions that permit this final step were met.

The genocide statutes were written with Nazi Germany's preoccupation with anti-Semitism in mind. This has had the practical effect of criminalizing only killing undertaken in the name of racial or ethnic superiority. By default, other types of mass killing became "not as bad," irrespective of how brutal or callous they were. Thus the genocide law is a poor legal fit for incidents like the Khmer Rouge policies in 1975–1978, which resulted in the deaths of millions; war and mass murder in countries such as Sierra Leone and Congo in the 1990s; the civil war in Colombia; the Cultural Revolution in China; and a host of other situations that were not genocide but were still extraordinarily lethal. The genocide law proved a better fit in places like Rwanda—where there was an explicitly racist ideology behind the killing of the Tutsi—and the former Yugoslavia, where allegiances and killing fell along ethnic lines.

Laws about war crimes and genocide in the late twentieth and early twenty-first centuries are still being resolved as tribunals are established to prosecute crimes in the former Yugoslavia, Rwanda, Cambodia, Liberia, Sierra Leone, and elsewhere. It can be expected that as with the development of laws against private feuding, enforcement will focus on weaker states unable to resist military and economic powers that are able to assert jurisdiction. In the same way that powerful clan leaders like Devil Anse Hatfield were exempt from prosecution, the elite of the international scene—that is, countries like the United States (in Vietnam and Iraq), Russia (in Afghanistan and Chechnya), China (Cultural Revolution), Great Britain (in Kenya and Malaya), and France (in Indochina and Algeria)—are exempt from review by international courts.

Nationalism and the Capacity to Command Killing

Most killing is done as a patriotic act in the name of a nation. Benedict Anderson (1991) wrote *Imagined Communities: Reflections on the Origin and Spread of Nationalism* about the nature of this nationalism, and why it is so important for understanding why people will kill on behalf of the modern nation-state. He defines a nation as "an imagined political community—and imagined as both inherently limited and sovereign" (p. 6).

Nationalism and Killing

Embedded in Anderson's definition are issues I have discussed with respect to whether killing is criminal or legitimate. *Legitimate killing* is rooted in the state's capacity to define execution as necessary to preserve its limits and sovereignty. What Anderson adds is that power must be "imagined" to be both limited to a particular area and sovereign. Imagining such power sounds very nebulous. But, in fact, Anderson points out that in the modern world the idea of the nation-state is very powerful. Indeed, love of country is so powerful that when the state and nation are combined to form a nation-state, it is this "imagined" entity that patriotic individuals offer their lives to defend. To protect their monopoly over the use of coercive force, nation-states use patriotism to form armies in which citizens both are willing to die and, more important, are ready to kill when commanded to do so. Killing for one's government becomes a form not only of patriotism but of right-eous sacrifice. The trick for the modern bureaucratic government is to get ordinary citizens to do this for them. Here the story becomes interesting because of what social psychology has to say. The good news is that, as psychologist Dave Grossman has written, most humans are reluctant to kill unless *personally* provoked and endangered. The bad news is that social psychologists developed techniques in the latter half of the twentieth century to get individuals to push past this reluctance in ever higher numbers. These techniques are readily adapted to the training programs of modern bureaucratic governments seeking to sustain a monopoly over the use of coercive force.

The Social Psychology of Killing
Strangers Who Do not Personally Threaten

Humans find it very difficult to kill a stranger in the predictable and rational fashion modern armies demand. In fact, humans kill on their own initiative only if there is an immediate threat to their own safety or to compatriots to whom they have an emotional tie. Most normal people are exceedingly reluctant to kill when the enemy is remote or is not an immediate lethal threat. This is why most people make poor snipers; they are reluctant to pull the trigger to kill a stranger sighted through a rifle scope. Indeed, as will be described, research has shown that as in the past, most soldiers aimed high or even failed to shoot at all unless there was an immediate personal threat.

Grossman writes about the role of military training in increasing the willingness of citizen soldiers to kill strangers on command. In his book *On Killing: The Psychological Cost of Learning to Kill in War and Society* (1996), he describes how humans can overcome a reluctance to kill strangers who are not an immediate threat to themselves or to those close to them. Quoting the military historian S.L.A. Marshall, Grossman points out that "the average and healthy individual . . . has such an inner and usually unrealized resistance towards killing a fellow man that he will not of his own volition take life if it is possible to turn away from that responsibility. . . . At the vital point [of pulling the trigger, the normal soldier] becomes a conscientious objector" (1996:29). This is because "looking another human being in the eye, making an independent decision to kill him, and watching as he dies due to your action come to form the single most basic, important, primal, and potentially traumatic occurrence of war" (ibid., 31).[7]

To emphasize how difficult this has been throughout history, Grossman notes that most soldiers in the US Civil War, World War I, and World War II never fired their weapons in battle, even when faced with hostile fire. Assessment of marksmanship, amount of ammunition fired, and number of enemy soldiers hit in fighting since the Civil War indicate that soldiers become instant conscientious objectors. Even in close-up trench warfare, many routinely did not fire their weapons or fired over the heads of their enemies. Indeed, as recently as World War II, only 15–20 percent of combat soldiers actually fired their weapons in battle. And this only happened in the context of close monitoring by supervisors moving through trenches, ordering soldiers to fire. In the absence of a supervisor (typically a noncommissioned officer), most soldiers instead found other things to do, some of which even involved great courage (carrying messages between trenches, assisting the wounded, loading weapons, etc.). But the actual act of firing at another human being was something they were reluctant to do, even though they were standing firm in the trenches during a battle.[8]

From World War I to World War II and the Vietnam War, the number of combat soldiers who actually fired their weapons at an enemy steadily increased. Why was this so? Because applied research and improved training techniques used since 1945 increased the willingness of soldiers to kill on command. The number of combat troops actually firing their weapons increased to 50 percent in the Korean War, and to 90 percent in the Vietnam War. Grossman attributes this increase to more systematic training that sought to break down normal impulses not to kill. In short, it was due to psychological conditioning.

Psychological conditioning techniques begun in basic military training, Grossman writes, are the key to understanding why soldiers in Vietnam were more willing to fire their weapons at humans. These conditioning techniques were broad. For example, basic military training no longer focused on shooting at bull's-eye targets, such as it did during World War II, but at humanlike cutouts that in a simulation of battle conditions would appear and disappear quickly. The "deification of killing" also became part of basic training. Unheard of in World War I, rare in World War II, and common during Vietnam were drills asking recruits to chant slogans about the glories of killing (Grossman 1995:252).

Cultural conditioning also emphasizes the superiority of the warriors' culture over that of the enemy; this was apparently particularly effective in the German army of World War II, which emphasized the racial superiority of the German people—and helped the Germans inflict 50 percent higher casualties (Grossman 1996:162). Cheap automatic weapons, with their bursts of bullets, also permitted more reflexive killing without requiring careful aim. For American soldiers in Vietnam, the conditioning emphasized the systematic dehumanization of the enemy, whether through use of epithets like "gook" or briefings comparing the "VC" to animals. The net result, Grossman writes, made for a more effective soldier, but also led to psychological damage in those trained to kill. This, of course, is a process similar to the moral panics described in Chapter 4 in which elites stimulate excitement in a public to generate lynch mobs. Such a moral panic is created in which a deviant group is identified as being venal, which in turn creates the conditions necessary for extreme violence.[9] By the same token, Grossman found, stereotypes of American soldiers as "monkeys" were important to the North Vietnamese effort. There is a great distance between the abstract love of country that Anderson marvels at and the mechanistic descriptions by Grossman of how killers are made. But the two phenomena are connected. For without a monopoly over the use of coercive force in a sovereign territory, the context to condition masses willing to kill and tolerate killing is missing.

Why the State Kills

Understanding that the state kills does not tell anything about why a country takes such extreme risks with its own political and even physical survival. What are the conditions that lead a nation to confront another nation or an internal group in a manner that leads to mass death? Does mass death become a necessary catharsis for those in power?

Scapegoating, moral panics, cultural conditioning, and demonization of enemies are important techniques used by governments to justify their own power, and by extension killing. Many books have been written about the dehumanization of an enemy, whether by casting it as "cockroaches" (as Radio Rwanda did in 1994), by attacking enemies of the people's revolution (as in Cambodia and China), or by dehumanizing military enemies (e.g., the United States in Vietnam). But this tells little about the miscalculations nations make as they saunter toward the catastrophes of war, mass execution, and genocide.

Wolfgang Schivelbusch (2003:5–6) points out that nations heading toward war do so because they believe extinction threatens them. This requires a self-confidence and hubris where both sides become convinced of their military superiority. That one side must necessarily be wrong is irrelevant. When a target group is defined, expropriation begins, righteousness is asserted, and a context for mass killing is created. The process Schivelbusch describes is one in which miscalculations and mistakes are systematically made. One's own capacity is overestimated as a public becomes drunk on patriotism; at the same time, the capabilities of an enemy are denigrated and, as a result, underestimated. In many respects, the lurch toward war, mass execution, and genocide is one of catastrophic miscalculations, not unlike two drunk miners in a Bodie bar. An intent to kill may not have been present when the eventual antagonists walked into the bar or into the international confrontation. But as insults are exchanged, sabers rattled, and shots fired, the intent and desire to kill by waging war emerge.

In short, ecological theories can be used to understand the stateless areas that exist between nation-states. As in bars, it is the insult, emotion, and the presence of weapons that make a lethal result more likely. For nations the intoxicating lubricant of patriotism, which, like alcohol, leads to lower levels of impulse control, accelerates a rush toward war. The lethal result may not be what either combatant intended when the confrontation started. Indeed, as with barroom confrontations, such situations usually do not end in war, mass death, or genocide. But it is here, particularly in the context of patriotism, that the probability increases that any such event will escalate to a lethal conclusion.

Ultimately, state power is both a two-edged sword and a two-party conflict. When the state initiates a moral panic to protect its role as an effective third party, there will be both intended and unintended consequences. The paradox is that the monopoly over the use of coercive force broadens the capacity for the preservation of peace, while at the same time increasing the ability to wreak further violence. This is because the means to control violence—the third party—is the same as the means to extend violence. By having a monopoly over the use of coercive force, the anarchic violence found in small egalitarian societies is controlled, but the violence of inequality—where some control the means of violence and others do not—emerges.

How Is State Killing Slowed?

This chapter is about killing that is not criminalized—or at least has yet to be criminalized. Throughout history, killing has been the prerogative of the powerful—especially those who control legitimated lethal power. International norms about national sovereignty have meant that much of this kind of killing is done without comment from a third party. Each of the permanent members of the United Nations Security Council has taken advantage of this chance to kill without regulation: the French in Algeria in the 1950s, the United States in Vietnam and Iraq, and the British in Kenya and Malaya in the 1950s. The Soviet Union did it in Afghanistan in the 1980s and in Chechnya in the 1990s. Most lethally, the Chinese killed millions during the Cultural Revolution and in the invasion of Vietnam in 1978. Such killing, no matter how justifiable, remains unevaluated by any powerful third party.

But a new international order is emerging that seeks to regulate the most lethal of human activities—genocide, war, and execution. Courts are now investigating weak defeated countries. The stirrings of new norms and conscience about human rights mean that unfettered military action even by the most powerful countries is slowly coming to be legitimately questioned. Disagreements are still a human by-product of an international order. But the presence of such a conscience may well mean that sabers will be rattled less frequently and the intoxicating qualities of virulent patriotism will be less lethal.

The limitations that international law has in controlling killing can be understood by looking at the decline in private killing during the past 500 years. Most important, this decline in private violence has occurred in a context in which the capacity of private citizens to take vengeance on their own behalf changed fundamentally. Thus, it seems significant that many small but prosperous countries (e.g., much of Western and Central Europe and Japan) have effectively disarmed, as decisions were made that neighbors no longer posed a significant threat of violence. For instance, France and Germany, Great Britain and Ireland, and Japan and South Korea no longer threaten each other militarily. This change has occurred despite the fact that these countries engaged in terrible wars during the twentieth century. Routine negotiations about trade, immigration, crime, and the like are no longer conducted by metaphorically armed individuals. Regular cross-border traffic makes nationalistic scapegoating campaigns between, say, Germany and France difficult to sustain. It is as if miners in Bodie were no longer armed and drunk when sitting together at the bar. Differences are still there, but they are unlikely to escalate to the level of lethal combat.

International courts are often considered to be the solution to many of the incidences of war crimes and genocide. And indeed, they are part of a solution. This is why the international community in recent years generously funded war crimes trials in places like Cambodia, Rwanda, the former Yugoslavia, Liberia, and Sierra Leone. But again, what is known of the decline of private violence tells us that such courts will be effective only if their power is perceived as legitimate by those policed. This legitimacy emerges not only out of the expression of military power but from the acquiescence of potential combatants. It also implies control of the broader social ecology of international relations. To a certain extent, the existing international order is developing this capacity. Even the most powerful countries, such as the United States, respond at least grudgingly to complaints about human rights violations, even while international courts have no coercive power to compel the United States to appear. If you take the analogy from the decline of elite private violence described by Cooney, this is perhaps not that surprising. After all, as the rule of law took hold around the world, the weak and powerless became more peaceful in their interpersonal relations even as the monarchies and chiefs maintained a violent culture of honor.

Controlling Private Violence, Controlling State Violence

However, theories about private violence should not be taken too far from the situations for which they were created. State-sponsored violence is different from private violence. First, it is always undertaken in the context of popular institutions, and frequently with the widespread acquiescence of a population. And while it is clear that states can be enormously effective in killing, the enormity of the killing is not merely the sum of each individual pulling a trigger, wielding a machete, or signing a paper. Rather, it is the result of group dynamics undertaken in the context of a formal state, a political network like al-Qaeda, or even a corporation. By way of example, look at the case study of King Leopold of Belgium, who organized the companies of the Congo Free State, which brutalized the population of the Congo on his behalf from the 1880s to 1908. Millions died as a result of his policies, even though he himself never even set foot in the Congo. Certainly some people held the pen or sword condemning millions, but the process itself was much bigger than these individuals, and the responsibility was diffused across the bureaucracies Leopold created. And so the orders Leopold's bureaucrats followed in the pursuit of legitimate profits ended in mass death. Likewise, as Lee Strobel (1980) wrote in the case of the Ford Pinto, the culture at Ford Motor Company emphasized economy and marketing deadlines over safety considerations, leading to the fiery deaths of the three Ulrich girls as well as many others. The two cases are very different, but the institutional callousness is similar. And this institutional callousness lies both within and beyond individuals. It is in the culture and social networks that such callousness emerges.

This means that it is not possible for nations simply to isolate the few deviants in a Durkheimian game of musical chairs; there are too many people in an organization that takes actions resulting in death, whether it be an explicit goal such as in Rwanda or the by-product of some legitimate activity, such as at the Ford Motor Company. Masses who kill as a result of mass psychological conditioning cannot all be incarcerated; incarceration only works in a functioning society where the deviants are few.

This points to possibilities for further controls not only on the callousness of nation-states but on other institutions. First, however, we need to be able to identify how institutions evaluate information. For example, what type of nationalism elevates risks for genocide, and what kind is expressed harmlessly at a soccer game? Which demands on elites create the conditions for war crimes, and which create pressure for better government? Such questions are not simply an issue of the legal intent of an individual but emerge out of certain types of groups and not others.

Notes

1. See Ermann and Lee (1999:30) for a discussion about how organizational decisionmaking affects potentially lethal situations. Ermann and Lee were writing about decisionmaking with respect to the Pinto gas tank explosions, but the same principles can be applied to situations that are even more lethal, like genocide.

2. Similar calculations are undoubtedly made by countries fighting insurgencies. The British fighting in Kenya in the 1950s, the French fighting in Algeria and Indochina in the 1950s and 1960s, and the Russians in Afghanistan in the 1980s all required foreign troops to make distinctions among combatants, potential combatants, and civilians. Effective killing in insurgent wars depends less on physical distance and more on the establishment of a social distance between the soldiers occupying the country and the population harboring the insurgents.

3. In Europe, which discontinued use of the death penalty after World War II, there is frequently strong criticism of the United States for continuing to administer it. The European Union requires all member states to renounce use of the death penalty as a condition for admission.

4. Ironically, the mortality rate for death row prisoners in California from natural causes is higher than from execution. Since the death penalty was reinstated in California in 1978, fourteen have died from execution and fifty-four as a result of other causes. The most common cause of death is suicide; thirteen of the fifty-four committed suicide. See State of California, Youth and Adult Correction Agency, available at www.yaca.state.ca.us.ReportsResearch/docs/CIWHD.pdf (accessed January 2007).

5. As Weber noted in his essay, this point is borrowed from Leon Trotsky, who was a political and military leader in Russia's Bolshevik Revolution in 1917 and was involved with peace negotiations with Germany at Brest-Litovsk. The conclusion of the talks was that Russia was able to withdraw from World War I in exchange for granting a number of Eastern European countries independence.

6. The term *genocide* itself was invented in 1943 to describe the systematic destruction of the Armenians of the Ottoman empire during World War I. It was quickly applied to the Jews targeted by German policies before and during World War II.

7. Grossman (1996:44, 180–185) also mentions the 2 percent of people (and soldiers) who due to "aggressive psychopathic personalities thrive in battle." In civilian life, such individuals often are arrested and incarcerated. In a military battle, they can become heroes.

8. Grossman calls this need for a command to kill "the centurion factor." A military innovation of the Romans was to develop a noncommissioned officer who did not himself fight, but would walk along the lines ordering soldiers to fire arrows, launch javelins, and throw spears. This was in contrast to the Greek phalanx leaders, who were spear-throwing comrades. They were not mobile within the ranks, as the Romans were. The Roman soldiers were more disciplined, more likely to fire at an enemy, more likely to hit the enemy, and, as a result, more lethal (see Grossman

1995:145–146). The difference was in leadership, not courage or fighting skill.

9. Most notably, Grossman attributes the high rates of posttraumatic stress disorder following the Vietnam War to the psychological manipulations that made so many soldiers into people willing to kill.

War Crimes Tribunals, Genocide, and Rwanda

Before World War II, there were no international war crimes trials or courts. Defeated wartime leaders were above personal culpability and were typically simply exiled or summarily executed by the victors. In many respects this reflects how elites have long been treated—as above the laws that they themselves made and enforced.

Following World War II, though, leaders of the German and Japanese war efforts were tried in tribunals created by the victorious allies. In their trials, the prosecution and defense presented evidence and questioned witnesses. The point of such trials was to demonstrate to the world that leaders are accountable before the law, even those who denied such rights to others when they ruled. Particularly from the perspective of the more idealistic American victors, such trials demonstrated that World War II was fought to guarantee the rule of law and the importance of rights for people accused of even the most heinous of crimes. In Nuremberg, twenty-four men were indicted for four new crimes: crimes against peace; planning, initiating, and waging wars of aggression; war crimes; and crimes against humanity (this includes laws against genocide). Sixteen of the leaders of Germany were convicted of these crimes and were hanged in October 1946. Others were sentenced to prison terms, and two were acquitted. Similar trials took place in Japan.

The post–World War II trials are sometimes called illegitimate because they were based on "after the fact" laws and were therefore victor's justice. Be that as it may, it is clear that worldwide there is now awareness that such crimes are illegal under international law and potentially prosecutable. In Cooney's terms, the justice system is moving into the stateless area previously occupied by the elite leaders of governments.

However, for almost fifty years after the close of the Nuremberg and Tokyo trials, there was no international court designed to try such crimes. This changed following the wars in the former Yugoslavia when the International Criminal Tribunal for the Former Yugoslavia was established in 1993 in The Hague, Netherlands, and the International Criminal Tribunal for Rwanda was established in Tanzania in 1995. Since then, international tribunals were established to try war crimes committed in Sierra Leone and Liberia. A more general court was also established in The Hague in 2002; it has jurisdiction over crimes committed in countries that acceded to a Rome

Statute for the International Criminal Court. By 2006, 102 countries had signed this treaty.

The three tribunals have had some successes in capturing and convicting high-ranking organizers of genocide from Rwanda and Yugoslavia. Recently Charles Taylor, the former president of Liberia, was arrested and extradited to the international court sitting in The Hague. A look at how this has worked in the case of Rwanda provides some insight into the strengths and weaknesses of such approaches.

Rwanda is a small central African country where about 8 million farmers and pastoralists lived in the early 1990s. A former Belgian colony, it achieved independence in 1961 along with many neighboring countries. But its independence movement was marred by violence. The Belgians had for decades favored the minority Tutsi in the awarding of positions in government, education, business, and the church. The majority Hutu, which formed about 85 percent of the population, were resentful, and when the Hutu assumed power at independence, many Tutsi were massacred, and survivors fled to neighboring countries.

The thirty or so years after Rwandan independence provided mixed blessings for ethnic relations. Peace was achieved under the Hutu-dominated government, and Rwanda by the 1980s acquired a reputation for being a well-managed if autocratic African country. Indeed, foreign aid donors were pleased with Rwanda because funds were often spent well, and the country had economic promise despite a rapidly growing population. The president, Juvenal Habyarimana, also had a reputation with donors for running a government that was responsive to the concerns of development economists. In this context the ethnic divisions were permitted to fester.

But, if Rwanda's predominantly Hutu population was growing rapidly, so was that of the Tutsi exiles living across the border in Uganda. In 1990, with the assistance of the Ugandan government, Tutsi exiles calling themselves the Rwanda Patriotic Front (RPF) invaded, pushing to within a few miles of the capital in Kigali before being pushed back toward the Uganda border by a combination of Rwandan and French troops. Then a diplomatic and military stalemate emerged. The RPF army remained in a small corner of the north while an ever more paranoid Hutu government dominated the rest of the country. As in the period at independence, massacres of Tutsi civilians occurred, even as the two sides negotiated in nearby Tanzania.

Nevertheless, in August 1993, an agreement was negotiated in which the Hutu and Tutsi shared government control. In preparation for the agreement, the RPF military was given a base near the capital in Kigali. This power-sharing agreement displeased radical elements of the Hutu government, who resisted further handover of power. Assassination and more attacks on the civilian population occurred in the night, and the Hutu government did little to respond. A small garrison of United Nations troops under the command of Canadian general Romeo Dallaire was established in Kigali in 1993 as part of the agreement. In January 1994, General Dallaire raised concerns about arms shipments that were arriving in the country in anticipation, he feared, of a possible resumption of killing. He requested permission from UN headquarters to seize the weapons. The permission was refused.

On April 8, 1994, President Habyarimana's plane was shot down as it approached Kigali Airport, returning from peace talks in Tanzania. Habyarimana, the president of Burundi, and the French crew were all killed. It has never been established who shot down the plane, but the events of the following days are well documented. Hutu militia carrying prepared lists began to kill their political opponents in particular, and Tutsi in general. Among the earliest victims was the prime minister, along with the eight Belgian soldiers who were guarding her. Within a few days, it was clear that both the militias and most elements of the Hutu-dominated regular military were involved in the killings. And indeed, within a few weeks, the scope of the genocide became clear. All Tutsi living in Rwanda were to be eliminated. Gangs of youths carrying machetes, grenades, and automatic weapons began killing all Tutsi, as well as any Hutu who opposed them. By the end of July 1994, at least 500,000 people would be dead. Tens of thousands of the dead were thrown into the Kagera River, where they could be filmed by the international press as the river passed through Tanzania and into Uganda. Two to three million people would flee to neighboring countries.

Because of the UN peacekeeping role, there emerged very quickly a demand that they "do their job" and stop the genocide. General Dallaire requested armed reinforcements to do this. However, instead of reinforcing the troops, a decision was taken to draw down the UN troop commitment. This was done in May and June 1994.

The genocide continued until August 1994, when the last of the Hutu military and rump government was expelled from the country by the victorious RPF forces. Bodies continued to arrive in Tanzania for at least another eight months, many of them apparently victims of military exactions undertaken by the victorious RPF military (Prunier 1995/1997:359–360).

The RPF installed a government in Kigali dominated by Tutsi who shared exile in Uganda before 1994. Rwanda again has a good reputation with donors because donor money is well spent. However, as in the past, the government is authoritarian. The Tutsi-dominated government also has undertaken military adventures in neighboring Congo, where it has followed its political enemies, as well as establishing economic interests in the mining sector in that country. This action by the RPF has also been called genocidal in nature (LeMarchand 2005).

There has been much recrimination since the Rwanda genocide by people like President Bill Clinton, Secretary of State Madeleine Albright, and

UN Secretary General Kofi Annan. All now believe that much of the genocide could have been prevented had the West taken military action as
Dallaire advised. It is, of course, speculative about whether this is the case.
Indeed, there is some doubt that given the military capabilities of the West
and the speed of the genocide, troops could have arrived in time to prevent
most of the killing (see Kuperman 2001; Waters 2001).

In part to compensate for this perceived failing, the West has funded a
court in Arusha, Tanzania, to try accused perpetrators of the genocide. More
than ninety cases have been made since 1994. The tribunals have been criti-
cized by the Rwandan government for their slow pace and inability to sentence defendants to the death penalty.

But, while the complaints by the Rwandan government may be justified, they do not address a broader question of whose conscience gets
catharsis as a result of the prosecution in Arusha. Certainly, Rwandans will
find satisfaction in seeing guilty people imprisoned for long terms, even if
they do not feel the penalty is strong enough. Perhaps more important for
the broader international community, though, is the catharsis demanded by a
developed world's concern that it did not "do enough" during the genocide
itself.

Further Reading

Dallaire, Romeo (2004). *Shake Hands with the Devil: The Failure of Humanity in
Rwanda*. New York: Carroll and Graf.
Des Forges, Alison (1999). *Leave None to Tell the Story: Genocide in Rwanda*. New
York: Human Rights Watch.
LeMarchand, Rene (2005). "Being Witness to Mass Murder." *African Studies
Review* 48, no. 3: 93–101.
Prunier, Gerard (1995/1997). *The Rwanda Crisis: History of a Genocide*. New York:
Columbia University Press.
Umutesi, Marie Beatrice (2004). *Surviving the Slaughter*. Madison: University of
Wisconsin Press.
Waters, Tony (2001). *Bureaucratizing the Good Samaritan*. Boulder, CO: Westview.

Death in the Congo Free State

Genocide is generally thought of as a twentieth-century phenomenon, perhaps because the word itself is new, used after World War II to describe Nazi Germany's systematic killing of Jews. But mass killing of civilian populations is actually an older phenomenon, carried out with varying degrees of thoroughness, brutality, and callousness. The extent of the brutality varies somewhat with the technology available (e.g., bombs, gas chambers, and machine guns), though such variation is not absolute. Quick and efficient mass killing has been achieved with simple tools, including machetes, hoes, fire, single-shot rifles, and axes.

One of the most sustained killing fields in recent history has been in Central Africa in what is today the Democratic Republic of Congo. The most sustained period of killing there was from 1890 to 1908, when 5–8 *million* people died as a result of military activity, hostage taking, disease, and neglect brought about by the companies that Belgian king Leopold II established to exploit the Congo.

The aggressive exploitation of the Congo by outsiders began in the mid-nineteenth century when Arab slavers arrived from the Indian Ocean coast. They established a short-lived mercantile state in the center of the Congo and introduced smallpox and other big killers to the area. In the 1870s, King Leopold II of Belgium began using his personal money to establish a company to exploit the wealth of the Congo from the Atlantic coast. To facilitate Leopold's control, the European powers granted him personal sovereignty over the area and agreed not to interfere with the policies his companies adopted to extract wealth from the people and forests. Thus a paradox emerged: King Leopold II was a constitutional monarch answerable to a parliament in Belgium, but in what became known as the "Congo Free State," he was an absolute monarch who personally assumed the right to make and enforce all laws. He and his companies designed the rules to serve their own business interests. He made laws about trading, taxation, where people could live, requirements to work for companies, payment for labor, and a host of other powers normally assumed by a government. He also sent armies and police to enforce the laws designed to make his companies rich.

Without ever setting foot in Africa, Leopold was absolute ruler of the Congo from 1886 to 1908, answerable only to himself and his investors. He and his backers wanted the profits from trade, particularly in the wild rubber that could be used in the emerging tire industry. To force the local people to collect rubber, the companies, backed by Leopold's police state, established quotas. Wives were held hostage to ensure that men brought in their allotment of rubber. Failure to meet the quota could result in the amputation of a hand. Failure of a village to fulfill its overall quota could result in raiding and burning the village and surrounding fields and even the massacre of the entire village (Hochschild 1998:226). Millions died of violence, disease, and starvation. Writer Joseph Conrad, then a ship captain, spent a period in the Congo Free State in 1890 and characterized it as "the vilest scramble for loot that ever disfigured the history of human conscience" (Hochschild 1998:4).

Leopold's downfall came at the hands of an accountant named Henri Morel, employed by one of the companies with which Leopold's Congo ventures contracted. Morel noticed that while large stocks of rubber and ivory were arriving from Leopold's business ventures in Africa, all that left Europe were soldiers and military equipment. In other words, there was no "trade" going on, only the looting of a land by unrestrained companies. Morel's investigations over the coming years revealed policies, diaries, and testimonies about the practices of Leopold's state and companies. Detailed was the systematic use of amputation, burning of villages, and military attacks as an explicit part of the companies' "employment" policies.

In response to the depredations in the Congo in the late 1890s, a range of missionaries and liberal thinkers began to attack the company. Unlike earlier campaigns against brutality, this one featured fast communication via telegraph, photography, and newspapers. Leopold's company responded in kind, taking government leaders and journalists on carefully controlled trips to the colony.

Leopold's control eroded after about 1905, as did his health. Forced to cede the Congo Free State to Belgium in 1908, the colony passed into the control of the Belgian parliament. To destroy the records of what had happened, the archives of the Congo Free State were ordered burned, a process that took eight days in August 1908 (Hochschild 1998:294–295). Belgian rule of the Congo lasted until 1959 and continued to be callous, though the greater excesses of the Free State were tempered.

Leopold cuts an ambiguous figure in Europe today. He is still honored for having been a king of Belgium, and statues of him remain in Brussels today. The Royal Museum of Central Africa that Leopold II founded remains a major repository for items taken from the Congo Free State during and after Leopold's time.

Nevertheless, Leopold's greed, cunning, duplicity, and charm made him a hated figure by the end of his life, even in his own Belgium. The criticism was bluntest when penned by writers like Mark Twain, who wrote "King

Leopold's Soliloquy," a satirical look at how King Leopold might view the deaths that were raised by his Congo business policies; and Joseph Conrad, whose book *Heart of Darkness* described the sickening rape of the Congo. Twain's pamphlet, published by the Congo Reform Society, even pointed out that the precedent for executing kings had been established in England in 1648 when Charles's head was chopped off, and made a plea for the hanging of King Leopold II.

Memories of the Congo killing have dulled in the past 100 years, and the atrocities are rarely featured in history books, despite what such excesses might teach about human capacity to kill callously and on a grand scale. Other massacres and genocides are now better known. And yet, it is with the now largely forgotten depredations in the Congo that the principles of humanitarian activism emerged. It was one of the first places that the art of using the press to tweak a broader conscience about how humans treat each other emerged.

Further Reading

Conrad, Joseph (1901). *Heart of Darkness.* http://www.cwrl.utexas.edu/~benjamin/316kfall/316ktexts/heart.html.

Emerson, Barbara (1979). *Leopold II: King of the Belgians.* New York: St. Martin's Press.

Hochschild, Adam (1998). *King Leopold's Ghost.* New York: Houghton Mifflin.

Twain, Mark (1905). "King Leopold's Soliloquy: A Defense of His Congo Rule." http://www.boondocksnet.com/congo/kls/.

CASE STUDY
The Milgram Experiment and Obedience

Psychologist Stanley Milgram is well-known for studying the conditions under which individuals can be ordered to kill. His experiments, which began in 1960, involved a simulation of a "learning experiment" that included three people: a "teacher" recruited through a newspaper ad, a learner who was in fact an actor, and the experimenter who was the authority figure in the lab coat. The teacher was instructed to administer an electric shock to the "learner" when he or she answered a question wrongly. The unwitting teacher was asked by the experimenter to administer ever greater amounts of electricity to the learner, who was strapped into a chair, whenever he made mistakes. As the "voltage" increased, the learner would begin to protest that the treatment was painful and ask the teacher to stop the experiment. The experimenter would insist that the experiment continue, instructing the teacher to ignore the learner's protestations. Thus, the unwitting "teacher" was presented with a moral dilemma: whether to continue with the experiment by being obedient to the authority figure or to side with the subordinated learner and walk away. The teachers would sweat, argue, fidget, and demonstrate other signs of stress and nervousness. Even so, Milgram found that in a normal population, he could induce 65 percent of the people to obey an authority figure to a point where the teacher believed that the level of shock was at least causing great pain and was possibly lethal.

The research question Milgram had in mind when designing his experiments was rooted in the nature of culture and the Holocaust. Milgram's original hypothesis was that the Holocaust was committed by Germans (rather than Americans) because the German culture fostered obedience whereas the American culture did not. By this way of reasoning, a high proportion of the American teachers would be expected to be disobedient to the experimenter and to walk away from the experiment when presented with the moral dilemma. In fact, Americans in the study continued to respond to the orders of the authority figure. This result was later replicated in a number of other countries around the world.

Milgram saw in his experiment not only the answer to the question of how ordinary Germans came to participate in the Holocaust but also how ordinary people become soldiers and kill at the command of an authority figure. He came to believe that obedience to authority is deeply embedded

(Top) The actor who played the "learner" in Milgram's experiments was actually a 47-year-old accountant. (Bottom) When asked to hold the "learner's" arm to get a good contact, many of the "teachers" in Milgram's experiment complied.

Photos from Stanley Milgram, *Obedience to Authority: An Experimental View.* Copyright © 1974 by Stanley Milgram. Reprinted by permission of HarperCollins Publishers.

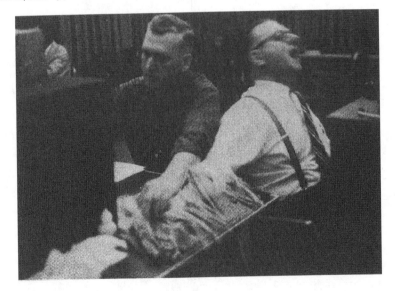

in human behavior, as we navigate our daily routines trying to decide whether to defy or submit. He concluded:

> Obedience is as basic an element in the structure of social life as one can point to. Some system of authority is a requirement of all communal living, and it is only the person dwelling in isolation who is not forced to respond, with defiance or submission, to the commands of others. For many people, obedience is a deeply ingrained behavior tendency, indeed a potent impulse overriding training in ethics, sympathy, and moral conduct. (Milgram 1974:1)

In essence, Milgram said that authority figures can and do override ethical impulses. Or to put it a slightly different way, obedience to authority and conformity are in and of themselves moral impulses.

Milgram's experiments explain why and how individuals do terrible things to other people not out of anger or aggression but out of respect for authority, which is seemingly necessary to social life. In this manner, they show how much of the death dealt out by governments during the twentieth century occurred. But Milgram's experiments also point to a broader truth than the fact that governments can order people to kill callously on their behalf. For authority emerges not only out of governments but also in the context of a faceless bureaucratic psychology laboratory. If Milgram could persuade a stranger to obey his commands and inflict great bodily harm within an hour of meeting that person, so can the leader of a street gang, cult leader, Mafia boss, or other such figure demand lethal obedience from followers.

Further Reading

Milgram, Stanley (1974). *Obedience to Authority*. New York: Harper and Row.

CHAPTER 6

Understanding the Sociology of Killing

THIS BOOK HAS LOOKED AT THE CRIMINALIZATION OF KILLING FROM three perspectives: that of the third party, the ecology of lethal incidents, and the manner in which governments and societies respond to killing. In this concluding chapter I will review why these theories are an effective way to think about killing, and speculate about what might happen in the future as the world seeks to continue limiting violence and killing.

By now, it should be clear that the long decline of *private* killing in society is a sociological phenomenon emerging out of new ways that humans organize their governments. Notably this sociological conclusion is different from that embedded in modern law and psychology and assumes that killing declines as a result of the deterrence and punishment of certain flawed individuals. In contrast, the sociological perspective points out that law and punishment are tools of a more general social process that underlies the decline in *private* killing. Law enforcement and criminal penalties by themselves are not the cause of this decrease. Rather, it is the sustained presence of legitimated law.

More relevant to understanding why *private* violence is decreasing are government, the ways the micro-ecology of potentially lethal situations is regulated, and the capacity of a society to react and adapt to changing norms, laws, and situations. Understanding such approaches leads to at least one optimistic conclusion for a book about killing: private unregulated killing declined in recent centuries as the monopoly over the use of legitimated coercive force expanded into ever wider areas. This has happened because the amount of unregulated feuding in stateless areas declined substantially. To the extent statelessness continues to decline, rates of private violence are also likely to continue decreasing.

Norbert Elias (1939) was among the sociologists describing this change as being part of the "civilizing process" in the sense that there has been a process over the past 500 or more years as relations between humans in general and strangers in particular have become more civil and genteel. Elias wrote that this happens as humans come to control desires and as they develop the norms and manners to deal civilly with strangers. The new habits mean that individuals restrain themselves even when no government agents are plausibly present. When this occurs in the context of the monopolization of coercive power by the state, private behavior becomes more predictably civil, and peaceful trade and commerce become more likely to succeed (see Elias 1939; Cooney 2003).

Understanding the sociology of killing therefore teaches that government is important for understanding how violence and killing are controlled. An effective justice system does this by seeking justice on behalf of victims, restricting feuding by the powerful, controlling extralegal lynching, and recognizing the inherent volatility of scapegoating. But here is where the other shoe drops. Such control emerges only in the context of a plausible powerful third party. And the concentration of power in a third party is a two-edged sword, because it also makes possible the application of bureaucratic principles to the project of violence and killing by the state. In other words, the same force that controls private violence and establishes norms for a modern civility also provides a means for modern states to kill faster and across a greater territory than ever before, as indeed nations did in the twentieth century. Admittedly, such killing is only rarely criminalized; it is in fact legal. But the body count for such killing, undertaken during the twentieth century in the name of nationalism and the state, far exceeds the chaotic and anarchic killing among groups like the Ju/' Hoansi, or even the Aztec.

So, before expressing too much optimism about the human condition, it is important to recall from Chapter 5 that while the use of lethal *private* violence has declined, violence has escalated through *legal* means, including mass execution, war, and genocide. Thirty-four million people died in twentieth-century conflicts, including World Wars I and II, Vietnam, Africa's Great Lakes wars, the Russian Revolution, Mexican Revolution, Sudanese civil wars, the Indian Partition, and the Chinese revolutions. An additional 129 million were executed by, among others, the Germans during the Holocaust, Japan during its occupation of China, the Khmer Rouge in Cambodia, and Stalin's purges before and after World War II. So, indeed, if the twentieth century offers positive lessons about the decline of private violence, it also presents negative ones about the dangers of granting states the capacity to kill. This is because the centralization of power leads to the decline of private killing as a result of the general civilizing process while making possible the ever more lethal excesses of a state that creates soldiers willing to kill with machetes, machine guns, long-distance artillery, airpower, and atom bombs.

This paradox of the civilizing process is modeled well by Mark

Cooney's U-shaped description of why people in democratic societies are relatively peaceful. This is because power claimed through legitimate elections is about the peaceful assertion of legitimate political change. Transparent and enforceable laws contribute to the willingness of a population to comply, even when election results may not please 49.9 percent of the population. Elections and law mean that the population can challenge the power of the government legitimately and peacefully, usually averting the danger of anarchic feuds.

Briefly, I would like to explain why I reached this conclusion before I suggest new ways of thinking about the criminalization of killing, whether by individuals or the state.

Using Sociological Theory to Think About Killing

Ultimately, this book is about how to use sociological theory to think about an interesting social problem, the criminalization of killing. In the process, each of what Lawrence Sherman (1992:xi) called the three parts of criminology—how rules are made, why rules are broken, and how rules are enforced—was explored. In terms of theoretical approaches, this can be thought of as (in succession) why societies make rules, the process by which human interaction becomes violent, and how the broader society goes about deciding which rules to enforce, and when to prosecute or not. This corresponds roughly to Chapters 2, 3, and 4, that is, role of third-party theories, ecological theories, and Durkheimian theories.

Why Sociological Theories Are Different from Traditional Explanations

Many academic fields investigate the origins of crime. Indeed, crime—the venal acts of others—is among the favorite subjects of discussion among academics as well as everyone else. What many of these conversations have in common is a focus on righteousness, which by its very nature evaluates motive and intent—that is, psychological conditions—rather than broader sociological patterns. As has been acknowledged, a great deal of work has emerged from this approach, including assessments of psychological risks for particular individuals such as repeat offenders (or those who at least are rearrested). This is why evaluations of aggression, impulsivity, conformity, and so forth are made by probation officers to evaluate arrestees.[1]

But again, this approach presupposes the presence of law and "a system" in a way that sociology does not. Killing becomes the crime of homicide only in the context of a powerful state. Tracking homicides as measured by the FBI is always interesting, particularly in the short run when public policy effectiveness is evaluated. But such official reports of homicide are not a consistent measure of violence when definitions of self-defense change, police gain access to previously stateless areas, and moral panics result in more aggressive policing and prosecution. In the United States, such differences even reflect changing attitudes toward lynching. For example, the death of Sam Hose would today be classified as homicide. But Hose's death in 1899 would not have made it into the official statistics had they been kept, although Hose's killing of Alfred Cranford probably would have.

Why These Theories but Not Others?

There are many criminological theories, and not every one is used in this book. In fact, few of the many theories used by criminologists are discussed here. This is because most theories explain only official statistics, meaning those people who come to the attention of the police for whatever reason. Again, this is perhaps important for understanding arrest patterns under existing law. Standard fare in a criminological theory class is to provide a chronological sequence of what theories were used in the past, and their strengths and weaknesses in explaining official data. Among the independent variables investigated during the previous 150 years are nationality, race, intelligence quotient, poverty, education, peer association patterns, parental characteristics, prior arrest rates, and a host of other variables useful for this task. Psychology has also done a great deal of applied research on arrested criminals in order to better understand the relationship between criminality and crime prevention. While these theories do explain arrest patterns, they still assume a particular set of laws, the presence of a government, and policing. By default, they hold these variables constant, which means that such theories have little to say about why societies make rules, why rules are broken, or how they are enforced.

So the traditional "whatever explains arrest statistics the best" approach still misses important points raised by Sherman's definition of criminology. The main point of social theory is to have a way of thinking about a specific problem in a generalizable fashion, and using official arrest statistics to explain violence limits such generalization. The fact of the matter is that law enforcement and legal codes themselves vary broadly. And as should be evident, even what is murder varies a great deal from place to place and culture to culture. Officially reported murder rates are not just a product of killing; rather, they are related to the strength of the state, efficiency of police tactics, culture, norms regarding honor, and the acceptability of violence, among other things. In short, murder is a subcategory of other phenomena, most of which lie outside formal legal codes. As a result, comparing homicide rates between jurisdictions across cultures, across time, between states, and so forth, always is like comparing apples and oranges:

useful (they are both fruits, after all) but still not addressing broader points about the variation.

To be useful, social theory must fits a wide variety of contexts. But no theory—including those used in this book—fits every situation. Some theories are better than others given the nature of a particular question. For example, there are outstanding theories about the rationalization of society that are used to explain industrial organization and economic productivity. These theories explain the decisions managers make about hiring and firing workers, picking product lines, and innovations in product development. But such theories are not so useful in explaining why the Ache of Paraguay are so violent. In the same way, third-party theories are great for understanding why the Ache are so violent, but they are not very useful for answering questions about why the American public focused on the Columbine High School killings and not on those at Red Lake High School in Minnesota. My warning to students is that any theory that claims to be a general theory or a pure theory is probably not. Students should be wary of overutilizing a favorite theory that reduces an intellectual question to a single explanation. Rather, they should evaluate critically how well a particular approach works for achieving a better understanding.

Social Theory and Public Policy

Laypeople often evaluate sociological theory based on its utility for "solving" a pressing social problem. Certainly, murder is a serious social problem—just how serious is described well by the many cases reviewed in this book. Every society seeks to protect its own status quo against unregulated violence, and seeks better ways to do so. But no society can indefinitely prevent all killing. There always remains the question of what the society does when a cultural or legal norm is violated and a death occurs as a result. Social theory is useful for understanding why such failures occur, which in turn points to plausible (and implausible) ways that the issue can be dealt with.

A frustration for readers is that the theories reviewed here point to limitations of policy in controlling killing, not short-term solutions to last year's increase in killing in New York City. There is no key that will solve the murder problem, or more generally the violence problem. Indeed, one of the conclusions drawn from Emile Durkheim is that crime—something that the public regards as venal—will always necessarily be with us. Such limitations are not something that someone seeking power to rule, particularly in a democratic society where politicians must seek approval of voters, wants to talk about with respect to venality and violence. The governed do not want to hear from those seeking power that there are limits to what government can do to prevent violence and other bad things from happening. And yet, this is the message that social theory delivers—that some things are beyond the capacity of the powerful third party that is the government. And the nasty unintended consequence of too much concentration of power is one of the prerequisites for state-organized mass executions and war, including those that lead to genocidal policies.

The Sociology of Killing

The decline in private violence is due to factors best explained by sociology, with the most important conditions being the role that legitimated law plays. The rule of law means that the state responds forcefully, predictably, and legitimately when illegal killing occurs. As a result, fewer people demand the private vengeance that fueled violence in older societies as roughly matched combatants sought an elusive reciprocity that could not be satisfied by negotiation.[2] Rather, it is resolved by a powerful third party whose authority is not easily challenged by either disputant because it controls both institutions of justice and legitimated use of violence. In short, as the capacity of the state to express outrage on behalf of potential disputants strengthens, the overall rates of violence decrease. Violent confrontations become less frequent because punches are not thrown, insults are withheld, brothers are not defended, brawls are not joined, challenges are ignored, and feuding is not pursued.

Contrast this with the violent heritage of horticultural communities like the Ache, where killing is the product of the small intimate group. When every group is potentially the lethal enemy of every other group, all human interaction beyond the immediate kin group is shaped by the potential for violence, and the greatest status is often found in the capacity to personally deliver violence. Or, even if status is not involved, a prudent assumption is that all strangers are potential enemies. In these groups every male stands an excellent chance of dying violently or of killing someone else. As Norbert Elias pointed out, the civilization brought by centralized rule is not possible in such circumstances. Perhaps the best illustration of how such dependence in kin loyalty disrupts civilization was seen with the case of the Albanian feuding in the 1990s, and Mark Twain's prescient description of feuds:

> "Well," says Buck, "a feud is this way: A man has a quarrel with another man, and kills him; then that other man's brother kills him; then the other brothers, on both sides, goes for one another; then the cousins chip in— and by and by everybody's killed off, and there ain't no more feud. But it's kind of slow, and takes a long time." (1882:144)

Sociologists point out that controlling this type of violence is part of a general civilizing process. This process means that strangers can trust each other in routine encounters, without resorting to a loyalty rooted in kin ties. The key is for each individual to believe that the other person is similar or even equal before a general law and thus unlikely to engage in an unprovoked attack. In short, the civilizing process engenders a general empathy that results in impulsive recoil when even strangers are denied their rights. Such empathy makes possible vast middle-class societies where strangers routinely interact without violence. The ironic result of this civilizing process is that only in the remote "virtually stateless" areas do homicide rates approach those of the early modern world.

But all is not well with the modern world, either. After all, the capacity for organized killing is nevertheless greater in the modern world, where there is a strong state. Indeed, as psychologist Dave Grossman points out, for most modern people, overcoming this impulse to preserve life is difficult—though, as Stanley Milgram illustrated, individuals are enormously malleable through psychological conditioning.

The greatest expression of this need to have empathy even for strangers is found within the vast, mass, middle-class nations of Western Europe, North America, and Asia (as well as Australia), where modern democratic society is strongest. Such societies recoil at the thought of even the least of their fellow citizens being drawn and quartered, publicly hanged, or broken on a wheel, no matter what terrible act they committed. This recoil is the consequence of civilization—the sustained rule of legitimated law.

Sociology's Challenge to Psychology and Law

But the sociological processes underlying the spread of law—be they called a civilizing effect or something else—do not underlie modern jurisprudence. Modern jurisprudence is founded on the assumption that individuals are responsible for their own behavior and should be held accountable before the law as individuals. In modern countries there are elaborate justice systems dedicated to the proposition that isolating certain individuals from society prevents future criminal acts by that individual and/or by deterring others who would consider doing the same thing. Much of this system is rooted in an assumption that some people are criminal and others are not, and that a legal system using modern investigative techniques can determine which is which, and who is who. Modern psychology has emerged as the arbiter for understanding the *why* and *how* of such criminals. Indeed, in the United States there is a cottage industry in identifying the "6 or 7 percent" who are habitually criminal in the belief that incapacitating them through incarceration will solve, or at least minimize, "the crime problem."

But these psycholegal assumptions do not reflect the fact that crime is not only the product of certain individuals. What Durkheimian theory, social ecology, and studies of the powerful third party all show is that individuals are violent in some contexts but not others. And what is more, violence is reprehensible at some times and not at others. Individual psychological predispositions have little to do with this, so that it is unlikely that "treating" individuals will solve the entire crime problem. People who commit crimes—criminals—do not generate violence or crime without reference to a broader society. In other words, the *legitimacy* of the law for the resolution of disputes is more important than its content.[3] Still, psycholegal constructs are useful in organizing a response in a manner that resonates with modern culture. After all, as Durkheim pointed out, crime, even homicide, is necessary for the maintenance of the established order. But ultimately, the law works only in a place where there is a legitimated third party.

In the case of modern murder laws, psychology is so important and legitimate that its assumptions are embedded in laws that evaluate issues like intent and malice. Psychological evaluations are routinely included in probation reports, and assumptions about the nature of evil individuals, sociopaths, or psychopaths generated by popular culture make their way into law enforcement. What sociology has to say about such legal concepts is that they are important social facts for what they tell us about a society's anxieties, and are important when evaluated as such. Law by definition is important for the operation of the legitimate legal order. But this reflects the underlying moral order, which is, again, rooted in understandings of individual responsibilities. Embedded in such laws and practices are assumptions about what type of offense will be responded to. In the modern United States this is likely to be drug offenses (our War on Drugs) and sex offenses (Megan's Law and the sex offender registry). In colonial Massachusetts it would have been blasphemy and witchcraft.

Issues of intent and malice may provide an effective organizing principle for modern jurisprudence, but such psychological approaches also serve the same function that the theological disputes and witchcraft accusations played in Puritan Massachusetts. By this, I mean that they are indicative of anxieties about social change. Neither the psychology of today nor the theology of the Puritans had much to do with the long-term homicide rate. Ultimately, the chances of dying violently are only tangentially related to the number of bad people incarcerated, banished, mutilated, committed to mental hospitals, or executed. If you want to know about your chances of dying violently, ask not about the formal mechanics of the legal and correctional system but about how legitimate the social order is, how effective the third parties are, and how small "virtually stateless" areas have become. In other words, ask about the social ecology of the legal order. When you do this, you will start to understand better why the odds of dying violently are greater in the United States than in Canada, Iceland, or Switzerland.

The Modern Era's Dark Underside:
Legitimated Killing on Behalf of State and Company

The previous discussion was about the decline of private killing—that is, killing that has already been criminalized. It is clear that as the state extends its control around the world, this type of killing declines. But the dirty secret of this success is that as private, extralegal killing declines, the capacity for mass killing by the same state increases. The same innovations in statecraft, technology, and weaponry that make the assertion of a legitimated monopoly over the use of coercive power possible also permitted mass killing by governments in places like Germany, Vietnam, Cambodia, the Soviet Union, Poland, Colombia, Rwanda, Sudan, Yugoslavia, China, Algeria, and many other places during the twentieth century. In the twenty-first century, the same issues frame fighting in Iraq, Sudan, Congo, Chechnya, and other places. In other words, the mechanisms by which the monopoly over the use of coercive force is established and brings peace are the same ones that can be used for mass execution, war, and genocide.

So today, most killing is done by large institutions in which callousness is generated by a bureaucracy. It is true that the principles of psycholegal jurisprudence can demonstrate that there are individuals who are more culpable than others. But the fact of the matter is that the large numbers killed, whether in the Holocaust, the Rwanda genocide, Iraq, or Darfur, occur only in the context of an organization. As Matthew Lee and M. David Erman's (1999) article about the decisionmaking that went into marketing the defective Ford Pinto point out, the dynamics within the organization and the way that organizations process information make possible the callousness that kills; in this case, it is not individuals with psycholegal intent. This is a type of callousness that does not fit well with modern legal systems because it is a product of group culpability, not individual culpability. As such, modern law is an imperfect response to actions rooted in corporate dynamics. There is still no way to righteously imprison, execute, or torture a limited-liability corporation, which is really something other than the sum of its shareholders.

An important challenge for the future is not to prevent further private violence but to focus on preventing collective groups—be they corporations or governments—from callously organizing mass bureaucratic killing. Instead of pacifying the stateless, the excesses of the strong state (or corporation) need effective regulation if violent death is to continue its rapid decline. To a certain extent, older statutes rooted in psycholegal constraints can be used; white-collar executives are notoriously sensitive to threats of imprisonment. But it should also be pointed out that this is not the solution. The solution lies in understanding the "ecological conditions" that put a nation or corporation at risk for killing on a mass scale. People like Raul Hilberg (1967), in his studies of how genocide is organized, have started to do this. And while the nascent international court system provides a good first step, the capacity to enforce international law is still hampered by the unwillingness of those who truly control the use of coercive power—the nation-states themselves—to surrender this authority to a larger legal entity.

The Criminalization of Killing and the Universal Need for Justice

At the beginning of this book it was noted that the need for justice—that is, reciprocity in human relations—is seemingly universal. Demands for justice, whether in a remote hunter-gatherer society or in a modern nation-state, are always rooted in the rhetoric of reciprocity. This applies even to the most heinous of human crimes, which is killing in all its forms. What is different in the case of killing is that reciprocity is not owed the victim, as in the case of wounding or theft, but the larger group. When these groups feel they are robbed of a member, they respond, demanding repayment in whatever currency makes sense in that society. In other words, if someone is wronged, someone else is responsible and must pay in order to reestablish a sense of righteousness. This payment can be insisted upon—and judged by—the person and his or her kin who feel wronged, or by an independent and powerful judge. The point is that righteousness needs to be achieved, and that this righteousness emerges out of a social context.

The social context, not the individuals concerned, is why some but not all killing is criminalized. Understanding this fact is of course a two-edged sword, because social contexts are manipulable. They can be manipulated for good—in this case to create conditions where killing becomes less likely. Or they can be manipulated for evil, as the organizations that have perpetrated the greatest massacres of the twentieth century demonstrated.

Notes

1. See Miethe and Regoeczi (2004) for a similar discussion.
2. Cooney (1998:10–11) notes that people can handle conflict in myriad ways, including fighting, talking, running away, seeking advice, ignoring the problem, shaming, spreading gossip, seeking a mediator or judge, seizing hostages, or community suicide. The responses that emerge can be more or less peaceful or violent. But the point here is that the dynamics of the technique chosen are different in a society that has a powerful central state than in one that does not.
3. To paraphrase Durkheim (1973:34–35), the psycholegal approach to criminality can be considered both a widely accepted historical statement about what peo-

ple believe and a scientific theory of society. As a description of what people believe, this has great significance. But as a scientific theory of crime rates, it is somewhat wanting in precision. Or, to quote Durkheim's reasoning about the French Revolution directly: "In a word, [French revolutionary principles of 1789] have been a religion which, after all, has given birth to great things." The psycholegal system is also the religion underlying our modern criminal justice system. Our criminal justice system, too, has sacred unquestioned principles that, while not testable scientifically, nevertheless have given birth to things great and not so great.

APPENDIX 1

The Statistics of Killing

THE STATISTICS PRESENTED IN THIS APPENDIX WERE COLLECTED IN THE context of certain assumptions and definitions with respect to killing and murder and need to be interpreted in this context. The tables are arranged to correlate with Chapters 2, 3, and 4. However, some tables can be used to think about questions raised in several of the chapters.

Chapter 2

Chapter 3

Chapter 4

A.2.1   Ache and Ju/' Hoansi Causes of Death

This table summarizes what is known about death among the Ache of Paraguay and the Ju/' Hoansi of Namibia from the time before they had systematic contact with outsiders. In both cases, death from violence was very high.

Cause of Death by Age	Ache Before 1971		Female	Male
	All	Percentage		
Under Age 15				
All illness	51	22.2	27	24
Degenerative	19	8.3	8	11
Accident	14	6.1	2	12
Violence	146	63.5	76	70
Total	230	100.0	113	117
Age 15–59				
All illness	35	28.0	9	26
Degenerative	4	3.2	4	0
Accident	29	23.2	6	23
Violence	57	45.6	19	38
Total	125	100.0	38	87
Age 60 and Over				
All illness	5	18.5	2	3
Degenerative	6	22.2	2	4
Accident	7	25.9	4	3
Violence	9	33.3	3	6
Total	27	100.0	11	16

Cause of Death by Age	Ju/' Hoansi Before 1973		Female	Male
	All	Percentage		
Under Age 15				
All illness	144	87.8	70	74
Degenerative	6	3.7	3	3
Accident and violence	14	8.5	7	7
Total	164	100.0	80	84
Age 15–59				
All illness	101	79.5	55	46
Degenerative	4	3.1	2	2
Accident and violence	22	17.4	5	17
Total	127	100.0	62	65
Age 60 and Over				
All illness	27	51.9	15	12
Degerative	21	40.5	12	9
Accident and violence	4	7.6	2	2
Total	52	100.0	29	23

Source: Hill and Hurtado 1996:174.

A.2.2   Ju/' Hoansi Causes of Violent Death, 1920–1955

This table summarizes what is known about the patterns of feuding among the Ju/' Hoansi of Namibia. There were a total of twenty-two deaths in a society that was gradually being incorporated into territory controlled by governments from British Botswana and southwest Africa (modern Namibia). Data reflect feuding that took place from the 1930s to 1950s and that was recalled by their informants. Note that toward the end of the period, the South African colonial government in southwest Africa and the British colonial government in Botswana began to make arrests for homicide.

1. *1930s:* In a general brawl over a woman, three men kill another man east of Xai xai.

2. *1930s:* By general agreement, the senior of the three killers in the earlier killing is killed in retaliation.

3. *1940:* A well-known fighter named /Twi kills a man in a spear fight.

4. *1940s:* /Twi kills another man.

5. *1940s:* While being fatally attacked by a large group, /Twi kills one man and wounds a woman.

6. *1940s:* Twi is ambushed by a large group and killed by collective action.

7. *1940s:* One man kills another in a sneak attack involving the victim's wife. The victim's wife runs off with the killer, but later returns.

8. *1930s:* A young man kills his uncle (father's brother) in a spear fight.

9. *1930s:* In a fight about adultery, the accused adulterer is killed and the aggrieved husband is wounded.

10. *1920s:* In a fight between a husband and wife about adultery, a man kills his wife and then flees.

11. *1930s:* Gau kills a man with a spear, which initiates a long feud, described in part in Chapter 2.[a]

12. *1930s:* Gau is attacked by his enemies but survives, even after killing one of his attackers.[a]

13. *1930s:* A relative of Gau's is killed in a fight that precedes killings 11 and 12. The anthropologists assume that the two fights are related.[a]

14. *1930s:* Gau is attacked again, but he kills one of his attackers. This is one of three deaths on the same day and in the same melee (see 15 and 16 below).[a]

15. *1930s:* One of the victims is a woman bystander from Gau's group who is killed with an arrow.[a]

16. *1930s:* The third victim that day is another man from Gau's group.[a]

17. *1940s:* A young man from a group outside the feud finally kills Gau in a sneak attack.[a]

18. *1950s:* The younger brother of Gau is attacked by another man. In the ensuing fight, the man's wife is killed. Gau's brother is arrested by the government of southwest Africa (Namibia), and goes to jail.

19. *1950s:* Returning from jail, Gau's younger brother is ambushed on the road and killed by relatives of his victim.

(continues)

A.2.2   continued

20. *1946:* A black settler is killed by a Ju/' Hoansi man after he is caught *in fla-grante delicto* with the Ju/' Hoansi man's wife. The Ju/' Hoansi man is later jailed in Botswana.

21. *1952:* A young man kills an older man in a brawl. The young man is jailed in Botswana.

22. *1955:* The last case of killing reported in the area studied by Richard Lee and his coworkers is the result of a general brawl in which a young man and his father kill another man. Both are taken to jail in Botswana.

Source: Adapted from Lee 1979:94.
Note: a. Denotes killings associated with Gau, described in Chapter 2.

Figure A.2.3 Homicide Rates in England, 1200–2000

Statistics are necessarily erratic in a time series of this nature, reflecting the changing nature of both definitions and statistical data from before 1900. In general, these
statistics reflect the long-term decline in homicide rates that has taken place in
England during the past 800 years.

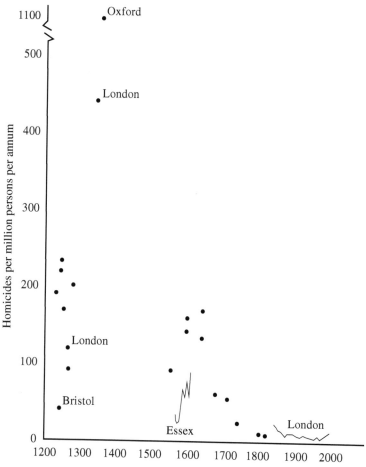

Source: Daly and Wilson 1988:276.
   Note: Each point represents an estimated homicide rate for a city or county over a few
years or decades.

A.2.4   Estimated Homicide Rates in Thirteenth-Century England

Reconstructions of records from early English eyre courts. Such data are of course difficult to interpret with any precision. But what this does show is that homicide rates in thirteenth-century England were notably higher than in the present day.

Eyre (Court)	Number of Victims in Sample	Estimated Rate (per 100,000 per year)
Bedford	321	22
Bristol	16	4
Kent	494	23
Norfolk	719	9
Oxford	309	17
Warwick	376	47
London	199	12

Source: Givens 1977:36.

A.3.1   Known Ages of Homicide Victims and Perpetrators in the United States, 2004

Age	Victims	Percentage of Victims	Offenders	Percentage of Offenders
Under 1	176	1.27	0	0
1 to 4	328	2.34	0	0
5 to 8	73	0.53	2	0.02
9 to 12	81	0.58	16	0.16
13 to 16	411	2.96	480	4.65
17 to 19	1,244	8.97	1,555	15.07
20 to 24	2,629	18.96	2,726	26.41
25 to 29	2,137	15.41	1,669	16.17
30 to 34	1,547	11.16	1,047	10.14
35 to 39	1,224	8.83	782	7.58
40 to 44	1,144	8.25	737	7.14
45 to 49	920	6.63	508	4.92
50 to 54	643	4.64	316	3.06
55 to 59	389	2.81	179	1.73
60 to 64	273	1.97	124	1.20
65 to 69	204	1.47	60	0.58
70 to 74	144	1.04	48	0.47
75 and over	299	2.16	72	0.70
Total	14,121		15,935	
Total age known	13,866		10,321	
Total age unknown	255		5,614	

Source: Uniform Crime Reports 2004, tables 2.4 and 2.5.
Notes: The ages of more than 5,000 perpetrators are unknown, presumably because no perpetrator has been identified by the police. More than 25 percent of perpetrators are from the ages of twenty to twenty-four. This is also the age at which a perpetrator is most likely to be a victim.

Figure A.3.2 Age and Gender of Homicide Victims and Offenders in Canada, 1974–1983

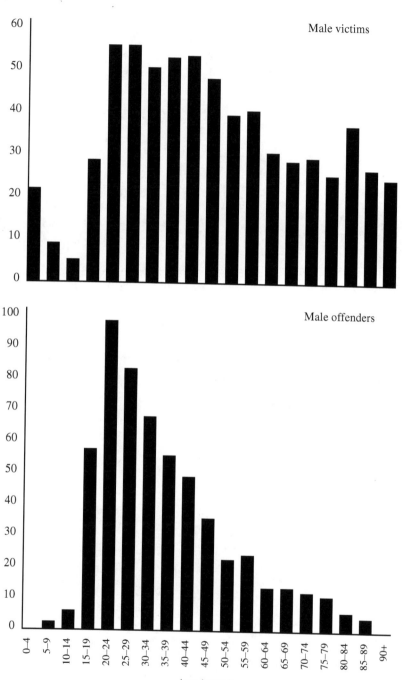

Figure A.3.2 continued

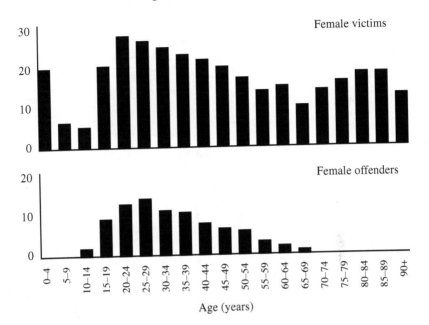

Age (years)

Source: Daly and Wilson 1988:169.

A.3.3   Race and Gender of Murder Victims in the United States, 2004

Race	Total	Male	Female	Unknown
White	6,929 (49.1%)	5,031	1,896	2
Black	6,632 (47.0%)	5,562	1,067	3
Other	365 (2.6%)	269	95	1
Unknown	195 (1.4%)	128	41	26
Total	14,121	10,990 (77.8%)	3,099 (21.9%)	32 (0.01%)

Source: Uniform Crime Reports 2004, table 2.3.

A.3.4   Race and Gender of Offender and Victims in the United States, 2004

Race of Victim	Total	Race of Offender				Gender of Offender		
		White	Black	Other	Unknown	Male	Female	Unknown
White victims	3,727	3,123	522	37	45	3,309	373	45
Black victims	3,067	228	2,784	7	48	2,738	281	48
Other race victims	177	42	23	110	2	159	16	2
Unknown race	68	34	15	1	18	40	10	18

Race of Victim	Total	Race of Offender				Gender of Offender		
		White	Black	Other	Unknown	Male	Female	Unknown
Male victims	5,050	2,253	2,613	110	74	4,488	488	74
Female victims	1,920	1,139	716	44	21	1,717	182	21
Unknown sex	69	35	15	1	18	41	10	18

Source: Uniform Crime Reports 2004, table 2.7.

Note: This table is based on incidents where some information about the offender is known by law enforcement. It excludes incidents reported with a value of "unknown offender."

A.3.5   Homicide Victimization by Race in the United States, Twentieth Century

Year	African American (rate per 100,000)	White (rate per 100,000)
1910	22.3	4.1
1920	28.8	4.8
1930	37.9	5.6
1940	33.9	3.2
1950	NA	NA
1960	21.9	2.5
1970	35.9	4.4
1980	37.7	6.3
1990	37.7	5.4
1999	20.6	3.5

Source: Beeghley 2004:72.
Note: Data from 1910–1930 are inferred from death registration data. After 1930, data are from the Bureau of Justice Statistics.

A.3.6 Murder by Circumstances, 2004

Circumstances	2000	2001	2002	2003	2004
Total	13,230	14,061	14,263	14,465	14,121
Felony type					
Total	2,229	2.364	2.340	2,385	2,089
Rape	58	61	44	43	36
Robbery	1,077	1,080	1,111	1,061	988
Burglary	76	80	97	94	77
Larceny/theft	23	17	16	21	14
Motor vehicle theft	25	22	15	32	38
Arson	81	71	59	77	28
Prostitution and commercialized vice	6	5	8	16	9
Other sex offenses	10	7	8	10	14
Narcotic drug laws	589	575	664	679	554
Gambling	12	3	5	6	7
Other/not specified	272	443	313	346	324
Suspected felony type	60	72	66	87	117
Other than felony					
Total	6,871	7,073	7,185	7,130	6,972
Romantic triangle	122	118	129	98	97
Child killed by babysitter	30	37	39	27	17
Brawl due to influence of alcohol	188	152	149	128	139
Brawl due to influence of narcotics	99	118	85	53	98
Argument over money or property	206	198	203	220	218
Other arguments	3,589	3,618	3,577	3,850	3,758
Gangland killings	65	76	75	114	95
Juvenile gang killings	653	862	911	819	804
Institutional killings	10	8	12	13	17
Sniper attack	8	7	10	2	1
Other/not specified	1,901	1,879	1,995	1,806	1,728
Unknown	4,070	4,552	4,672	4,863	4,943

Source: Uniform Crime Reports 2004, table 2.13.

A.3.7 Murder Victims by Weapon, 2000–2004

Weapon	2000	2001	2002	2003	2004
Total	13,230	14,061	14,263	14,465	14,121
Firearms					
Total	8,661	8,890	9,528	9,659	9,326
Handguns	6,778	6,931	7,294	7,745	7,265
Rifles	411	386	488	392	393
Shotguns	485	511	486	454	507
Other guns	53	59	75	76	117
Type not stated	934	1,003	1,185	992	1,004
Knives or cutting instruments	1,782	1,831	1,776	1,828	1,866
Blunt objects (e.g., clubs, hammers)	617	680	681	650	663
Personal weapons (hands, fists, feet)	927	961	954	962	933
Poison	8	12	23	9	11
Explosives	9	4	11	4	1
Fire	134	109	103	170	114
Narcotics	20	37	48	44	76
Drowning	15	23	20	17	15
Strangulation	166	153	145	184	155
Asphyxiation	92	116	100	131	105
Other/unknown	799	1,245	874	807	856

Source: Uniform Crime Reports 2004, table 2.9.

A.3.8   Murder Weapons in the United States and England/Wales, 1999 (percentage)

	United States	England/Wales
Firearms	65	9
Knives or cutting instruments	13	30
Hands, feet, or fists	7	22
Other methods/unknown	15	39

Source: Beeghley 2004:116.

A.3.9   US Homicides by Month, 2000–2004 (percentage)

	2000	2001	2002	2003	2004
January	8.4	7.9	8.2	7.7	7.9
February	7.3	6.2	6.8	6.8	6.7
March	7.6	7.1	7.8	8.0	8.4
April	7.7	7.9	7.7	8.3	8.0
May	8.5	8.3	8.0	8.7	8.8
June	8.5	8.5	8.1	8.3	8.3
July	9.3	9.5	9.7	9.3	9.5
August	9.4	9.0	9.2	9.1	9.4
September	8.3	8.6	9.7	8.6	8.6
October	8.7	9.3	8.4	8.3	8.3
November	7.7	8.5	7.9	7.8	7.9
December	8.7	9.2	8.6	9.0	8.1

Source: Uniform Crime Reports 2004, table 2.2.

Note: If time of year did not matter, each month should have 1/12 of the homicides (i.e., 8.3 percent of homicides each year). However, time of year does matter, which is why the summer months of July and August, when people are more likely to be outside, have consistently higher rates of homicide than other months.

A.3.10   Murder by US Region, 2004

	Homicide Rate per 100,000	Percentage of US Population	Percentage of Murders	Percentage by Firearms
Northeast	4.2	18.6	14.1	61.3
Midwest	4.7	22.4	19.3	66.5
South	6.6	36.1	43.0	66.6
West	5.7	23.0	23.7	67.7
Total	5.5	100.0	100.0	66.0

Source: Uniform Crime Reports 2004:15 and table 2.8.

A.3.11   Murder by US Urban Status, 2004

	Percentage of US Population	Homicide Rate per 100,000
Urban areas[a]	82.9	5.9
Suburban areas	6.5	3.5
Nonurban counties	10.4	3.6
Cities over 250,000 people		12.5
Cities under 10,000 people		2.4

Source: Uniform Crime Reports 2004.
Note: a. Urban areas include people living both within metropolitan service areas (MSAs) and outside the MSAs, typically in suburban areas.

A.3.12   Killer-Victim Relationship in Relation to Final Case Disposition, Houston, Texas, 1969

Case Disposition	Relatives	Friends	Strangers
No charges/no bill/no prosecution	40	37	24
Dismissed	4	3	2
Not guilty	6	4	4
Probation	10	9	7
Death penalty	0	0	9
Outcome undetermined/charge pending	13	3	11
Life sentence	1	3	2
Sentenced to determinant jail time	21	37	42
Adjusted average sentence (years)	8	10	28

Source: Lundsgaarde 1977:232.

A.3.13   Number of Homicides in Houston, Texas, Each Day of the Week in 1969

Day	Number of Homicides
Monday	27
Tuesday	21
Wednesday	21
Thursday	18
Friday	29
Saturday	70
Sunday	46
Total	232

Source: Lundsgaarde 1977:237.
Note: Virtually everywhere in the United States, weekends are the most likely time for killing.

A.3.14   Time of Day of Homicides, Houston, Texas, 1969

Time	Number of Homicides
6 P.M.	14
7	4
8	14
9	19
10	24
11	24
Midnight	24
1 A.M.	15
2	16
3	7
4	1
5	2
6	3
7	3
8	0
9	6
10	2
11	7
Noon	13
1	3
2	4
3	6
4	12
5	8

Source: Lundsgaarde 1977:182.

A.3.15 Fourteen US Birth-Year Cohorts and Their Characteristics

These two tables describe the relationships among year of birth, size of the birth cohort relative to all adult males, homicide rates, and number of children born out of wedlock. The tables contain a great deal of interesting information, although they can be difficult for the student to read. The point of these tables is to highlight the relationships between the size of the at-risk cohort of males and the proportion of boys raised by single mothers. For ecological theorists, both variables are indicators of how many impulsive young males will enter the at-risk age for crime at the same time. This in turn raises the propensity for violence in a society, and therefore the number of incidents that will be potentially lethal.

To start, familiarize yourself with the characteristics of, for instance, cohort 7. Cohort 7 members were born in the years 1940–1944, their percentage of nonmarital births (%NB) was a fairly low 3.62 percent, and their relative cohort size (RCS) was 12.43 percent when the cohort reached the ages of 15–19. This means that relatively few boys were born to unwed mothers, and the cohort size born from 1940 to 1944 was relatively small.

Now look at the second table to understand what this meant for the rates of homicide as this cohort aged. Find cohort 7 and you will see that when cohort 7 reached the ages of 15–19 (in 1960), their RCS was 12.43 percent, and their homicide rate was 8.98 per 100,000. You can trace cohort 7's homicide rates and RCS throughout their lifespan by moving downward diagonally. Notice that the homicide rate for cohort 7 members rises and peaks when this cohort reaches the ages of 25–29 (when their homicide rate is 20.09 homicides per 100,000). After that age, cohort 7's homicide rate falls throughout the rest of their lifespan.

Next, look at cohort 8 and trace the RCS and homicide rates for that cohort over time. You'll see some striking differences, though the general trend of rising and falling homicide rates as they age beyond 24 years matches the pattern of cohort 7. Compare again the different characteristics of cohorts 7 and 8.

This first table can be read horizontally to determine the homicide rates for each cohort in each year (e.g., look at the row for 1995, where extreme differences in homicide rates among the different-aged cohorts are very clear), or vertically to determine the homicide rates of each of the different cohorts when they were at the same age. Look at the column under 15–19 years and note the nearly uninterrupted increase in homicide rates for each succeeding group of 15- to 19-year-olds. In other words, 15- to 19-year-olds became more violent during the twentieth century. Compare this with the column under 45–49 years, where the homicide rates are uniformly low and far more stable across the twentieth century.

The researchers who gathered the data for these tables found that a large RCS and a large %NB were strongly correlated to a larger homicide rate for cohorts when they became 15–24 years old. In general, it is accepted that younger males commit the lion's share of crimes and homicides, and that criminality decreases with age.

(continues)

A.3.15 continued

However, O'Brien, Stockard, and Isaacson (1999) show that the size of each cohort relative to all adults aged 15–64 can have a very marked impact on homicide rates, even during the more criminally active teen years and early twenties. Study the vertical rows under ages 15–19 and 20–24. Note that a higher RCS nearly always correlates positively to a higher homicide rate. Now look at the %NB in seemingly outlandish rises in homicide rates, such as those that occur in 1990 and 1995. Though criminologists theorize that these very large spikes in homicide rates in 1990 and 1995 may be connected to the crack cocaine epidemic in inner cities, the %NB has also been shown to be a determining factor.

Characteristics	Cohort 1	Cohort 2	Cohort 3	Cohort 4	Cohort 5	Cohort 6	Cohort 7
Birth years	1910–1914	1915–1919	1920–1924	1925–1929	1930–1934	1935–1939	1940–1944
%NB[a]	Not available	2.10	2.57	2.93	3.92	4.08	3.62
RCS[b]	14.40	13.89	13.69	12.39	10.80	10.87	12.43

Characteristics	Cohort 8	Cohort 9	Cohort 10	Cohort 11	Cohort 12	Cohort 13	Cohort 14
Birth years	1945–1949	1950–1954	1955–1959	1960–1964	1965–1969	1970–1974	1975–1979
%NB	3.82	4.06	4.82	5.99	8.97	12.11	15.59
RCS	14.62	15.27	15.33	14.03	11.72	10.82	10.53

(continues)

A.3.15 continued

	15–19 years	20–24 years	25–29 years	30–34 years	35–39 years	40–44 years	45–49 years
1960	Cohort 7	Cohort 6	Cohort 5	Cohort 4	Cohort 3	Cohort 2	Cohort 1
%NB[a]	3.62	4.08	3.92	2.93	2.57	2.10	n/a
RCS[b]	12.43	10.14	10.09	11.10	11.64	10.85	10.17
Homicide rate[c]	8.98	14.00	13.45	10.73	9.37	6.48	5.71
1965	Cohort 8	Cohort 7	Cohort 6	Cohort 5	Cohort 4	Cohort 3	Cohort 2
%NB	3.82	3.62	4.08	3.92	2.93	2.57	2.10
RCS	14.62	11.58	9.70	9.54	10.32	10.70	9.81
Homicide rate	9.07	15.18	14.69	11.70	9.76	7.41	5.56
1970	Cohort 9	Cohort 8	Cohort 7	Cohort 6	Cohort 5	Cohort 4	Cohort 3
%NB	4.06	3.82	3.62	4.08	3.92	2.93	2.57
RCS	15.27	13.16	10.80	9.14	8.80	9.50	9.64
Homicide rate	17.22	23.76	20.09	16.00	13.13	10.10	7.51
1975	Cohort 10	Cohort 9	Cohort 8	Cohort 7	Cohort 6	Cohort 5	Cohort 4
%NB	4.82	4.06	3.82	3.62	4.08	3.92	2.93
RCS	15.33	13.96	12.41	10.21	8.37	8.07	8.51
Homicide rate	17.54	25.62	21.05	15.81	12.83	10.52	7.32
1980	Cohort 11	Cohort 10	Cohort 9	Cohort 8	Cohort 7	Cohort 6	Cohort 5
%NB	5.99	4.82	4.06	3.82	3.62	4.08	3.92
RCS	14.03	14.25	13.09	11.82	9.38	7.81	7.35
Homicide rate	18.02	23.95	18.91	15.22	12.31	8.79	6.76

(*continues*)

A.3.15 continued

	15–19 years	20–24 years	25–29 years	30–34 years	35–39 years	40–44 years	45–49 years
1985	Cohort 12	Cohort 11	Cohort 10	Cohort 9	Cohort 8	Cohort 7	Cohort 6
%NB	8.97	5.99	4.82	4.06	3.82	3.62	4.08
RCS	11.72	13.27	13.74	12.81	11.19	8.88	7.36
Homicide rate	16.32	21.11	16.79	12.59	9.60	7.50	5.31
1990	Cohort 13	Cohort 12	Cohort 11	Cohort 10	Cohort 9	Cohort 8	Cohort 7
%NB	12.11	8.97	5.99	4.82	4.06	3.82	3.62
RCS	10.82	11.66	12.94	13.35	12.18	10.84	8.42
Homicide rate	36.52	29.10	17.99	12.44	9.38	6.81	5.17
1995	Cohort 14	Cohort 13	Cohort 12	Cohort 11	Cohort 10	Cohort 9	Cohort 8
%NB	15.59	12.11	8.97	5.99	4.82	4.06	3.82
RCS	10.53	10.43	11.08	12.75	12.97	11.79	10.17
Homicide rate	35.24	32.34	16.75	10.05	7.27	5.48	3.67

Notes: a. %NB is the number of nonmarital births per 100 live births occurring in that cohort's five-year birth span.
b. RCS (relative cohort size) is the size of each cohort at each age, relative to all adults aged 15–64.
c. Homicide rate is per 100,000 people in that cohort at that age.

A.3.16 Domestic Disturbance Calls and Homicides in Minneapolis by Year, 1985–1989

This table, compiled by Michael Buerger from Minneapolis Police Department records, shows that homicides are more likely to occur at addresses where at least one domestic disturbance call has been recorded than they are at addresses with no disturbance calls. However, as Lawrence Sherman (1992) points out, there is a "hindsight fallacy" at work here. Even though the differences in homicide rates between these two categories of household are statistically significant (meaning that the differences are not likely due to chance), they are not *substantially* significant as predictors of who will kill whom, or when. In essence, these data cannot assist the police in predicting homicide in particular households. Although the differences in the rates of homicide are statistically meaningful, the overall rates of homicide in either type of household (from 0.03 to 0.82 per 1,000 residents) are exceedingly low. Sherman calls homicide "an extremely rare event in any population, even among couples engaged in domestic violence" (Sherman 1992:232). Rare events, such as lightning strikes or lottery wins, are certain to happen, yet predicting *where* these rare events will happen is nearly impossible. Sherman points out that even at addresses with at least one domestic disturbance call, the homicide rates are so low (less than 1 homicide per 1,000 residents) that these data would give police no assistance whatsoever in predicting or preventing domestic homicides.

Year	A Addresses with One or More Domestic Calls	Addresses in A with a Domestic Homicide	Homicides per 1,000 Addresses in A	B Addresses with No Domestic Calls	Addresses in B with a Domestic Homicide	Homicides per 1,000 Addresses in B
1985	9,083	2	0.22	105,917	3	0.03
1986	9,518	3	0.32	105,482	7	0.06
1987	9,970	5	0.50	105,030	4	0.04
1988	9,599	4	0.42	105,401	9	0.08
1989	9,712	8	0.82	105,288	7	0.06

This table on first glance would also seem to suggest a predictive correlation between domestic disturbance calls and domestic homicides. The lowest five-year rate of homicide (0.28 per 1,000 residents) belongs to addresses where no domestic disturbance calls were recorded, whereas the highest five-year homicide rate (16.83 per 1,000 residents) belongs to addresses that logged nine or more domestic disturbance calls per calendar year. However, a "hindsight fallacy" is at work here as well: Sherman points out that "with foresight rather than hindsight, a prediction of homicide from chronic domestic disturbance calls would be wrong 997 times out of 1000" (Sherman 1992:233–236).

(continues)

A.3.16 continued

Number of Domestic Disturbance Calls	Mean Yearly Addresses with That Many Calls	Number of Domestic Homicides at Addresses with That Many Calls in the Calendar Year	· Five-Year Rate of Domestic Homicides per 1,000 Addresses
0	105,424	30	0.28
1	5,520	9	1.63
2	1,670	0	0
3	812	3	3.69
4	457	0	0
5	284	2	7.04
6	194	1	5.15
7	131	0	0
8	102	0	0
9 or more	416	7	16.83

A.4.1 Disposition of Cases in Thirteenth-Century England

Disposition	Number Accused	Percentage of Total
Acquitted	944	27.0
Executed	247	7.1
Killed by victim or pursuers	20	0.6
Transferred to church court	78	2.2
Pardoned	56	1.6
Outlawed	1,444	41.4
Abjured	258	7.4
Fled	49	1.4
Escaped from jail	7	0.2
Died before trial	93	2.7
Other	137	3.9
None given	159	4.6
Total	3,492	

Source: Givens 1977:93.
Notes: Trials were conducted under a system in which both juries and judges played a role. The most common punishment for homicide was expulsion from the community as an "outlaw." Only 7.1 percent of those tried were eventually hanged.

A.4.2   Justifiable Homicides, 2000–2004

The rates of justifiable homicide increased in number for the five years in this table. However, as a phenomenon, it has become rarer as laws requiring combatants to withdraw from a potentially lethal confrontation have become more strict. Justifiable homicide has become exceedingly rare in the United States.

	Law Enforcement Officers	Private Citizens
2000	309	164
2001	378	222
2002	341	233
2003	373	247
2004	437	229

Source: Uniform Crime Reports 2004, tables 2.15, 2.16.

Figure A.4.3 US Homicide Victimization Rates, 1990–2000 (A), and Homicide Rates in the United States and England/Wales, 1990–2000 (B)

These two figures represent two interpretations of variations in the rate of homicide in the twentieth century. Both utilize official FBI data for the period after 1933. However, before 1930 the best estimates vary a great deal because of different definitions of homicide and variations in local reporting. According to Beeghley (2003), an important element in the variation resulted in the improvement in investigative techniques, which meant that deaths previously labeled as "natural" became more likely to be classified as homicide.

A

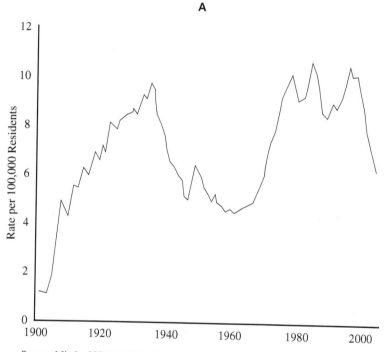

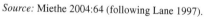

Source: Miethe 2004:64 (following Lane 1997).

Figure A.4.3 continued

B

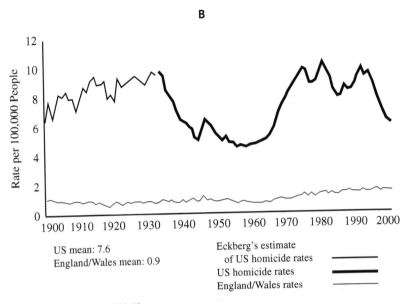

US mean: 7.6
England/Wales mean: 0.9

Eckberg's estimate
  of US homicide rates ────────
US homicide rates ━━━━━━
England/Wales rates ────────

Source: Beeghley 2003:63.

A.4.4 Disposition of Cases, Houston, Texas, 1969 (status of killer relative to those killed, by eventual disposition of the case)

	No Bill, no Charges, or Suicide	Dismissed	Probation	Not Guilty	Under 1 year	1.1–5 years	5.1–10 years	10.1–20 years	20.1–40 years	40.1 years–life	Death Penalty	Unknown	Total
Husband, boyfriend	4	15	2	1	2	3	3	1	0	1	0	5	37
Wife, girlfriend	1	15	0	0	1	1	0	0	0	0	0	2	20
Sibling	0	3	0	0	0	1	0	0	0	0	0	1	5
Other relative	0	3	2	2	0	0	1	0	0	0	0	4	12
Close Friend	0	8	1	0	1	3	1	0	0	0	0	2	16
Acquaintance	0	23	5	1	4	14	4	3	1	3	0	6	64
Stranger	0	11	2	2	1	3	2	3	3	7	5	5	44
Unknown	2	18	2	1	2	2	2	1	0	0	0	2	32
Total	7	96	14	7	11	27	13	8	4	11	5	27	230

Source: Compiled from Lundsgaarde 1977:224–229.

A.4.5 Killer-Victim Relationships and Final Case Disposition for 246 Murders in Houston, Texas, 1969

This table was compiled from the book *Murder in Space City* (1977), Henry Lundsgaarde's study of homicides, killer-victim relationships, and final case dispositions in Houston, Texas, in 1969. At the time, Texas had the highest murder rate in the United States. Note that of the 246 murders for which data were available, 165 occurred between people who knew one another, while only 81 occurred between strangers. Also note that punishments tend to grow more severe as the strength of acquaintanceship decreases. For instance, the death penalty was assigned five times, but only in cases where the killer and the victim were strangers.

Disposition	Blood Kin	Nonblood Kin[a]	Acquaintance[b]	Stranger or Unknown[c]
Killer commits suicide	—	3 (5%)	3 (3%)	2 (2%)
No charge or dismissal	6 (50%)	23 (41%)	36 (37%)	29 (36%)
Not guilty	—	5 (9%)	3 (3%)	4 (5%)
Probation only	—	5 (9%)	11 (12%)	7 (9%)
Prison sentence	5 total (42%)	10 total (18%)	37 total (38%)	27 total (33%)
Less than 1 year		1	4	2
1–5 years	2	4	20	5
6–24 years	1	4	7	9
25 years–life	2	1	6	11
Death penalty	—	6 (11%)	5 (5%)	5 (6%)
Sentence undetermined	1 (8%)	4 (7%)	2 (2%)	3 (4%)
Charge pending	—	—	—	4 (5%)
Total	12	56	97	81

Notes: a. Nonblood kin includes ex-spouses and common-law spouses. b. Acquaintances include unmarried boyfriends and girlfriends. c. Thirty-seven cases where the relationship between killer and victim was unknown were added to the forty-four cases of stranger killings (making 81 total in this category). It is certain that family ties (blood kin or nonblood kin) or close acquaintanceships were not involved in these cases (close relationships would have been uncovered during the case). There is a small possibility, however, that minor acquaintanceship existed but was concealed by the killer.

A.4.6   Justifications for Known Lynchings in the United States, 1882–1968

	Number	Percentage
Homicides	1,937	40.84
Felonious assault	205	4.32
Rape	912	19.22
Attempted rape	288	6.07
Robbery and theft	232	4.89
Insult to white person	85	1.79
All other causes	1,084	22.85
Total	4,743	100.00

Source: Charles Chesnutt Digital Archive, available at faculty.berea.edu/browners/chesnutt/ classroom/lynchingstat.html.

APPENDIX 2

Laws and Norms About Murder

An effective way to look at what a society thinks is important about life, killing, and punishment at a particular time is by seeing how they define murder in the law. Modern criminal law requires a judge, prosecutor, or jury to infer motivation and intention of the killer in assessing culpability. Particularly in a system using citizen jurors, such as that in the United States, this is determined in the context of culturally grounded understandings of motivation, psychology, and law. Note that there is much more of an emphasis on psychology than sociology. Thus, most modern US statutes follow California's definition of law, which emphasizes "malice" and "forethought." The definition is: "Murder is the unlawful killing of a human being, or a fetus, with malice aforethought."

The legal meaning of *malice* is that someone must have "intent" to kill, and *forethought* means that he or she will have planned to kill. Out of these elements, the crimes of first-degree murder, second-degree murder, and manslaughter emerge. First-degree murder is, in a general way, a killing that has both malice and forethought, while second-degree murder is killing that has only malice, but no planning (e.g., a brawl that is unexpected but during which the assailant becomes angry and kills intentionally). Killing without malice or forethought is manslaughter; this is what happens when someone is so reckless that he knew he could kill but did not have anyone in mind (i.e., no malice) and hoped that the reckless action would not result in an accident. Examples of the latter are firing a gun in the air at a crowded fair and driving a vehicle so recklessly that a fatality is likely.

While such a definition of intent and malice is seemingly straightforward, the devil is in the details. Legislatures, courts, and juries all play roles in defining the details. When specific cases emerge, what is important to the underlying social fabric also becomes apparent. For example, California's ambivalence about abortion is revealed in the second sentence and second clause of Penal Code Section 187, which specifies that killing a fetus is also murder, except when done by a licensed physician. Thus, someone who killed a pregnant woman can be tried for a double murder. In California this meant that a defendant like Scott Peterson, who killed his pregnant wife in late 2002, could be tried for double murder and was therefore subject to the death penalty instead of only life without parole. The fact that some types of killing are regarded as worse than others are seen in the legislature's insistence that if a person kills in the course of a robbery while using armor-piercing bullets (see Penal Code Section 189), the defendant cannot claim that he did not have "intent." Such a killing is always first-degree murder even if the robber did not fire the shot. In other words, if your partner kills a bartender in the course of a robbery, it is worse than killing the same bartender because he refused you a drink, which in turn led to a lethal fight in which the bartender died. In the former, intent is assumed, while in the latter it might be assumed that it was the "heat of the moment" that led to the death, making it second-degree murder (unless armor-piercing bullets were used).

The law as written by the California legislature also specifies that peace officers are more important than others in the event of second-degree murder. Thus, even in a nonpremeditated murder, the penalty for killing a peace officer is life without parole, while for the killing of the rest of us it is twenty-five years to life.

The point here is that the underlying values and controversies that are important to a society—the sociology of its laws—can be seen in the paragraphs where crimes are defined and specified by a legislature, and in how judges and juries are called on to make a determination of what intent and malice mean. A good way to think about this is to contrast California's laws, in which there is a strong emphasis on malice, forethought, and abortion, with Texas's statutes in the 1960s. Texas at that time was concerned with other issues, including those of honor, marital relations, and self-defense, which are missing from both states' contemporary statutes.

Penal Code Section 187 may be typical of US homicide laws at the beginning of the twenty-first century, but it is also the result of a long "evolution" of law that has occurred in state legislatures throughout the country. Texas today has laws against homicide similar to California's, but in earlier years, this was not necessarily the case.

California Penal Code Sections 187–190.1

Section 187

(a) Murder is the unlawful killing of a human being, or a fetus, with malice aforethought.

(b) This section shall not apply to any person who commits an act that results in the death of a fetus if any of the following apply:

(1) The act complied with the Therapeutic Abortion Act, Article 2 (commencing with Section 123400) of Chapter 2 of Part 2 of Division 106 of the Health and Safety Code.

(2) The act was committed by a holder of a physician's and surgeon's certificate, as defined in the Business and Professions Code, in a case where, to a medical certainty, the result of childbirth would be death of the mother of the fetus or where her death from childbirth, although not medically certain, would be substantially certain or more likely than not.

(3) The act was solicited, aided, abetted, or consented to by the mother of the fetus.

(c) Subdivision (b) shall not be construed to prohibit the prosecution of any person under any other provision of law.

Section 188

Such malice may be express or implied. It is express when there is manifested a deliberate intention unlawfully to take away the life of a fellow creature. It is implied, when no considerable provocation appears, or when the circumstances attending the killing show an abandoned and malignant heart.

When it is shown that the killing resulted from the intentional doing of an act with express or implied malice as defined above, no other mental state need be shown to establish the mental state of malice aforethought. Neither an awareness of the obligation to act within the general body of laws regulating society nor acting despite such awareness is included within the definition of malice.

Section 189

All murder which is perpetrated by means of a destructive device or explosive, knowing use of ammunition designed primarily to penetrate metal or armor, poison, lying in wait, torture, or by any other kind of willful, deliberate, and premeditated killing, or which is committed in the perpetration of, or attempt to perpetrate, arson, rape, carjacking, robbery, burglary, mayhem, kidnapping, train wrecking, or any act punishable under Section 206, 286, 288, 288a, or 289, or any murder which is perpetrated by means of discharging a firearm from a motor vehicle, intentionally at another person outside of the vehicle with the intent to inflict death, is murder of the first degree. All other kinds of murders are of the second degree.

As used in this section, "destructive device" means any destructive device as defined in Section 12301, and "explosive" means any explosive as defined in Section 12000 of the Health and Safety Code.

To prove the killing was "deliberate and premeditated," it shall not be necessary to prove the defendant maturely and meaningfully reflected upon the gravity of his or her act.

Section 190

(a) Every person guilty of murder in the first degree shall be punished by death, imprisonment in the state prison for life without the possibility of parole, or imprisonment in the state prison for a term of 25 years to life. The penalty to be applied shall be determined as provided in Sections 190.1, 190.2, 190.3, 190.4, and 190.5.

Section 190.03

(a) A person who commits first-degree murder shall be punished by imprisonment in the state prison for life without the possibility of parole, if the defendant intentionally killed the victim because of the victim's disability, gender, or sexual orientation or because of the defendant's perception of the victim's disability, gender, or sexual orientation.

(b) The term authorized by subdivision (a) shall not apply unless the allegation is charged in the accusatory pleading and admitted by the defendant or found true by the trier of fact. The court shall not strike the allegation, except in the interest of justice, in which case the court shall state its reasons in writing for striking the allegation.

(c) For the purpose of this section, "because of" means the bias motivation must be a cause in fact of the offense, whether or not other causes also exist. When multiple concurrent motives exist, the prohibited bias must be a substantial factor in bringing about the particular result. This subdivision does not constitute a change in, but is declaratory of, existing law as set forth in In Re M.S. (1995) 10 Cal.4th 698, 716–720 and *People v. Superior Court of San Diego County* (Aishman) (1995) 10 Cal.4th 735.

(d) Nothing in this section shall be construed to prevent punishment instead pursuant to any other provision of law that imposes a greater or more severe punishment.

Section 190.1

A case in which the death penalty may be imposed pursuant to this chapter shall be tried in separate phases as follows:

(a) The question of the defendant's guilt shall be first determined. If the trier of fact finds the defendant guilty of first degree murder, it shall at the same time determine the truth of all special circumstances charged as enumerated in Section 190.2 except for a special circumstance charged pursuant to paragraph (2) of subdivision (a) of Section 190.2 where it is alleged that the defendant had been convicted in a prior proceeding of the offense of murder in the first or second degree.

(b) If the defendant is found guilty of first degree murder and one of the special circumstances is charged pursuant to paragraph (2) of subdivision (a) of Section 190.2 which charges that the defendant had been convicted in a prior proceeding of the offense of murder of the first or second degree, there shall thereupon be further proceedings on the question of the truth of such special circumstance.

(c) If the defendant is found guilty of first degree murder and one or more special circumstances as enumerated in Section 190.2 has been charged and found to be true, his sanity on any plea of not guilty by reason of insanity under Section 1026 shall be determined as provided in Section 190.4. If he is found to be sane, there shall thereupon be further proceedings on the question of the penalty to be imposed. Such proceedings shall be conducted in accordance with the provisions of Section 190.3 and 190.4.[1]

Summary of Contemporary Texas Homicide Laws

Homicide is unlawfully causing the death of an individual. There are four types of homicide: murder, capital murder, manslaughter, and criminally negligent homicide. Most forms of homicide are felonies.

Murder is causing the death of an individual under any of the following circumstances:

- By intentionally or knowingly causing the death.
- By intending to cause serious bodily injury and committing an act that clearly endangers human life.
- While committing a felony and committing an act that clearly endangers human life.
- While fleeing from committing a felony and committing an act that clearly endangers human life.

Murder is divided into subcategories by degree of seriousness. If the defendant commits any of the above acts, he or she will be charged with murder. At the sentencing stage of the trial, if the defendant is able to prove he or she committed the murder while immediately influenced by sudden passion, and that the passion arose from an adequate cause, the defendant will be sentenced for murder of the second degree. Otherwise, the sentence is for murder of the first degree.

A Schematic View of Texas Homicide Statutes
Before 1974

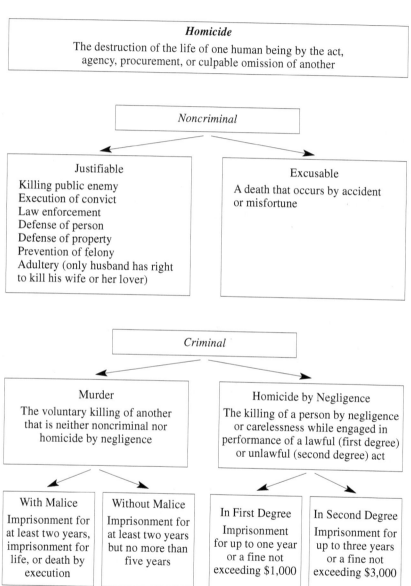

Homicide

The destruction of the life of one human being by the act, agency, procurement, or culpable omission of another

Noncriminal

Justifiable

Killing public enemy
Execution of convict
Law enforcement
Defense of person
Defense of property
Prevention of felony
Adultery (only husband has right to kill his wife or her lover)

Excusable

A death that occurs by accident or misfortune

Criminal

Murder

The voluntary killing of another that is neither noncriminal nor homicide by negligence

Homicide by Negligence

The killing of a person by negligence or carelessness while engaged in performance of a lawful (first degree) or unlawful (second degree) act

With Malice

Imprisonment for at least two years, imprisonment for life, or death by execution

Without Malice

Imprisonment for at least two years but no more than five years

In First Degree

Imprisonment for up to one year or a fine not exceeding $1,000

In Second Degree

Imprisonment for up to three years or a fine not exceeding $3,000

A Schematic View of Texas Homicide Statutes
After 1974

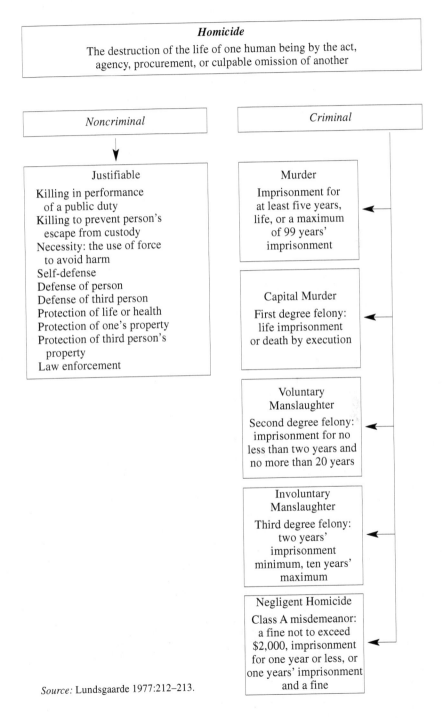

Homicide

The destruction of the life of one human being by the act, agency, procurement, or culpable omission of another

Noncriminal

Criminal

Justifiable

Killing in performance
  of a public duty
Killing to prevent person's
  escape from custody
Necessity: the use of force
  to avoid harm
Self-defense
Defense of person
Defense of third person
Protection of life or health
Protection of one's property
Protection of third person's
  property
Law enforcement

Murder

Imprisonment for
at least five years,
life, or a maximum
of 99 years'
imprisonment

Capital Murder

First degree felony:
life imprisonment
or death by execution

Voluntary
Manslaughter

Second degree felony:
imprisonment for no
less than two years and
no more than 20 years

Involuntary
Manslaughter

Third degree felony:
two years'
imprisonment
minimum, ten years'
maximum

Negligent Homicide

Class A misdemeanor:
a fine not to exceed
$2,000, imprisonment
for one year or less, or
one years' imprisonment
and a fine

Source: Lundsgaarde 1977:212–213.

Capital murder is similar to murder. A person convicted of capital murder will receive a death sentence. Capital murder is murder under any of the following circumstances:

- Murder of someone the defendant knows is a peace officer or firefighter acting in his or her official capacity.
- Murder committed intentionally during an aggravated sexual assault, arson, burglary, kidnapping, obstruction, retaliation, or robbery.
- Murder for pay.
- Paying another to commit murder.
- Murder while escaping from prison.
- Murder while incarcerated, if the victim is a prison guard or the defendant is incarcerated for aggravated robbery, aggravated sexual assault of a child, or murder.
- Murder of more than one person at once or during the same scheme or course of conduct.
- Murder of a child under the age of six.

If the jury in a capital homicide case does not find the defendant guilty beyond a reasonable doubt, the charge may be reduced to murder or another lesser offense.

Manslaughter is defined as recklessly causing the death of a person. Manslaughter is a felony of the second degree. *Criminally negligent homicide* is a state jail felony, and is defined as causing the death of an individual by criminal negligence.[2]

Notes

1. See http://caselaw.lp.findlaw.com/cacodes/pen/187-199.html.
2. See http://www.weblocator.com/attorney/tx/law/c13.html.

Bibliography

Anderson, Benedict (1991[1983]). *Imagined Communities: Reflections on the Origin and Spread of Nationalism.* New York: Verso.

Anderson, Elijah (1999). *Streetwise: Race, Class, and Change in an Urban Community.* Chicago: University of Chicago Press.

Anderson, Scott (1999). "The Curse of Blood and Violence." *New York Times Magazine,* December 26.

Anderson, David (2005). *Histories of Hanged: The Dirty War in Kenya and the End of Empire.* New York: W. W. Norton.

Archer, Dane, and Rosemary Gartner (1976). "Violent Acts and Violent Times: A Comparative Approach to Postwar Homicide Rates." *American Sociological Review* 41: 937–963.

Bates, Robert H. (2001). *Prosperity and Violence: The Political Economy of Development.* New York: W. W. Norton.

Baumgartner, M. P. (1988). *The Moral Order of a Suburb.* Oxford: Oxford University Press.

Becker, Howard (1963). "Moral Entrepreneurs: The Creation and Enforcement of Deviant Categories." In *The Outsiders.* London: Free Press of Glencoe.

Beeghley, Leonard (2003). *Homicide: A Sociological Explanation.* Lanham, MD: Rowman and Littlefield.

Benton, Thomas [1826?]. "In Defense of Dueling." http://www.civilwarstlouis.com/History/benton.htm.

Billacois, François (1990). *The Duel: Its Rise and Fall in Early Modern France.* Edited and translated by Trista Selous. New Haven, CT: Yale University Press.

Black, Donald (1976). *The Behavior of Law.* New York: Academic.

——— (1993). *The Social Structure of Right and Wrong.* New York: Academic.

Blumer, Herbert (1956). "Race Prejudice as a Sense of Group Position." *Pacific Sociological Review* 1, no. 1: 3–7.

Bradley, James (2003). *Flyboys: A True Story of Courage.* New York: Back Bay Books.

Brearly, H. C. (1932). *Homicide in the United States.* Chapel Hill: University of North Carolina Press.

Brundage, Fitzhugh (1993). *Lynching in the New South: Georgia and Virginia, 1880–1930.* Chicago: University of Illinois Press.

Bugliosi, Vincent (1994). *Helter Skelter: 25th Anniversary Edition.* New York: W. W. Norton.

237

Cohen, Lawrence E., and Kenneth Land (1987). "Age Structure and Crime: Symmetry Versus Asymmetry and the Projection of Crime Rates Through the 1990s." *American Sociological Review* 52: 170–183.

Collins, Randall (1973). "Three Faces of Cruelty." *Theory and Society* 1: 415–440.

Conrad, Joseph (1901). *Heart of Darkness.* http://etext.virginia.edu/toc/modeng/public/ConDark.html.

Cook, Phillip J. (1979). "The Effects of Gun Availability on Robbery and Robbery Murder: A Cross-section Study of Fifty Cities." In *Policy Studies Review Annual*, vol. 3, edited by Robert H. Haveman and B. Bruce Zellner. Beverly Hills, CA: Sage, 743–781.

Cooney, Mark (1997a). "From Warre to Tyranny." *American Sociological Review* 62: 316–338.

——— (1997b). "The Decline of Elite Homicide." *Criminology* 35, no. 3: 381–407.

——— (1998). *Warriors and Peacemakers: How Third Parties Shape Violence.* New York: New York University Press.

——— (2003). "The Privatization of Violence." *Criminology* 41, no. 4: 1377–1406.

Cronon, William (1983). *Changes in the Land.* New York: Hill and Wang.

Curran, Daniel (1993). "King Coal Rules." In *Dead Laws for Dead Men: The Politics of Federal Coal Mine Health and Safety.* Pittsburgh: University of Pittsburgh Press.

Daly, Martin, and Margo Wilson (1988). *Homicide.* New York: Aldine de Gruyter.

——— (1982). "Homicide and Kinship." *American Anthropologist* 84, no. 2: 372–377.

de Tocqueville, Alexis. *Democracy in America,* vol. 2, part 3. http://xroads.virginia.edu/~Hyper/detoc/.

Diamond, Jared (1992). *The Third Chimpanzee: The Evolution and Future of the Human Animal.* New York: W. W. Norton.

——— (1999). *Guns, Germs, and Steel: The Fates of Human Societies.* New York: W. W. Norton.

——— (2005). *Collapse: How Societies Choose to Fail or Succeed.* New York: W. W. Norton.

Dowie, Mark (1977). "Pinto Madness." *Mother Jones,* September/October.

Drake, Ross (2004). "Duel." *Smithsonian,* March.

Dray, Philip (2002). *At the Hands of Persons Unknown.* New York: Random House.

Durkheim, Emile (1938[1895]). *The Rules of the Sociological Method.* 8th ed., translated by Sarah A. Solovay and John H. Mueller. New York: Free Press.

——— (1973). *On Morality and Society.* Edited and with an Introduction by Robert Bellah. Chicago: University of Chicago Press.

Economist (1999). "The Cruel and Ever More Unusual Punishment." *The Economist,* May 15.

Elias, Norbert (1939). *The Civilizing Process.* Oxford: Blackwell.

Emerson, Barbara (1979). *Leopold II: King of the Belgians.* New York: St. Martin's.

Englehart, Joshua. (2005). "Why Prisons Can't Integrate." *Los Angeles Times,* March 11, p. B13.

Erikson, Kai (1966). *Wayward Puritans: A Study in the Sociology of Deviance.* Boston: Allyn and Bacon.

——— (1976). *Everything in Its Path: Destruction of Community in the Buffalo Creek Flood.* New York: Simon and Schuster.

Faderman, Anne (1998). *I Begin My Life All Over Again.* Boston: Beacon.

Farrell, Harry (1992). *Swift Justice.* New York: St. Martin's.

Fisiy, Cyprian (1998). "Containing Occult Practices: Witchcraft Trials in the Cameroon—The People Versus Betta Samuel and Adama Epongo." *African Studies Review* 41, no. 3: 152–155.

Fisiy, Cyprian, and Peter Geschiere (1990). "Judges and Witches, or How Is the State to Deal with Witchcraft? Examples from Southeastern Cameroon." *Cahiers d'études africaines* 118: 135–156.

Foucault, Michel (1976). *Discipline and Punish: The Birth of the Prison.* New York: Vintage.

Furfey, Paul (1966). *The Respectable Murderers: Social Evil and Christian Conscience.* New York: Herder and Herder.

Gelernter, Daniel (1998). "What Do Murderers Deserve?" *Commentary,* April, pp. 21–24.

Givens, James Buchanan (1977). *Society and Homicide in Thirteenth-Century England.* Palo Alto: Stanford University Press.

Gottfredson, Michael, and Travis Hirschi (1990). *A General Theory of Crime.* Palo Alto: Stanford University Press.

Gourevitch, Phillip (1998). *We Wish to Inform You That Tomorrow We Will Be Killed with Our Families: Stories from Rwanda.* New York: Farrar, Straus Giroux.

Grossman, Dave (1995). *On Killing: The Psychological Cost of Learning to Kill in War and Society.* New York: Back Bay.

Gurr, Ted Robert, and Hugh Davis Graham (1979). *Violence in America: Historical and Comparative Perspectives.* Thousand Oaks, CA: Sage.

Hall, John R. (1987). *Gone from the Promised Land.* New York: Transaction.

Hilberg, Raul (1967). *The Destruction of the European Jews.* Chicago: Quadrangle.

——— (1992). *Perpetrators, Victims, and Bystanders.* New York: Harper.

Hill, Kim, and A. Magdalena Hurtado (1996). *Ache Life History: The Ecology and Demography of a Foraging People.* New York: Aldine de Gruyter.

Hobbes, Thomas (1651). *Leviathan.* http://www.gutenberg.org/etext/3207.

Hochschild, Adam (1998). *King Leopold's Ghost.* New York: Houghton Mifflin.

Holmes, Ronald M., and Stephen T. Holmes (2000). "Serial Murder in the United States." In *Serial Murder,* 2nd ed. Thousand Oaks, CA: Sage, 29–32.

Howell, Nancy (1979). *The Demography of the Dobe !Kung.* New York: Academic.

Jones, Ann (1980) *Women Who Kill.* New York: Holt, Rinehart, and Wilson.

Kane, Harnett T. (1951). *Gentlemen, Swords, and Pistols.* New York: William Morrow.

Katz, Jack (1988). *Seductions of Crime.* New York: Perseus.

Kiernan, V. G. (1988). *The Duel in European History: Honour and the Reign of Aristocracy.* Oxford: Oxford University Press.

Klein, Malcolm (1995). *The American Street Gang.* New York: Oxford University Press.

——— (2004). *Gang Cop: The Words and Ways of Officer Paco Domingo.* Walnut Creek, CA: Alta Mira.

Kotlowitz, Alex (1999). "The Unprotected." *New Yorker,* February 8, pp. 42–53.

Krajicek David (n.d.). "Ken McElroy." *Court TV Crime Library.* http://www.crimelibrary.com/notorious_murders/classics/ken_mcelroy/index.html.

Kuperman, Alan (2001). *The Limits of Humanitarian Intervention.* Washington, DC: Brookings Institution.

LaFree, Gary (1999). "A Summary and Review of Comparative Studies of Homicide." In *Homicide: A Sourcebook of Social Research,* edited by M. Dwayne Smith and Margaret A. Zahn. Thousand Oaks, CA: Sage, 138–143.

Lane, Roger (1997). *Murder in America: A History.* Columbus: Ohio State University Press.

LeBlanc, Steven (2003). *Constant Battles: The Myth of the Noble Savage.* Cambridge, MA: Harvard University Press.

Lee, Matthew T., and M. David Ermann (1999). "Pinto 'Madness' as a Flawed Landmark Narrative: An Organizational and Network Analysis." *Social Problems* 46, no. 1: 30–47.

Lee, Richard (1979). "Homicide Among the Dobe !Kung." In *The Dobe !Kung.* New York: Holt, Rinehart, and Winston.

LeMarchand, Rene (2005). "Being Witness to Mass Murder." *African Studies Review.* 48, no. 3: 93–101.

Levitt, Steven D., and Sudhir Alladi Venkatesh (2000). "An Economic Analysis of a Drug-Selling Gang's Finances." *Quarterly Review of Economics* 115, no. 3: 755–789.

Lundsgaarde, Henry P. (1977). *Murder in Space City.* Oxford: Oxford University Press.

MacClintock, S. S. (1901). "The Kentucky Mountains and Their Feuds." *American Journal of Sociology* 7: 1–28, 171–187.

MacLean, Harry D. (1988). *In Broad Daylight: A Murder in Skidmore, Missouri.* New York: Dell.

Mauss, Marcel (2000). *The Gift: The Form and Reason for Exchange in Archaic Societies.* New York: W. W. Norton.

McGrath, Roger (1984). *From Gunfighters, Highwaymen, and Vigilantes.* Berkeley: University of California Press.

McMahan, Jeff (2002). *The Ethics of Killing: Problems at the Margins of Life.* Oxford: Oxford University Press.

Miethe, Terrance D., and Wendy C. Regoeczi (2004). *Rethinking Homicide.* Cambridge: Cambridge University Press.

Milgram, Stanley (1974). *Obedience to Authority.* New York: Harper and Row.

Monkkonen, Eric (2001). *Murder in New York City.* Berkeley: University of California Press.

Montopoli, Brian (2005). "A Long Way from Columbine." *Columbia Journalism Review Daily,* March 29. http://www.cjrdaily.org/behind_the_news/a_long_way_from_columbine.php.

Myers, Jim. (2000). "Notes on the Murder of Thirty of My Neighbors." *Atlantic Monthly,* March, pp. 72–86.

O'Brien, Robert M., Jean Stockard, and Lynne Isaacson (1999). "The Enduring Effects of Cohort Characteristics on Age-Specific Homicide Rates, 1960–95." *American Journal of Sociology* 104, no. 4: 1061–1095.

O'Meara, James (1881). *Broderick and Gwin: The Most Extraordinary Contest for a Seat in the Senate of the United States Ever Known.* San Francisco: Bacon.

Oppenlander, Nan (1982). "Copping or Copping Out." *Criminology* 20: 449–465.

Paciotti, Brian, and Monique Borgerhoff Mulder (2004). "Sungusungu: The Role of Preexisting and Evolving Social Institutions Among Tanzanian Vigilante Organizations." *Human Organization* 63: 112–124.

Pearce, John Ed (1994). *Days of Darkness: The Feuds of Eastern Kentucky.* Lexington: University of Kentucky Press.

Prunier, Gerard (1995/1997). *The Rwanda Crisis: History of a Genocide.* New York: Columbia University Press.

Robarchek, Clayton A. (1989). "Hobbesian and Rousseauan Images of Man: Autonomy and Individualism in a Peaceful Society." In *Societies at Peace:*

Anthropological Perspectives, edited by Signe Howell and Roy Willis. London: Routledge, 31–44.

Robarchek, Clayton A., and R. K. Dentan (1987). "Blood Drunkenness and the Bloodthirsty Semai: Unmasking Another Anthropological Myth." *American Anthropologist* 89, no. 2: 356–365.

Roberts, Simon (1979). *Order and Dispute: An Introduction to Legal Anthropology.* New York: St. Martin's.

Rosenthal, A. M. (1999[1964]). "Introduction." In *Thirty-Eight Witnesses: The Kitty Genovese Case.* Berkeley: University of California Press.

Schivelbusch, Wolfgang (2003). *The Culture of Defeat: On National Trauma, Mourning, and Recovery.* New York: Metropolitan.

Shawcross, William (1985). *The Quality of Mercy.* New York: Simon and Schuster.

Sherman, Lawrence (1992). *Policing Domestic Violence.* New York: Free Press.

Sloan, Henry D., Arthur Kellerman, Donald T. Reav, et al. (1988). "Handgun Regulations, Crime, Assaults, and Homicide: A Tale of Two Cities." *New England Journal of Medicine* 319: 1256–1262.

Smith, Adam (1776). *The Wealth of Nations.* http://www.econlib.org/LIBRARY/Smith/smWN.html.

Strobel, Lee Patrick (1980). *Reckless Homicide? Ford's Pinto Trial.* South Bend, IN: And Books.

Twain, Mark (1882). *Huckleberry Finn.* http://etext.virginia.edu/twain/huckfinn.html.

——— (1906[1961]). *King Leopold's Soliloquy.* Includes "Ought King Leopold Be Hanged?" Interview by Mr. W. T. Stead with the Rev. John H. Harris. Berlin: Seven Seas, 80–85.

Umutesi, Marie Beatrice (2005). *Surviving the Slaughter: The Ordeal of a Rwandan Refugee in Zaire.* Madison: University of Wisconsin Press.

Uniform Crime Reports, Homicide (various years). Federal Bureau of Investigation, Washington, DC.

Van Biema, David (1999). "Should All Be Forgiven?" *Time,* April 5, pp. 55–58.

Vigil, Diego (2002). *A Rainbow of Gangs.* Austin: University of Texas Press.

Waller, Altina (1988). *Feud: Hatfields, McCoys, and Social Change in Appalachia, 1860–1890.* Chapel Hill: University of North Carolina Press.

Waters, Tony (1997). "Beyond Structural Adjustment: State and Market in a Rural Tanzanian Village." *African Studies Review* 40, no. 2: 59–89.

——— (1999). *Crime and Immigrant Youth.* Thousand Oaks, CA: Sage.

——— (2001). *Bureaucratizing the Good Samaritan.* Boulder, CO: Westview.

Waters, Tony, and Lawrence E. Cohen (1993). *Laotians in the Criminal Justice System.* Berkeley: California Policy Seminar.

Weber, Max (1948). *From Max Weber.* Translated and edited by H. H. Gerth and C. Wright Mills. New York: Oxford University Press.

Wells-Barnett, Ida (1899). *Lynch Law in Georgia, Chapter II.* http://afroamhistory.about.com/library/blidabwells_lynchlawingeorgia2.htm.

Westermeyer, Joseph (1972). "Comparison of Amok and Other Homicide in Laos." *American Journal of Psychiatry* 129: 79–85.

White, Walter (1969). *Rope and Faggot.* New York: Arno.

Wright, George C. (1990). *Racial Violence in Kentucky, 1865–1940.* Baton Rouge: Louisiana State University Press.

Yablonsky, Lewis (1997). *Gangsters: Fifty Years of Madness, Drugs, and Death on the Streets of America.* New York: New York University Press.

Zahn, Margaret A., and Patricia L. McCall (1999). "Trends and Patterns of Homicide in the 20th Century United States." In *Homicide: A Sourcebook of Social Research,* edited by M. Dwayne Smith and Margaret A. Zahn. Thousand Oaks, CA: Sage, 9–21.

Zangrando, Robert (1980). *The NAACP Campaign Against Lynching.* Philadelphia: Temple University Press.

Index

243

About the Book

TAKING ANOTHER PERSON'S LIFE IS THE CRIME FOR WHICH EVERY SOCIETY reserves the strongest of punishments. But why (and when) is the act of killing sometimes defined as murder—as inexcusable—and other times considered a justifiable, or even righteous, act? Grappling with this ambiguity, Tony Waters sheds light on the sociology of murder.

This innovative text draws on wide-ranging case studies of killing—from urban gangs in Washington, DC, to the Salem witchcraft trials, from the "Wild West" to blood feuds in modern Albania, from dueling gentlemen to government-orchestrated mass executions—to illustrate the process of criminalization. Along the way, it looks at both the micro-sociological level of the violent act itself and the macro level of society's reaction. *When Killing Is a Crime* will leave students with a clear understanding of how differences in culture, status, power, technology, and legal systems pattern violence and murder.

Tony Waters is professor of sociology at California State University, Chico. He is author of *Crime and Immigrant Youth, The Persistence of Subsistance Agriculture,* and *Bureaucratizing the Good Samaritan.*